MICROPROCESS

AUTHOR

Dr. Yogendra Kumar Gupta
Associate Professor,
Dept. of Computer Science & Engineering,
Swami Keshvanand Institute of Technology Management & Gramothan, Jaipur, Rajasthan

REVIEWER

Prof. Shaik Rafi Ahamed
Professor,
Dept. of Electronics and Electrical Engineering,
Indian Institute of Technology, Guwahati

KHANNA BOOK PUBLISHING CO. (P) Ltd.
4C/4344, Ansari Road, Darya Ganj,
New Delhi, India

All India Council for Technical Education
Nelson Mandela Marg, Vasant Kunj,
New Delhi, India

Dear Readers,

To prevent the piracy, this book is secured with HIGH SECURITY HOLOGRAM on the front title cover. In case you don't find the hologram on the front cover title, please write us to at contact@khannabooks.com or whatsapp us at +91-99109 09320 and avail special gift voucher for yourself.

Specimen of Hologram on front Cover title:

Moreover, there is a SPECIAL DISCOUNT COUPON for you with EVERY HOLOGRAM.
How to avail this SPECIAL DISCOUNT:
Step 1: Scratch the hologram
Step 2: Under the scratch area, your "coupon code" is available
Step 3: Logon to www.khannabooks.com
Step 4: Use your "coupon code" in the shopping cart and get your copy at a special discount
Step 5: Enjoy your reading!

ISBN: 978-93-5538-608-3
Book Code: UG483EN

Microprocessors

by Dr. Yogendra Kumar Gupta

First Edition: 2026

Originally Published by:
All India Council for Technical Education, Ministry of Education, GOI

Exclusively Published & Distributed by:
Khanna Book Publishing Co. (P) Ltd.
4C/4344, Ansari Road, Daryaganj,
New Delhi (INDIA)

Visit us at: **www.khannabooks.com**
Write us at: **contact@khannabooks.com**

To view complete list of books, Please scan the QR Code:

KPH

Printed in Bharat.

प्रो. टी. जी. सीताराम
अध्यक्ष
Prof. T. G. Sitharam
Chairman

सत्यमेव जयते

आज़ादी का अमृत महोत्सव

अखिल भारतीय तकनीकी शिक्षा परिषद्
(भारत सरकार का एक सांविधिक निकाय)
(शिक्षा मंत्रालय, भारत सरकार)
नेल्सन मंडेला मार्ग, वसंत कुंज, नई दिल्ली-110070
दूरभाष : 011-26131498
ई-मेल : chairman@aicte-india.org

ALL INDIA COUNCIL FOR TECHNICAL EDUCATION
(A STATUTORY BODY OF THE GOVT. OF INDIA)
(Ministry of Education, Govt. of India)
Nelson Mandela Marg, Vasant Kunj, New Delhi-110070
Phone : 011-26131498
E-mail : chairman@aicte-india.org

FOREWORD

Engineers are the backbone of any modern society. They are the ones responsible for the marvels as well as the improved quality of life across the world. Engineers have driven humanity towards greater heights in a more evolved and unprecedented manner.

The All India Council for Technical Education (AICTE), have spared no efforts towards the strengthening of the technical education in the country. AICTE is always committed towards promoting quality Technical Education to make India a modern developed nation emphasizing on the overall welfare of mankind.

An array of initiatives has been taken by AICTE in last decade which have been accelerated now by the National Education Policy (NEP) 2020. The implementation of NEP under the visionary leadership of Hon'ble Prime Minister of India envisages the provision for education in regional languages to all, thereby ensuring that every graduate becomes competent enough and is in a position to contribute towards the national growth and development through innovation & entrepreneurship.

One of the spheres where AICTE had been relentlessly working since past couple of years is providing high quality original technical contents at Under Graduate & Diploma level prepared and translated by eminent educators in various Indian languages to its aspirants. For students pursuing 2nd year of their Engineering education, AICTE has identified 87 books, which shall be translated into 12 Indian languages - Hindi, Tamil, Gujarati, Odia, Bengali, Kannada, Urdu, Punjabi, Telugu, Marathi, Assamese & Malayalam. In addition to the English medium, books in different Indian Languages are going to support the students to understand the concepts in their respective mother tongue.

On behalf of AICTE, I express sincere gratitude to all distinguished authors, reviewers and translators from the renowned institutions of high repute for their admirable contribution in a record span of time.

AICTE is confident that these outcomes based original contents shall help aspirants to master the subject with comprehension and greater ease.

(Prof. T. G. Sitharam)

ACKNOWLEDGEMENT

I would like to express my deep gratitude to the leadership of AICTE, especially Prof. T.G. Sitharam, Chairman; Dr. Abhay Jere, Vice-Chairman; Prof. Rajive Kumar, Member Secretary; and Dr. Sunil Luthra, Director, and Reena Sharma, Hindi Officer Training and Learning, for their visionary support in planning the publication of this book on "Microprocessors." I am particularly thankful to Prof. Shaik Rafi Ahamed, Professor of Electronics & Electrical Engineering at Indian Institute of Technology Guwahati, for his meticulous review of the manuscript. His insightful feedback and suggestions for improvement have significantly enhanced the quality of the content. I would also like to extend heartfelt appreciation to my wife, Monika, whose unwavering encouragement has fueled my efforts in writing this book. This work is the result of numerous contributions from AICTE members, experts, and fellow authors who provided invaluable feedback to further the development of engineering education in our country. I am deeply indebted to all contributors, researchers, and professionals in this field whose published works, articles, papers, photographs, and references have enriched my understanding and informed the content of this book.

Yogendra Kumar Gupta

PREFACE

In electronic system design, microcontrollers have become a very important component. Digital systems interacting with the environment need computation power for signal processing or for executing a control algorithm. As an electronic system designer, particularly in the digital domain, one should have a good grasp on the features, architectures, programming techniques and interfacing requirements of various microcontrollers, available in the market. Though it is a difficult task to have very good knowledge on each of the alternatives available, one should be able to select the best possible solution for a given application and go ahead with the design and development task without much inconvenience.

To address the issue of application development using microcontrollers, this book attempts to provide a deep understanding for the microcontroller 8051. In order to introduce the concepts related to microcontrollers, first some basic topics on computer organization, 8085 and 8086 microprocessors have been discussed. This will help the reader to prepare the background to initiate the study on microcontrollers. The features of generic microcontrollers have been elaborated to establish their requirement, over and above the existing microprocessors. The architecture, programming and interfacing issues of the 8051 have been elaborated in sufficient detail. Connecting keyboard, LEDs, 7-segment displays, LCDs to the 8051 have been illustrated. To interact with the world, which is analog in nature, analog-to-digital and digital-to-analog converter (ADC and DAC) interfacing techniques have been enumerated. The 8051 supports both the parallel and the serial modes of communication. Both the modes have been illustrated for data transfer to/from the 8051 chip. Apart from assembly language programming for interfacing and control algorithms, Embedded C language has been explored.

The book is an outcome of the author's experience of handling the theory and laboratory courses on subjects like Microprocessors, Microcontrollers and Embedded Systems for more than six years. It is expected that the book will be highly useful to the students and the subject teachers, for whom it has been primarily meant for.

Yogendra Kumar Gupta

OUTCOME BASED EDUCATION

For the implementation of an outcome-based education the first requirement is to develop an outcome-based curriculum and incorporate an outcome-based assessment in the education system. By going through outcome-based assessments, evaluators will be able to evaluate whether the students have achieved the outlined standard, specific and measurable outcomes. With the proper incorporation of outcome-based education there will be a definite commitment to achieve a minimum standard for all learners without giving up at any level. At the end of the programme running with the aid of outcome-based education, a student will be able to arrive at the following outcomes:

PO1. Engineering knowledge: Apply the knowledge of mathematics, science, engineering fundamentals, and an engineering specialization to the solution of complex engineering problems.

PO2. Problem analysis: Identify, formulate, review research literature, and analyze complex engineering problems reaching substantiated conclusions using first principles of mathematics, natural sciences, and engineering sciences.

PO3. Design / development of solutions: Design solutions for complex engineering problems and design system components or processes that meet the specified needs with appropriate consideration for the public health and safety, and the cultural, societal, and environmental considerations.

PO4. Conduct investigations of complex problems: Use research-based knowledge and research methods including design of experiments, analysis and interpretation of data, and synthesis of the information to provide valid conclusions.

PO5. Modern tool usage: Create, select, and apply appropriate techniques, resources, and modern engineering and IT tools including prediction and modeling to complex engineering activities with an understanding of the limitations.

PO6. The engineer and society: Apply reasoning informed by the contextual knowledge to assess societal, health, safety, legal and cultural issues and the consequent responsibilities relevant to the professional engineering practice.

PO7. Environment and sustainability: Understand the impact of the professional engineering solutions in societal and environmental contexts, and demonstrate the knowledge of, and need for sustainable development.

PO8. Ethics: Apply ethical principles and commit to professional ethics and responsibilities and norms of the engineering practice.

PO9. Individual and team work: Function effectively as an individual, and as a member or leader in diverse teams, and in multidisciplinary settings.

PO10. Communication: Communicate effectively on complex engineering activities with the engineering community and with society at large, such as, being able to comprehend and write effective reports and design documentation, make effective presentations, and give and receive clear instructions.

PO11. Project management and finance: Demonstrate knowledge and understanding of the engineering and management principles and apply these to one's own work, as a member and leader in a team, to manage projects and in multidisciplinary environments.

PO12. Life-long learning: Recognize the need for, and have the preparation and ability to engage in independent and life-long learning in the broadest context of technological change.

COURSE OUTCOMES

By the end of the course the students will be able to:

CO-1: Understand and Compare Fundamentals of Microprocessors and Microcontrollers.

CO-2: Implement Assembly and C- Language Programs for Data Manipulation and Interfacing.

CO-3: Interface I/O and Peripheral Devices with 8051 Microcontroller.

CO-4: Implement Communication Standards and Protocols.

CO-5: Design systems using different microcontrollers.

Mapping of Course Outcomes with Program Outcomes to be done according to the matrix given below:

Course Outcomes	Expected Mapping with Program Outcomes *(1-Weak Correlation; 2-Medium correlation; 3-Strong Correlation)*											
	PO1	**PO2**	**PO3**	**PO4**	**PO5**	**PO6**	**PO7**	**PO8**	**PO9**	**PO10**	**PO11**	**PO12**
CO-1	3	2	1	1	2	1	1	1	1	2	1	3
CO-2	3	3	2	2	3	1	1	1	1	2	1	2
CO-3	3	2	3	2	3	2	1	1	1	2	1	2
CO-4	3	2	3	3	3	2	1	1	2	2	1	2
CO-5	3	3	3	3	3	2	2	2	3	2	3	3

GUIDELINES FOR TEACHERS

To implement Outcome Based Education (OBE) knowledge level and skill set of the students should be enhanced. Teachers should take a major responsibility for the proper implementation of OBE. Some of the responsibilities (not limited to) for the teachers in OBE system may be as follows:

- Within reasonable constraint, they should manoeuvre time to the best advantage of all students.
- They should assess the students only upon certain defined criterion without considering any other potential ineligibility to discriminate them.
- They should try to grow the learning abilities of the students to a certain level before they leave the institute.
- They should try to ensure that all the students are equipped with the quality knowledge as well as competence after they finish their education.
- They should always encourage the students to develop their ultimate performance capabilities.
- They should facilitate and encourage group work and team work to consolidate newer approach.
- They should follow Blooms taxonomy in every part of the assessment.

Bloom's Taxonomy

Level	Teacher should Check	Student should be able to	Possible Mode of Assessment
Create	Students ability to create	Design or Create	Mini project
Evaluate	Students ability to justify	Argue or Defend	Assignment
Analyse	Students ability to distinguish	Differentiate or Distinguish	Project/Lab Methodology
Apply	Students ability to use information	Operate or Demonstrate	Technical Presentation/ Demonstration
Understand	Students ability to explain the ideas	Explain or Classify	Presentation/Seminar
Remember	Students ability to recall (or remember)	Define or Recall	Quiz

GUIDELINES FOR STUDENTS

Students should take equal responsibility for implementing the OBE. Some of the responsibilities (not limited to) for the students in OBE system are as follows:

- Students should be well aware of each UO before the start of a unit in each and every course.
- Students should be well aware of each CO before the start of the course.
- Students should be well aware of each PO before the start of the program.
- Students should think critically and reasonably with proper reflection and action.
- Learning of the students should be connected and integrated with practical and real life consequences.
- Students should be well aware of their competency at every level of OBE.

LIST OF ABBREVIATIONS

AC	Auxiliary Carry
ADC	Analog to Digital Converter
ALE	Address Latch Enable
ALU	Arithmetic Logic Unit
AVR	Advanced Virtual RISC
CISC	Complex Instruction Set Computer
CLK	Clock
CPU	Central Processing Unit
CS	Code Segment
CY	Carry
DAC	Digital to Analog Converter
DB	Define Byte
DI	Destination Index
DS	Data Segment
EA	External Access
EOC	End of Conversion
ES	Extra Segment
EU	Execution Unit
FIQ	Fast Interrupt Processing
GPR	General Purpose Register
GUI	Graphical User Interface
IDE	Integrated Development Environment
IE	Interrupt Enable
IIC, I2C	Inter Integrated Circuit
IP	Instruction Pointer, Interrupt Priority
IR	Instruction Register
kB	Kilobytes
kHz	Kilohertz
LCD	Liquid Crystal Diode
LED	Light Emitting Diode
LSB	Least Significant Bit
MHz	Megahertz
MSB	Most Significant Bit
OE	Output Enable
PC	Program Counter
PCB	Printed Circuit Board
PIC	Programmable Interface Controller
PPI	Programmable Peripheral Interface
PSEN	Program Strobe Enable
PWM	Pulse Width Modulation
RAM	Random Access Memory
RD	Read
RISC	Reduced Instruction Set Computer
ROM	Read Only Memory
RS	Register Select
SC	Start Conversion
SCI	Serial Communication Interface
SI	Source Index
SID	Serial Input Data
SoC	System-on-Chip
SOD	Serial Output Data
SP	Stack Pointer
SPI	Serial Peripheral Interface

LIST OF FIGURES

LIST OF TABLES

CONTENTS

1 Fundamentals of Microprocessors

UNIT SPECIFICS

Through this unit we have discussed the following aspects:

- *Fundamentals of Microprocessor Architecture*
- *8-bitMicroprocessor and Microcontroller architecture*
- *Comparison of 8-bit microcontrollers, 16-bit and 32-bit microcontrollers*
- *Definition of embedded system and its characteristics*
- *Role of microcontrollers in embedded Systems*
- *Overview of the 8051 family*

The practical applications of the topics are discussed to spark curiosity, enhance creativity, and improve problem-solving skills. In addition to offering multiple-choice questions, short and long answer questions are categorized according to Bloom's taxonomy, addressing both lower and higher-order thinking. Assignments include numerous numerical problems, and a list of references and suggested readings is provided for further practice. To access more information on specific topics, QR codes have been included in various sections, which can be scanned for relevant supplemental knowledge.

After the practical content, there is a "Know More" section designed to provide additional useful information to readers. This section covers initial activities, interesting facts, analogies, and the history of the subject's development, emphasizing key observations and findings. It includes timelines tracking the topic's evolution up to the present day, real-life and industrial applications, case studies related to environmental, sustainability, social, and ethical issues, where relevant, and topics that foster inquisitiveness and curiosity.

RATIONALE

This unit on Fundamentals of Microprocessors helps students to get a primary idea about microprocessor and microcontroller architecture. This unit also discuss about basics of embedded systems and role of microcontrollers in embedded systems.

PRE-REQUISITES

Basic understanding of digital electronics.

UNIT OUTCOMES

List of outcomes of this unit is as follows:

U1-O1: Understand fundamentals of microprocessors.

U1-O2: Compare and contrast microprocessors and microcontrollers.

U1-O3: Comparison of 8-bit, 16- bit and 32- bit microcontrollers.

U1-O4: Discuss criteria for considering a microcontroller.

U1-O5: Explain the concept of embedded systems.

Unit-1 Outcomes	***EXPECTED MAPPING WITH COURSE OUTCOMES*** *(1-Weak Correlation;2-Medium Correlation;3-Strong Correlation)*				
	CO-1	***CO-2***	***CO-3***	***CO-4***	***CO-5***
U1-O1	*3*	*1*	*1*	*1*	*1*
U1-O2	*3*	*1*	*1*	*1*	*1*
U1-O3	*3*	*1*	*1*	*1*	*2*
U1-O4	*2*	*1*	*1*	*2*	*3*
U1-O5	*3*	*1*	*2*	*1*	*2*

1.1 A Historical Background

Welcome to the rapidly evolving world of modern technology. Drones, autonomous cars, smartphones, RFID sensors, augmented reality, and your favorite shopping website are just the beginning! Soon, you will be the driving force behind new additions to this list. The main driving force behind all these inventions is the "Microprocessor" (μP). A microprocessor is a central processing unit (CPU) fabricated on a single integrated circuit (IC) or chip. It functions as the brain of a computer, performing arithmetic, logic, control, and input/output (I/O) operations specified by instructions in programs. Microprocessors are found in a wide range of devices, including computers, smartphones, appliances, vehicles, and more. They interpret instructions, execute tasks, and manage the flow of data within a computing system. Microprocessors come in various architectures and are essential components in modern electronics. This chapter we will discuss historical milestones that paved the way for the evolution of microprocessors, including the emergence of highly important and contemporary models such as the 80X86 series, Pentium, Pentium Pro, Pentium III, Pentium 4, and multicore processors. The world's first microprocessor, the Intel 4004, launched in 1971 was a 4-bit microprocessor.

In 1972, Intel recognized the commercial potential of microprocessors and released the 8008, an enhanced 8-bit version of the 4004 microprocessor. However, engineers quickly realized that the 8008 had limitations in memory, speed, and instruction set, making it unsuitable for more complex tasks. To overcome these challenges, Intel introduced the 8080 microprocessor in 1973, marking the advent of modern 8-bit processors. Tasks that took 20 microseconds (50,000 instructions per second) on an 8008 system were completed in just 2 microseconds (500,000 instructions per second) on the 8080. Moreover, the 8080 was compatible with transistor-transistor logic (TTL), making interfacing simpler and more cost-effective compared to the 8008.

In 1977, Intel released the 8085, an upgraded version of the 8080 and the company's last 8-bit general-purpose microprocessor. Although only slightly more advanced, the 8085 ran software faster than the 8080. Its key improvements included an internal clock generator, an internal system controller, and a higher clock frequency, making it more affordable and practical. With over 100 million units sold, the 8085 became Intel's most successful 8-bit microprocessor.

1.2 The Modern Microprocessor

In 1978, Intel released the 8086 microprocessors, followed by the 8088 about a year later. Both were 16-bit microprocessors that could execute instructions in just 400 nanoseconds (2.5 MIPs, or 2.5 million instructions per second), significantly faster than the 8085. They could also address 1 megabyte of memory, 16 times more than 8085, which allowed them to replace smaller minicomputers in many applications. Additionally, the 8086 and 8088 featured a small instruction cache or queue of 4 or 6 bytes that prefetch instructions before execution, speeding up the process. This concept laid the foundation for larger instruction caches in modern microprocessors. The increased memory size and additional instructions, such as multiply and divide, enabled more advanced applications for microprocessors.

1.2.1 Microprocessor Architecture

A microprocessor is a versatile, programmable, clock-driven electronic device that contains Memory, Control Unit (CU) and ALU (Arithmetic and Logic Unit). It reads binary instructions from memory, accepts binary data as input, processes it according to those instructions, and provides outputs the results. At a basic level, we can compare a microprocessor to the human brain, which also processes information based on instructions stored in its memory. Both microprocessors and the brain have memory systems. Microprocessors use various types of memory, like cache and RAM, to temporarily store data for processing. Similarly, the brain has short-term and long-term memory for storing and retrieving information for cognitive tasks. Just as a microprocessor processes information in a computer, the brain processes sensory information and generates responses. The brain gets input from the eyes and ears and sends processed information to output devices like the face, hands, or feet. However, the complexity of the human brain and its memory is far greater than of a microprocessor and its memory. A typical programmable machine consists of four main components: the microprocessor, memory, input, and output, as shown in Figure 1.1.

The microprocessor, also known as the CPU, is the brain of the machine. It executes instructions, performs calculations, and coordinates all system operations. It reads instructions stored in memory and performs tasks accordingly. Memory, such as RAM (Random Access Memory), provides temporary storage for data and instructions that the microprocessor needs quickly. This includes the program being run and any relevant data required during the operation. Memory allows the microprocessor to quickly access and manipulate information during operation. There is also ROM (Read-Only Memory) that stores permanent instructions or firmware. Firmware is a type of software that provides low-level control for a device's hardware. In our general-purpose computers bootloader is an example of firmware. It is typically stored in **non-volatile memory** like ROM, EPROM, or flash memory, and it remains there even when the device is powered off. Unlike general-purpose software, which can be easily changed or updated by the user, firmware is often embedded into the hardware and is designed to perform specific functions related to the operation of the device.

The input component lets the machine receive data or instructions from external sources. This includes devices like keyboards, mice, touchscreens, sensors, and more. Input devices convert physical or digital signals into a format the machine can understand and process. The output component allows the machine to communicate results or display information to users or other systems. Common output devices include displays, monitors, printers, and speakers. Output devices convert the data processed by the microprocessor into a human-readable or machine-readable format. These four components collaborate to perform tasks, forming a complete system. The physical elements of this system are referred to as hardware. A series of instructions written for the microprocessor to execute a specific task is called a program, and a collection of these programs is known as software. The system illustrated in Figure 1.1 can be programmed to control traffic lights, perform mathematical computations, or operate a guidance system. Based on its application, the system can vary in complexity and is named according to its intended purpose. Microprocessor applications are generally classified into two main categories: reprogrammable systems and embedded systems. Here's an explanation of each:

Reprogrammable Systems

Reprogrammable systems are characterized by their flexibility and versatility. These systems use microprocessors that can be programmed to perform a wide range of tasks. Because the microprocessor can be reprogrammed, it can adapt to different functions as needed. Examples of reprogrammable systems include:

- Personal Computers: These can run various software applications, from word processing to gaming, because the microprocessor can execute different programs.
- Digital Pianos: A microprocessor in a digital piano can generate sounds, process user inputs, and control various functions, demonstrating its ability to perform multiple tasks based on the instructions given.
- Smartphones: These devices can run numerous apps, perform calculations, manage communications, and more, thanks to their reprogrammable microprocessors.

Embedded Systems

Embedded systems are designed to perform specific tasks and are often built into other devices. The microprocessor in an embedded system is programmed to handle particular functions and typically does not change once it is set. These systems are optimized for their specific tasks, making them efficient and reliable. Examples of embedded systems include:

- Automotive Control Systems: Microprocessors in cars control functions like engine management, braking, and climate control.
- Home Appliances: Devices such as microwaves, washing machines, and refrigerators use embedded microprocessors to manage their operations.
- Medical Devices: Equipment like pacemakers and insulin pumps have embedded systems that monitor and regulate bodily functions.

In summary, reprogrammable systems offer flexibility and can be adapted for various tasks, while embedded systems are specialized, dedicated to performing specific functions within a larger system.

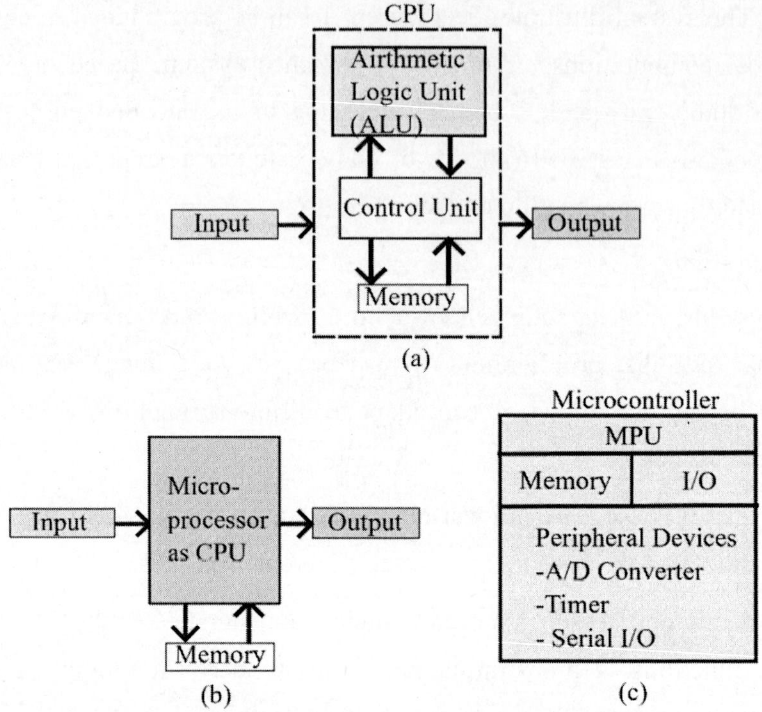

Figure 1.1 Block diagram of a computer [R. S. Gaonkar,1996]

Central Processing Unit (CPU)

We can also view the microprocessor as a critical component of a computer. A block diagram of a digital computer is shown in Figure 1.1(a), illustrating that a computer consists of four main components: memory, input, output, and the central processing unit (CPU). The CPU comprises the arithmetic/logic unit (ALU) and the control unit. It contains various registers for data storage, the ALU for performing arithmetic and logical operations, instruction decoders, counters, and control lines. The CPU reads instructions from memory and executes the specified tasks, communicating with input/output devices to either receive or send data. These input/output devices, also known as peripherals, interact with the CPU, while the control unit manages the timing of these communications.

In the late 1960s, the CPU was built from separate components on different boards. However, with the advancement of integrated circuit technology, the entire CPU could be placed on a single chip. This single-chip CPU became known as a microprocessor, transforming the traditional block diagram in Figure 1.1(a) to the one shown in Figure 1.1(b). When a computer uses a microprocessor as its

CPU, it is referred to as a microcomputer. The terms "microprocessor" and "microprocessor unit" (MPU) are often used interchangeably, with MPU referring to a complete processing unit that includes all necessary control signals. Due to the limited number of pins on a microprocessor package, certain signals, like control and multiplexed signals, need to be generated using additional devices to fully function as an MPU. As semiconductor technology improved, manufacturers were able to integrate not only the MPU but also memory and input/output interfacing circuits onto a single chip, known as a microcontroller or microcontroller unit (MCU). A microcontroller functions like a complete computer on a single chip. As shown in Figure 1.1(c), a microcontroller chip includes additional features such as an A/D converter, serial I/O, and timers, which will be discussed in later chapters.

The microprocessor works with binary digits, which are 0s and 1s, also called bits. A bit stands for "binary digit." Binary digits, also known as bits, are the fundamental building blocks of computing and represent the smallest unit of digital data. Inside the microprocessor's circuits, these 0s and 1s are interpreted as electrical signals, usually shown as two voltage levels: high (1) and low (0). Every microprocessor handles a group of bits called a word. Microprocessors are grouped based on the length of their word. For example, an 8-bit microprocessor works with words that are 8 bits long, and a 32-bit microprocessor works with words that are 32 bits long. When we talk about an 8-bit microprocessor, it means that the data bus, which is like the pathway for data between the microprocessor and other parts of the system, is 8 bits wide. This means the microprocessor can deal with data in 8-bit pieces at a time. In an 8-bit microprocessor, instructions and data are usually in 8-bit binary format. This allows the microprocessor to do basic math, logic, and data manipulation with 8-bit binary numbers.

1.3 8085 Microprocessor

The 8085 microprocessor is an example of an 8-bit microprocessor. It's a chip that processes data in 8-bit chunks at a time. Introduced by Intel in 1976, the 8085 was widely used in early computing devices and embedded systems due to its affordability and versatility. Despite being relatively basic compared to modern processors, the 8085 could handle a variety of tasks, including basic arithmetic, logic operations, and data manipulation. Its architecture included features like an 8-bit data bus, 16-bit address bus, and various registers for storing data and instructions. Overall, 8085 played a significant role in the development of early microprocessor technology and paved the way for more advanced processors in the future. An 8-bit microprocessor has an 8-bit data bus, meaning it can transmit 8 bits of data simultaneously between the CPU and memory or peripherals. The address bus determines the maximum amount of memory that the microprocessor can access. In 8085 microprocessor, the address bus is typically 16 bits wide, allowing it to address up to 64KB of memory (2^16 = 64K locations). The 8085 Architecture is shown in Figure 1.2.

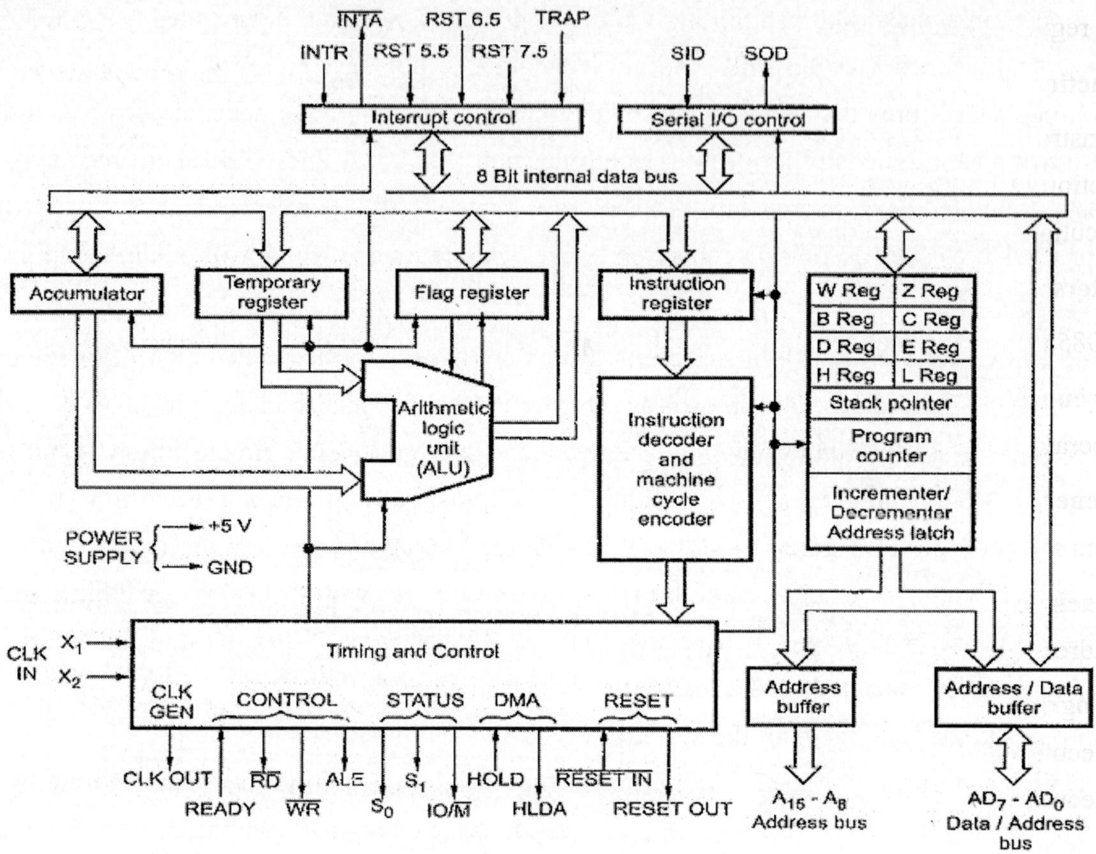

Figure 1.2 8085 Microprocessor Architecture [R. S. Gaonkar,1996]

8085 Architecture

1.3.1 Functional Units of 8085 Microprocessor

Arithmetic Logic Unit (ALU)

The Arithmetic Logic Unit (ALU) executes arithmetic and logical operations on data, handling tasks like addition, subtraction, logical AND, and logical OR. It operates on 8-bit data and sets flags to signal conditions such as zero, carry, sign, and parity after each operation.

Control Unit (CU)

The Control Unit coordinates and manages the operations of the other functional units within the microprocessor. It produces timing and control signals to ensure the proper execution of instructions and to regulate data transfer between different units, maintaining synchronization across the system.

Instruction Decoder

The Instruction Decoder interprets instructions fetched from memory, identifying the type of instruction being executed. It then generates the required control signals to direct the microprocessor in executing the specified operations based on the decoded instructions.

Registers

The 8085 microprocessor contains several registers, each serving specific functions:

- **Accumulator (A):** An 8-bit register used for arithmetic and logical operations. It holds one of the operands during calculations and stores the result.
- **General-Purpose Registers (B, C, D, E, H, L):** These six 8-bit registers are versatile, used for data storage and manipulation.
- **Stack Pointer (SP):** A 16-bit register those points to the top of the stack, which stores return addresses for subroutine calls, local variables, and other data.
- **Program Counter (PC):** A 16-bit register holding the memory address of the next instruction to execute. It automatically increments after each instruction fetch, enabling sequential program execution.
- **Flag Register (F):** An 8-bit register containing flags that represent the status after executing arithmetic and logical instructions. The flags include:
    - **Carry Flag (C):** Set if a carry or borrow occurs in arithmetic operations.
    - **Zero Flag (Z):** Set if the result of an operation is zero.
    - **Sign Flag (S):** Set (1) if the result is negative (MSB set) and cleared (0) for positive results.
    - **Parity Flag (P):** Set for even parity in the operation result, and cleared for odd parity.
    - **Auxiliary Carry Flag (AC):** Set if there is a carry or borrow from bit 3 to bit 4 during arithmetic operations.

Timing Control

Timing control in the 8085 microprocessor is crucial for synchronizing its operations with the external input/output devices and memory. The 8085 uses a clock signal, typically generated by an external crystal oscillator, to regulate the timing of all its internal operations. The microprocessor has a control unit that generates various timing and control signals, such as RD (Read), WR (Write), ALE (Address Latch Enable), and IO/M (Input/Output or Memory), to coordinate the data transfer and synchronization between the CPU, memory, and I/O devices. The timing diagram for each instruction cycle, machine cycle, and T-state helps ensure proper execution and sequencing of instructions, enabling the 8085 to perform accurate and efficient data processing and communication with external devices.

Interrupt Control

Interrupt control in the 8085 microprocessor manages the handling of external and internal events that require immediate attention, allowing the CPU to respond swiftly to changes in the system. The 8085 features five interrupt lines: TRAP, RST7.5, RST6.5, RST5.5, and INTR, with TRAP having the highest priority and INTR the lowest. These interrupts can be maskable or non-maskable, enabling selective enabling or disabling based on the system's requirements. When an interrupt is acknowledged, the microprocessor suspends its current operations, saves its state, and executes an interrupt service routine (ISR) to address the event. After completing the ISR, the CPU restores its previous state and resumes normal execution, ensuring efficient and timely response to critical events while maintaining overall system stability.

1.4 Microcontroller Architecture

A microcontroller is essentially a microprocessor combined with memory and I/O components, all integrated in a single chip. It's a compact and integrated computer system, containing a CPU, RAM (Random Access Memory), EPROM (Erasable Programmable Read Only Memory), as well as input/output interfaces. Additionally, it includes timers and an interrupt controller. For instance, the Intel 8051 is an example of an 8-bit microcontroller, while the Intel 8096 is a 16-bit microcontroller. The Basic Microcontroller Architecture is shown in Figure 1.3. A **microcontroller architecture** consists of a central processing unit (CPU), memory (ROM/flash for program storage and RAM for temporary data), input/output (I/O) ports for interfacing with external devices, and various peripherals, timers and serial communication port. The CPU handles instruction execution, while timers, counters, and interrupts manage precise timing and event-driven tasks. A clock source synchronizes operations, and specialized peripherals like analog-to-digital converters (ADC) and communication modules (e.g., UART, SPI, I2C) enable data processing and interaction with sensors, actuators, and other devices.

CPU	RAM	ROM
I/O	Timer	Serial COM port

Figure 1.3 Basic Microcontroller Architecture

1.5 Microcontroller versus general-purpose microprocessor

The distinction between a general-purpose microprocessor and a microcontroller lies in their architecture and intended applications. General-purpose microprocessors, such as Intel's x86 family (including the 8086, 80286, 80386, 80486, and Pentium), do not include RAM, ROM, or I/O ports on the chip itself, which is why they are referred to as general-purpose microprocessors. When designing a system using a general-purpose microprocessor like the Pentium or 68040, additional external components like RAM, ROM, I/O ports, and timers must be integrated to make the system functional. Although this adds bulk and expense to the system, it allows for versatility, enabling the designer to choose the specific amount of RAM, ROM, and I/O ports needed for the task.

In contrast, a microcontroller combines a CPU (a microprocessor) with a fixed amount of RAM, ROM, I/O ports, and a timer all on a single chip. This integration means that the processor, RAM, ROM, I/O ports, and timer are embedded together, preventing the addition of external memory, I/O, or timers. The predetermined amount of on-chip RAM, ROM, and I/O ports in microcontrollers makes them ideal for applications where cost and space are critical. For instance, in a TV remote control, the extensive computing power of an 80486 or even an 8086 microprocessor is unnecessary; instead, considerations like space, power consumption, and cost per unit are more important. Such applications typically require I/O operations to read signals and control certain functions, making microcontrollers a suitable choice.

1.6 Comparison of 8-bit microcontrollers, 16-bit and 32-bit microcontrollers

The main difference between 8-bit, 16-bit, and 32-bit microcontrollers lies in their data word size. This word size refers to the number of bits that the microcontroller or microprocessor can process at a time. Here's a comparison across various aspects:

Table 1.1 Comparison of 8-bit microcontrollers, 16-bit and 32-bit microcontrollers

Parameter	8 Bit	16 Bit	32 Bit
Word size	Processes 8 bits of data at a time	Processes 16 bits of data at a time.	Processes 32 bits of data at a time.
Instruction set complexity	Simpler instruction set due to the limited data handling.	More complex instruction set to handle wider data and perform more complex operations.	More complex instruction set to handle wider data and perform more complex operations.
Data handling capability	limited data handling capabilities, good for basic tasks.	better data handling capabilities, suitable for moderately complex tasks.	excellent data handling capabilities, ideal for complex calculations and data processing.
Processing speed	slower processing speed due to smaller word size.	faster processing speed than 8-bit microcontrollers.	fastest processing speed among the three.
Power consumption	lower power consumption due to simpler design.	higher power consumption due to increased complexity.	highest power consumption due to increased complexity.
Cost	generally lower cost due to simpler design and lower manufacturing complexity.	more expensive than 8-bit microcontrollers	more expensive than 16-bit microcontrollers

Choosing the right microcontroller for your project depends on your specific needs. Here's a general guideline: 8-bit microcontrollers: ideal for simple tasks like basic control systems, sensor data reading, and low-power applications. 16-bit microcontrollers: suitable for moderately complex tasks like motor control, data acquisition systems, and embedded user interfaces. 32-bit microcontrollers: well-suited for complex applications like image processing, communication protocols, and high-performance embedded systems.

1.7 Embedded System and Its Characteristics

In discussions about microprocessors, the term "embedded system" often comes up. Microprocessors and microcontrollers are widely used in embedded system products, which utilize them to perform a specific task. For example, a printer is considered an embedded system because its internal processor is dedicated solely to receiving data and printing it. This is in contrast to a Pentium-based PC (or any x86 IBM-compatible PC), which can handle multiple applications such as word processing, print serving, bank teller operations, video gaming, network serving, or internet browsing. A PC can run various software applications due to its RAM and an operating system that loads application software into RAM for execution by the CPU. In contrast, an embedded system typically runs a single application that is stored in ROM.

An x86 PC contains or connects to various embedded products, such as keyboards, printers, modems, disk controllers, sound cards, CD-ROM drives, and mice. Each of these peripherals features a microcontroller that performs a specific function. For instance, every mouse has a microcontroller that detects its position and sends that information to the PC. An embedded system is a computer system comprising both hardware and software designed to perform a specific task. These systems can function independently or be integrated into a larger system, often operating with minimal or no human intervention. Here are some key characteristics of embedded systems:

- **Task-specific**: Embedded systems are designed to excel at a particular function. This focus allows them to be optimized for efficiency and reliability in accomplishing that task. For instance, a vending machine is an embedded system.
- **Real-time operation:** Many embedded systems operate within specific time constraints. This means they need to process data and respond to events promptly to maintain functionality. An anti-lock braking system in a car is a prime example, where response time is crucial.
- **Limited resources:** Unlike general-purpose computers, embedded systems typically have restricted resources in terms of memory, processing power, and power consumption. This is because they are optimized for a specific task and don't require the general capabilities of a personal computer.
- **Small size and low power consumption:** Due to their focused nature, embedded systems are often compact and designed to use minimal power. This makes them suitable for integration into portable devices and battery-powered applications.
- **Minimal user interface:** Embedded systems may have very basic user interfaces, or no interface at all, depending on the application. They are programmed to function autonomously based on sensor data or pre-defined instructions.

- **Programmability:** While some embedded systems have fixed functionality, many are programmable. This allows for customization and updates to adapt to changing requirements.

1.8 Role of Microcontrollers in Embedded Systems

Microcontrollers play a critical role in embedded systems, acting as the brain or CPU. They are responsible for the following tasks:

- **Control:** Microcontrollers interpret data received from sensors and other inputs, make decisions based on programmed instructions, and control the overall functionality of the embedded system. This control can involve sending signals to actuators, turning components on or off, or regulating system behavior.
- **Data processing:** Microcontrollers can perform calculations and data manipulation based on the information they receive. This processing capability allows them to analyze sensor data, perform basic mathematical operations, and prepare data for transmission or storage.
- **Communication:** Many embedded systems communicate with external devices or networks. Microcontrollers handle this communication by interfacing with communication peripherals and following pre-defined protocols to transmit and receive data.
- **Program execution:** Embedded systems rely on programs to define their behavior. Microcontrollers fetch, decode, and execute these programs, carrying out the programmed instructions in a step-by-step manner.
- **Real-time operation:** As embedded systems often operate within time constraints; microcontrollers need to respond to events and data promptly. Their design ensures efficient processing to meet these real-time requirements.

In essence, microcontrollers provide the processing power and decision-making capabilities that enable embedded systems to function as intended. Their compact size, low power consumption, and programmability make them ideal for a wide range of embedded applications.

1.9 Overview of 8051 family

The 8051 family, also known as MCS-51, is a group of widely used 8-bit microcontrollers introduced by Intel in 1981. These microcontrollers are renowned for their versatility and are designed to perform specific tasks within a larger system. The 8051 family members typically include CPU with an ALU for performing calculations and an accumulator for temporary data storage. Program memory (ROM or Flash) to store the program instructions. Data memory (RAM) for storing temporary data during operation. Input/Output (I/O) ports for communication with external devices like sensors and actuators. Timers for generating delays or timing events. Serial communication interface for data transmission and reception.

Key Features of the 8051 Microcontrollers:

- **Clock Frequency:** The 8051 microcontrollers typically operate at a clock frequency of 11.0592 MHz This frequency is particularly chosen because it makes it easy to generate standard baud rates for serial communication.
- **Architecture 8-bit CPU:** The central processing unit (CPU) of the 8051 family is 8-bit, meaning it can process 8 bits of data at a time.
- **Registers:** It includes a number of general-purpose and special-function registers, including an accumulator (A), a B register for multiplication and division, and a set of registers organized in banks.
- **Memory:** The 8051 architecture typically features 128 bytes of RAM, 4 KB of ROM, and 34 general-purpose registers. Additionally, it has separate address spaces for program memory and data memory.
- **I/O Ports:** The microcontroller includes four parallel I/O ports (each 8 bits wide) that can be used for interfacing with external devices.
- **Timers/Counters:** The 8051 microcontrollers come equipped with two 16-bit timers/counters, which can be used for various timing and counting operations, such as generating time delays or counting events.
- **Serial Communication:** The 8051 includes a full-duplex UART for serial communication, making it capable of interfacing with other serial devices and supporting various serial communication protocols.
- **Interrupts:** It has five interrupt sources, providing flexibility in handling various events and making it suitable for real-time applications.
- **Power and Performance:** These microcontrollers are designed to be power-efficient while providing sufficient performance for many embedded applications.

Table 1.2 Features of the 8051

Feature	Quantity
ROM	4K bytes

Feature	Quantity
RAM	128 bytes
Timer	2
I/O pins	32
Serial port	1
Interrupt sources	6

1.9.1 Other members of the 8051 family

There are two other members in the 8051 family of microcontrollers. They are the 8052 and the 8031. 8-bit architecture: The core characteristic is the ability to process 8 bits of data at a time.

Table 1.3: Comparison of 8051 Family Members

Feature	8051	8052	8031
ROM (on-chip program space in bytes)	4K	8K	0K
RAM (bytes)	128	256	128
Timers	2	3	2
I/O pins	32	32	32
Serial port	1	1	1
Interrupt sources	6	8	6

Popularity and variants: The original Intel 8051 gained immense popularity due to its ease of use, relatively low cost, and robust instruction set. Seeing this success, other manufacturers were licensed to produce compatible variants. These variants offer variations in memory capacity, additional features like on-chip Analog-to-Digital Converters (ADC) and may differ slightly in instruction sets while maintaining compatibility with the core 8051 architecture. Some notable family members include the 8031 (ROM-less version) and the 8052 (with more RAM and timers).

1.10 Applications of 8051 Microcontrollers

The 8051 family is used in a wide range of applications due to its simplicity, reliability, and the extensive support it has received over the years. Some common applications include:

- **Consumer Electronics:** Used in devices like washing machines, microwave ovens, and remote controls.

- **Automotive:** Employed in engine control systems, airbag controllers, and dashboard instrumentation.
- **Industrial Control:** Utilized in process control systems, robotics, and automation equipment.
- **Communication:** Found in modems, network devices, and other communication equipment.
- **Healthcare:** Integrated into medical devices such as glucose meters, blood pressure monitors, and patient monitoring systems.

UNIT SUMMARY

In this unit we have studied Microprocessor architecture which forms the foundation of digital computing, defining how data is processed, stored, and controlled within a system. An 8-bit microprocessor handles data in 8-bit chunks, while microcontrollers integrate processor, memory, and I/O on a single chip for embedded applications. In contrast, 16-bit and 32-bit microcontrollers offer broader data handling and enhanced performance, suitable for complex tasks. An embedded system is designed for specific functions, emphasizing reliability, real-time operation, and compact design. Microcontrollers, especially the versatile 8051 family, play a critical role in embedded systems by providing efficient control for dedicated tasks across industries.

EXERCISES

Multiple Choice Questions (1 to 8)

1. What is the primary function of the Arithmetic Logic Unit (ALU) in a microprocessor?

   a) Store data b) Perform arithmetic and logic operations

   c) Manage input/output operations d) Control system timing

2. Which of the following is an example of an 8-bit microcontroller?

   a) Intel 8051 b) Intel 8086

   c) ARM Cortex-M3 d) Motorola 68000

3. Which of the following components are typically integrated into a microcontroller chip?

   a) RAM b) ROM

   c) I/O d) all of the above

4. Which of the following components typically need to be connected to a general-purpose microprocessor?

a) RAM
b) ROM
c) I/O
d) all of the above

5. In an 8-bit microcontroller, the data bus width is:

a) 4 bits
b) 8 bits
c) 16 bits
d) 32 bits

6. Which of the following microcontrollers can handle the largest amount of data at once?

a) 8-bit microcontroller
b) 16-bit microcontroller
c) 32-bit microcontroller
d) 4-bit microcontroller

7. Which characteristic typically differentiates a 16-bit microcontroller from an 8-bit microcontroller?

a) Number of I/O ports
b) Word size
c) Clock speed
d) Power consumption

8. An embedded system is designed to:

a) Perform multiple tasks simultaneously
b) Perform a specific task
c) Replace general-purpose computers
d) Execute various application software

Short Answer Questions (9 to 14)

9. An embedded system is also called a dedicated system. Why?
10. What does the term *embedded system* mean?
11. Calculate the maximum addressable memory for an 8-bit microcontroller with a 16-bit address bus.
12. A 32-bit microcontroller has a clock speed of 80 MHz, what is its clock period?
13. What role do microcontrollers play in embedded systems?
14. What are the advantages of using a 32-bit microcontroller over an 8-bit microcontroller?

Long Answer Questions (9 to 14)

15. Compare and contrast 8-bit, 16-bit, and 32-bit microcontrollers in terms of performance and applications.

16. Define an embedded system and list its main characteristics.
17. Explain the basic components of a microprocessor and their functions.
18. Describe the role of microcontrollers in embedded systems and explain how they contribute to the functionality and efficiency of these systems.
19. Provide an overview of the 8051-microcontroller family, highlighting its architecture, features, and common applications.

MCQ answers

1. (b) 2. (a) 3. (d) 4. (d) 5. (b) 6. (c) 7. (b) 8. (b)

KNOW MORE

In the 1970s, Gary Boone of Texas Instruments developed a revolutionary single integrated circuit chip capable of housing all essential components for a calculator, needing only a keypad and display to complete the device. This chip, named TMS1802NC, contained around 5000 transistors, offering 3000 bits of program memory and 128 bits of data memory. Recognizing diverse user needs, TI continued refining this innovation, leading to the commercial release of the TMS1000 microcontroller in 1974. Meanwhile, Intel launched its first microcontroller, the 8048, in 1976 and introduced the highly successful 8051 in 1980. The 1990s saw the advent of electrically erasable flash memories, prompting companies like Microchip and Atmel to incorporate this technology into their microcontrollers. Subsequent advancements have given rise to sophisticated microcontrollers, such as those based on ARM architecture, now integral to numerous aspects of daily life, including automobiles, lighting, communication devices, low-power handheld gadgets like smartphones, and even toothbrushes and toys.

REFERENCES AND SUGGESTED READINGS

1. R. S. Gaonkar, ", Microprocessor Architecture: Programming and Applications with the 8085", Penram International Publishing, 1996
2. Muhammad Ali Mazidi , Janice G. Mazidi, Rolin D. McKinlay 8051 Microcontroller, The: A Systems Approach: Pearson New International Edition 1st Edition, 2013

QR Code for further reading:

NPTEL
Microprocessor

2 The 8051 Architecture

UNIT SPECIFICS

Through this unit we have discussed the following aspects:

- *Internal Block Diagram of 8051 Microcontroller*
- *Address, Data and Control bus*
- *Special Function Register of 8051 Microcontroller*
- *Clock and RESET circuits*
- *Stack and Stack Pointer, Program Counter*
- *I/O ports, Memory Structures, Data and Program Memory*
- *Timing diagrams and Execution Cycles.*

The practical applications of the topics are discussed to foster curiosity, creativity, and enhance problem-solving skills. In addition to providing numerous multiple-choice questions and both short and long answer questions categorized by lower and higher-order levels of Bloom's taxonomy, the unit includes assignments featuring several numerical problems, as well as a list of references and suggested readings for further practice. To facilitate access to additional information on various topics of interest, QR codes have been included in different sections, allowing readers to scan them for relevant supportive knowledge.

Following the practical content, there is a "Know More" section designed to provide supplementary information that benefits users of the book. This section highlights initial activities, interesting facts, analogies, and the historical development of the subject, emphasizing key observations and findings. It includes timelines tracking the evolution of the topics up to the present day, as well as applications relevant to everyday life and industrial contexts across various aspects. Additionally, it covers case studies related to environmental, sustainability, social, and ethical issues where applicable, and concludes with topics that encourage inquisitiveness and curiosity related to the unit.

RATIONALE

This unit on the 8051 architecture illustrates the understanding the internal block diagram of a CPU, including its key components such as the Arithmetic Logic Unit (ALU), address, data and control buses, working registers, Special Function Registers (SFRs), clock and reset circuits, stack and stack pointer, program counter, I/O ports, memory structures, and the distinction between data and program memory, is fundamental to grasping computer architecture. These elements are integral to the CPU's functionality, enabling efficient data processing and instruction execution. Timing diagrams and execution cycles illustrate the synchronization and sequential operations of the CPU, highlighting how instructions are fetched, decoded, and executed.

PRE-REQUISITES

Unit 1st of this book.

UNIT OUTCOMES

List of outcomes of this unit is as follows:

U2-O1: Draw block-level diagram of internal architecture of the 8051.

U2-O2: Enumerate the registers and their functionalities.

U2-O3: State the operation of clock and reset circuitry of the 8051.

U2-O4: Discuss memory organization of 8051.

U2-O5: Draw the timing diagram.

Unit-2 Outcomes	**EXPECTED MAPPING WITH COURSE OUTCOMES** (1-Weak Correlation;2-Medium Correlation;3-Strong Correlation)				
	CO-1	**CO-2**	**CO-3**	**CO-4**	**CO-5**
U2-O1	3	2	2	1	2
U2-O2	3	3	2	1	2
U2-O3	3	2	2	1	1
U2-O4	3	2	2	1	2
U2-O5	3	2	1	1	1

2.1 The 8051 Microcontroller Architecture

In 1981, Intel Corporation introduced the 8051, an 8-bit microcontroller. This microcontroller featured 128 bytes of RAM, 4K bytes of on-chip ROM, two timers, one serial port, and four 8-bit ports, all integrated on a single chip (as illustrated in Figure 2.1). Known at the time as a "system on a chip," the 8051 is an 8-bit processor, meaning the CPU processes only 8 bits of data at once. Data larger than 8 bits must be divided into 8-bit segments for processing by the CPU. Although the 8051 can support up to 64K bytes of on-chip ROM, most manufacturers included only 4K bytes. Further details will be discussed later.

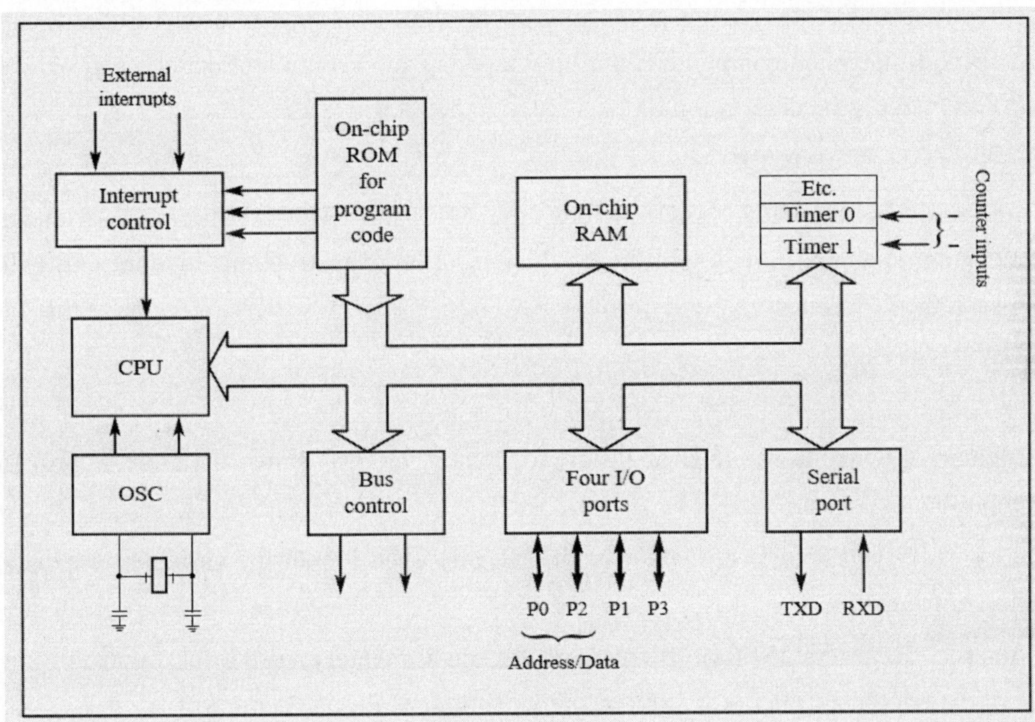

Figure 2.1 Inside 8051 Microcontroller [Mazidi, 2013]

8051 Architecture

The 8051 gained widespread popularity after Intel permitted other manufacturers to produce and market their own variations of the 8051, provided they remained code-

compatible with the original model. As a result, numerous versions of the 8051 have been released, featuring different speeds and varying amounts of on-chip ROM, by more than half a dozen manufacturers. Next, we will review some of these variations. It's important to note that, despite the differences in speed and on-chip ROM, all versions of the 8051 are instruction-compatible with the original model. This means that if you write a program for one version, it will run on any other version, regardless of the manufacturer.

Figure 2.1 shows the block diagram of 8051 microcontroller. The 8051-microcontroller architecture consists of several integrated components working together to execute instructions and manage data efficiently. Following is the description of each block in detail.

1. Central Processing Unit (CPU)

Central to its design is the CPU, which includes the ALU and CU. ALU performs arithmetic and logical operations. The control unit coordinates the execution of instructions by controlling the flow of data between the CPU, memory, and peripherals. The 8051 has a variety of registers that the CPU uses to perform operations.

2. Memory

Program Memory (ROM/Flash): 4KB of Program Memory (ROM) stores the code or program that the microcontroller executes.

Data Memory (RAM): 128 bytes of Data Memory (RAM) Used for storing variables and data during the execution of programs.

Special Function Registers (SFRs): A part of the data memory, used for controlling various operations of the microcontroller (e.g., timers, serial communication, I/O ports).

3. Oscillator and Clock Circuit

Provides the clock signals required for the operation of the CPU and other peripherals. The frequency of the oscillator determines the speed at which the microcontroller operates.

4. I/O Ports

Port 0, Port 1, Port 2, and Port 3: Each port consists of 8 pins, which can be configured as input or output. These ports are used for interfacing the microcontroller with external devices.

5. Timers/Counters

Timer 0 and Timer 1: 16-bit timers/counters that can be used to generate time delays, measure time intervals, or count external events.

6. Interrupts

The 8051 microcontroller has 5 interrupt sources: 2 external interrupts, 2 timer interrupts, and a serial communication interrupt. These allow the microcontroller to respond to external or internal events quickly.

7. Serial Communication Interface (UART)

Provides the capability to communicate with other devices serially (using the TXD and RXD pins).

8. Oscillator and Clock Circuit

Generates the clock pulses required to synchronize all internal operations of the microcontroller.

9. Power Supply

Power-On Reset: Ensures that the microcontroller starts executing the program from the beginning when it is powered on.

2.2 8051 Microcontroller Pin Diagram

The 8051 microcontroller is a popular 8-bit microcontroller used in embedded systems. It has 40 pins, each serving different functions as shown in Figure 2.2. Here's a detailed description of the pin configuration and functions:

Power Supply Pins:

- Vcc (Pin 40): Power supply (+5V).
- GND (Pin 20): Ground.

Oscillator and Clock Pins:

- XTAL1 (Pin 19) and XTAL2 (Pin 18): A crystal of 12 MHz (recommended) is connected between the pins with two 30 pF disc capacitors.

Reset Pin:

- RST (Pin 9): This pin is used to reset processor, RAM and I/O ports. The content of ROM is retained. The Program Counter starts execution from location 0000H. This is an active high reset input for the 8051. The **contents of ROM** (where the program code is stored) are retained because ROM is non-volatile memory.

Port Pins:

The 8051 microcontroller has four parallel I/O ports: Port 0, Port 1, Port 2, and Port 3. Figure 2.3 shows 8051 Microcontroller pins direction.

- Port 0: P0.0 - P0.7 (Pins 32-39): Multipurpose: Acts as both a general-purpose I/O port and a multiplexed address and data bus (AD0-AD7). Open drain: Requires external pull-up resistors to function as a general I/O port. The detailed discussion on multiplexing address and data bus, open drain port is discussed later in this chapter.

- Port 1: P1.0 - P1.7 (Pins 1-8) Dedicated I/O: These pins are used solely for general-purpose I/O.
- Port 2: P2.0 - P2.7 (Pins 21-28) Multipurpose: Acts as both a general-purpose I/O port and the high-order address bus (A8-A15).
- Port 3 (Pins 10-17): P3.0 - P3.7 (Pins 10-17) Multipurpose: Each pin has an alternate function as follows:

  P3.0 (Pin 10): RXD (Serial input for UART).

  P3.1 (Pin 11): TXD (Serial output for UART).

  P3.2 (Pin 12): $\overline{INT0}$ (External interrupt 0).

  P3.3 (Pin 13): $\overline{INT1}$ (External interrupt 1).

  P3.4 (Pin 14): T0 (Timer 0 external input).

  P3.5 (Pin 15): T1 (Timer 1 external input).

  P3.6 (Pin 16): $\overline{WR}$ (External memory write strobe).

  P3.7 (Pin 17): $\overline{RD}$ (External memory read strobe).

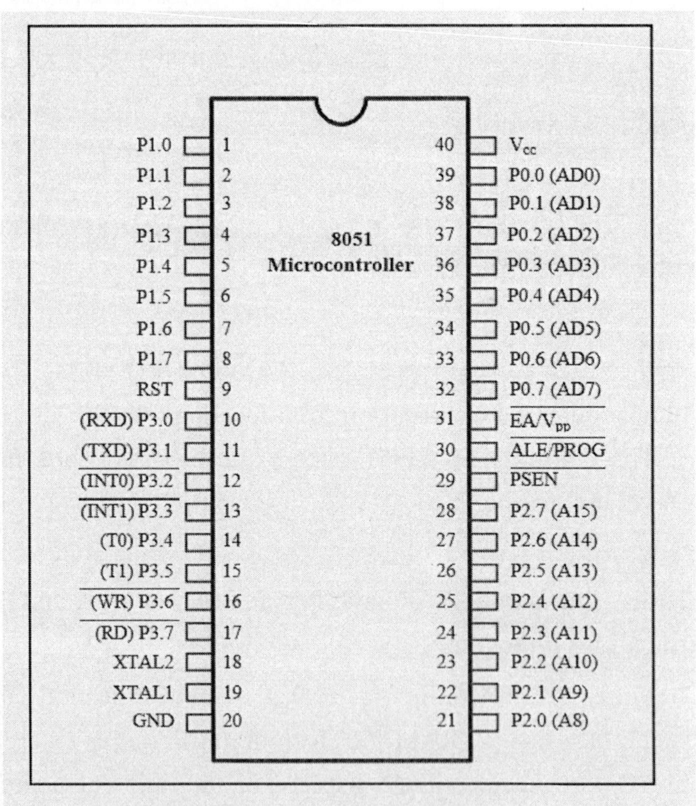

Figure 2.2 Pin Diagram of 8051 Microcontroller [Mazidi, 2013]

Special Function Pins:

- ALE (Pin 30): Address Latch Enable. Used to de-multiplex the address-data bus (AD0-AD7).

  ALE=1, The bus acts like an Address bus.

  ALE=0, The bus acts like a Data bus.

- $\overline{PSEN}$ (Pin 29): Program Store Enable. This is the read strobe to external program memory (ROM).

Function of PSEN:

External Program Memory Access:

The PSEN pin is used to enable the external program memory (such as external ROM or EPROM) during the execution of code stored in that memory. When 8051 executes instructions from external memory, it activates the PSEN pin by pulling it low to signal the external memory to place the contents of the addressed memory location on the data bus. During the fetch cycle, when the microcontroller fetches an instruction from external program memory, the PSEN pin goes low (active).

The external memory recognizes this signal and provides the corresponding byte from the addressed location to the microcontroller.

- $\overline{EA}$ (Pin 31): External Access Enable. When held high, the 8051 executes code from internal memory. When held low, it fetches code from external memory.

When $\overline{EA}$ = 0, External ROM address starts from 0000H and microcontroller discards internal ROM.

When $\overline{EA}$ = 1, External ROM address starts from 1000H. The internal ROM is 4 KB. 4 KB in hexadecimal is 1000H (since 4 * 1024 = 4096 in decimal, and 4096 = 1000H in hexadecimal). The internal ROM occupies addresses from 0000H to 0FFFH (0 to 4095 in decimal). The external ROM address starts from the next address after the internal ROM. Therefore, the external ROM starts from address 1000H (4096 in decimal).

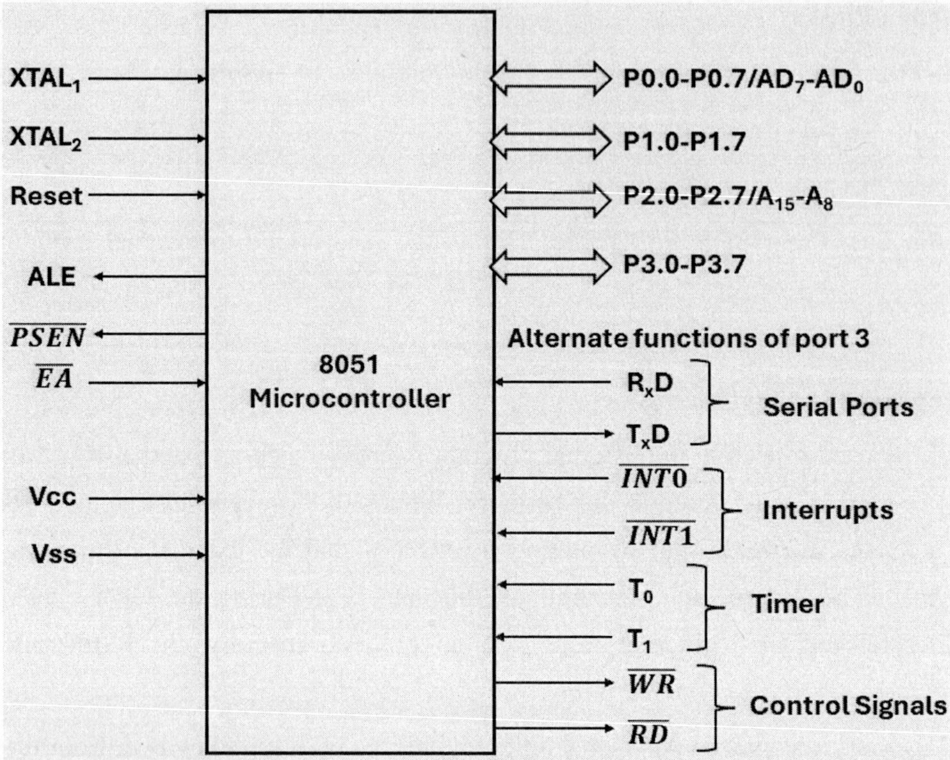

Figure 2.3 8051 Microcontroller pins direction

2.2.1 De-multiplexing of Address and Data Bus

To de-multiplex the address and data bus, the 8051 uses a latch (typically the 74LS373 or 74HC373 latch) and the ALE (Address Latch Enable) signal. ALE is a signal generated by the 8051 to indicate when the address is present on the AD0-AD7 lines. ALE goes high during the first part of the machine cycle, indicating that AD0-AD7 contain the lower byte of the address.

Steps for De-multiplexing:

Address Phase: At the beginning of the machine cycle, ALE goes high. AD0-AD7 lines carry the lower 8 bits of the address. The latch (74LS373) is enabled by the ALE signal to capture and hold these lower 8 bits of the address.

Data Phase: After the address is latched, ALE goes low. AD0-AD7 lines now carry the data. Once **ALE** goes low, it signifies the end of the address phase. The address is now latched, and the microcontroller can proceed to the data phase. During the data phase, the **AD0-AD7** lines, which are multiplexed lines (used for both address and data), carry the actual data to be written to or read from the external memory. The latched address (held by the 74LS373) and the data on AD0-AD7 can be used simultaneously to access external memory. This means that while the microcontroller has access to the specific address stored in the latch, it can also read the data that is present on the data lines. This efficient use of time allows for quicker data transfers, as it eliminates the need for separate cycles to handle address and data.

2.3 CPU

The Central Processing Unit (CPU) of the 8051 microcontroller is the core component responsible for executing instructions and managing various tasks within the system. There are two key Components of the 8051 CPU:

Arithmetic Logic Unit (ALU)

The ALU in the 8051 is an 8-bit unit that performs arithmetic and logic operations. The operations include:

- Arithmetic Operations: Addition, subtraction, multiplication, and division.
- Logic Operations: AND, OR, XOR, and NOT.
- Bit Manipulation: Rotate, shift, set, clear, and complement.

```
ADD A, R0     ; Adds contents of A register and R0 register and stores the result in A.
ANL A, R0     ; Logical AND between register A and R0 register and stores the result in A.
CPL P0.0      ; Complements the value of P0.0 pin.
```

Control Unit (CU)

The Control Unit (CU) orchestrates the execution of instructions by generating the necessary control signals. It fetches instructions from the program memory, decodes them, and then executes them by coordinating with the ALU and other components.

2.3.1 Address, Data and Control Bus of 8051

The 8051 microcontroller uses three primary buses to communicate internally and with external devices: the address bus, the data bus, and the control bus. Each bus has a specific role in the operation of the microcontroller. Here is an overview of each bus and its function in the 8051 architecture:

- **Address Bus**

Purpose: The address bus is used to specify the memory addresses from where the data or instructions are to be read from or written.

Width: The 8051 has a 16-bit address bus, allowing it to address up to 64KB (2^16 locations) of memory. This can split into internal and external memory spaces.

Operation: The address bus carries the address information from the microcontroller to the memory or I/O devices. For example, when the CPU wants to read a byte from memory, it places the address of that byte on the address bus.

- **Data Bus**

Purpose: The data bus is used to transfer data between the microcontroller, memory, and I/O devices.

Width: The 8051 has an 8-bit data bus, meaning it can transfer 8 bits of data at a time.

Operation: Data read from memory or received from an I/O device is placed on the data bus and transferred to the CPU or vice versa. For example, when the CPU reads data from memory, the data at the specified address is placed on the data bus and transferred to the CPU.

- **Control Bus**

Purpose: The control bus carries control signals that coordinate and manage the various operations of the microcontroller. The control bus includes several key signals, such as:

Read: Indicates that the CPU is reading data from memory or an I/O device.

Write: Indicates that the CPU is writing data to memory or an I/O device.

Program Store Enable ($\overline{PSEN}$): Used to enable the external program memory.

ALE (Address Latch Enable): Used to de-multiplex address and data bus.

$\overline{EA}$ (External Access): Determines whether the 8051 accesses internal or external memory. When $\overline{EA}$ is low, the microcontroller fetches code from external memory; when high, it uses internal memory.

2.3.2 Memory, Working Register and SFR (Special Function Register)

The 8051 chip has 4KB on-chip program memory implemented using EPROM/flash technology. It also has 128-byte data memory (RAM). Thus, the RAM location addresses range from 00H to 7F H. However, beyond 7F H (and till FF H), some RAM addresses are defined to correspond to some special function registers. It may be noted that only a few of the address locations between 80 H and FF H are used for this purpose, the rest of the locations are not usable. The internal RAM organization has been shown in Figure 2.4. It consists of the following components.

Addressing in the 8051:

Binary Representation: Each address in the RAM is represented by a 7-bit binary number (2^7=128 locations). The smallest 7-bit binary number is 000 0000, which corresponds to 00H in hexadecimal. The largest 7-bit binary number is 111 1111, which corresponds to 7FH in hexadecimal.

1. **Register Banks (00H to 1FH):** These are the lowest 32 bytes of RAM space grouped into 4 banks of 8 locations each. Each bank consists of registers R0, R1, R2, R3, R4, R5, R6 and R7. At a time, only one bank of registers is active that can be used by the instruction being executed. Activation of banks is controlled by two status bits in the Processor Status Word (PSW) register. Instructions can use the name of a register or a memory address to refer to an operand. For example, the RAM address 04H and register R4 in Bank-0 refer to the same memory location.

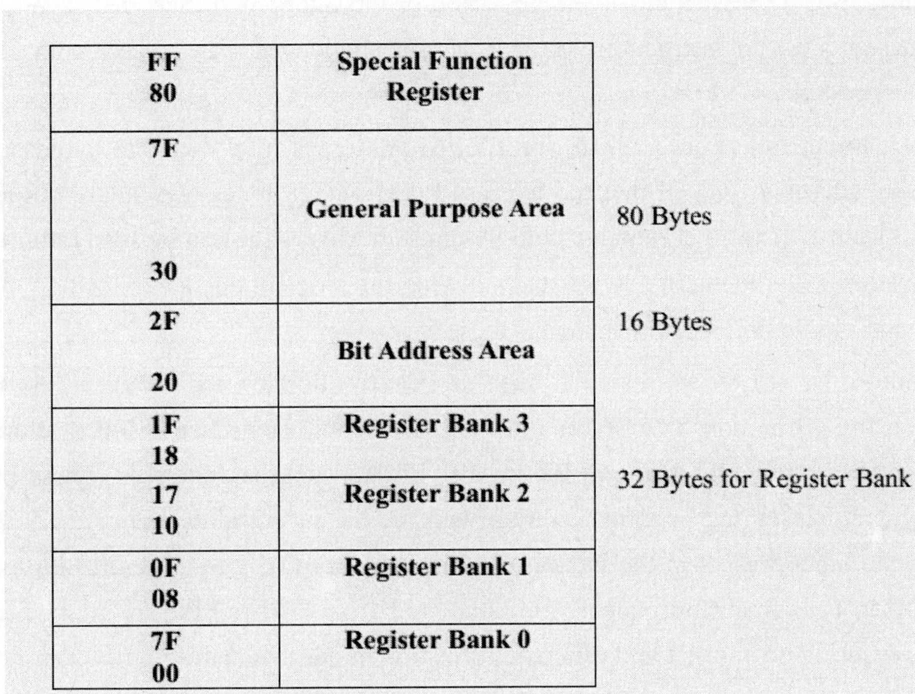

Figure 2.4: RAM Address organization

2. **Bit-Addressable RAM (20H to 2FH):** These are 16 memory locations of which individual bits can be referred to by the bit-manipulating instructions. Such instructions can set/clear a bit, complement it or check the value. Some of the Special Function Registers (SFRs), noted later, are also bit-addressable.

3. **General Purpose RAM (30H to 7FH):** These 80 bytes of RAM locations could be used as general-purpose storage space by the programs. It may be noted that for most of the applications, a stack space is needed for subprograms and interrupt handlers. The stack is also sometimes implemented in this region.

4. **Special Function Registers (SFRs):** Several addresses in the range of 80H to FFH are dedicated for SFRs. Out of the total 128 locations available in this range, only 21 have been used and the

remaining addresses are undefined. A user program should not try to access those addresses, as the result may be unpredictable. SFRs are 8-bit registers. Each SFR has its own special function. They are used by the programmer to perform special functions like controlling the timers, the serial port, the I/O ports etc. Special Function Registers (SFRs) are a critical part of many microcontroller architectures, including the 8051 microcontroller. They are used to control specific functionalities of the microcontroller, such as timers, serial communication, and I/O ports. While SFRs are essential for the operation of the microcontroller, their availability to the programmer and use in instructions present certain challenges, particularly with regard to the number of opcodes.

To reduce the number of opcodes, SFRs are allotted addresses in a way that avoids clashes with existing memory addresses. Given that the internal RAM of 128 bytes uses addresses from 00H to 7FH, the range from 80H to FFH remains entirely unused. This range can be freely allotted to SFRs, ensuring no overlap with the internal RAM and allowing for efficient opcode utilization by leveraging a distinct and non-conflicting address space for these special registers.

Moreover, some SFRs are bit addressable, such as Port 0, allowing individual access to its 8 bits (P0.0 to P0.7) using instructions like SETB and CLR. This could significantly increase the number of opcodes, but to avoid this, bits of the SFRs are also allotted unique addresses. These bit addresses differ from byte addresses and must not overlap with the bit addressable area of the internal RAM. Conveniently, the bit addresses in the internal RAM range from 00H to 7FH (128 bits), leaving the range from 80H to FFH free. Consequently, bit addresses from 80H to FFH are allotted to the bits of various SFRs, ensuring no conflict and efficient utilization of address space.

Accumulator (E0H): Also referred to as A register in the instructions, the accumulator is used in all arithmetic and logic instructions. It holds one of the source operands and acts as destination for such instructions. It is 8-bit bit-addressable register.

B Register (F0H): This is another general purpose 8-bit register, which is also bit addressable. The primary use of B register is as an operand and a destination of multiplication and division instructions.

Stack Pointer (81H): It points to the top of the stack. The stack is implemented in the on-chip RAM. On reset, the 8-bit stack pointer is initialized with 07H. It is not a bit addressable.

Data Pointer (82H – 83H): This is a 16-bit register consisting of two 8-bit parts – Data Pointer High (DPH) with RAM address 83H and Data Pointer Low (DPL) with memory address 82H. It is typically used by the programmer to transfer data from External RAM. It can also be used as a pointer to a look up table in ROM, using Indexed addressing mode. The register is not bit-addressable.

Interrupt Related: Two registers Interrupt Enable Control (IE) and Interrupt Priority Control (IP) are available at RAM addresses A8H and B8H respectively, both being bit addressable. The IE register is used for enabling/disabling certain interrupts while the IP is used to define the relative priorities between the enabled interrupts.

Timer/Counter Related: The current values of timers/counters are held in a few 8-bit registers. For timer-0, the lower byte is stored in register TL0 (memory address 8AH), higher byte in TH0 (8CH). For timer-1, the corresponding registers are TL1 (8BH) and TH1 (8DH). Apart from that, TCON register at 88H controls the operation of the timers/counters. Mode set register TMOD at 89H configures the modes of the timers/counters. Out of all these, only the TCON register is a bit-addressable.

Serial I/O Related: A bit-addressable register SCON at RAM address 98H controls the serial I/O operations. The SBUF register at 99H contains the data received/transmitted serially.

2.3.3 PSW Register (Program Status Word)

It is an 8-bit register known as the "Flag register," primarily containing status flags, as illustrated in Figure 2.5. These flags indicate the status of the current result and are updated by the ALU after each arithmetic or logic operation. Additionally, the programmer can modify these flags. The PSW (Program Status Word) is a bit-addressable register, allowing each bit to be individually set or reset by the programmer. The bits can be referenced either by their bit numbers (e.g., PSW.4) or by their names.

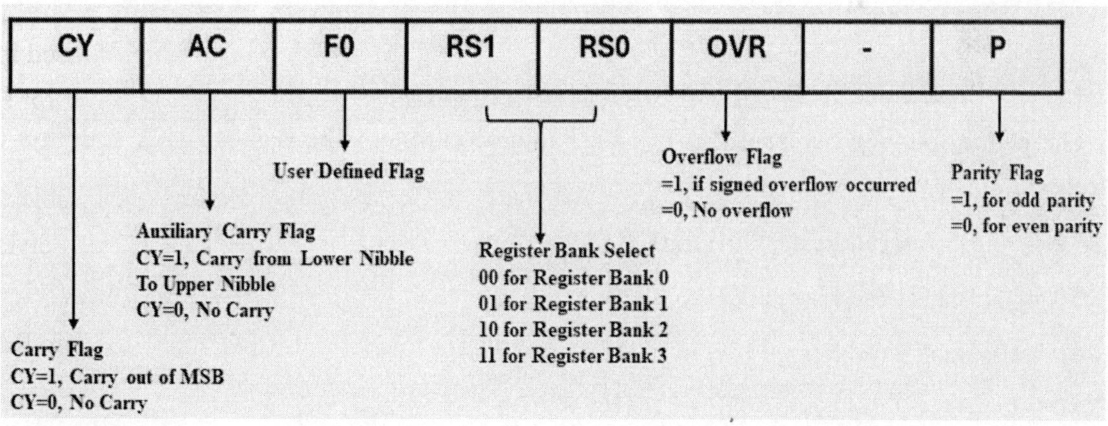

Figure 2.5: Program Status Word Register

Here is a description of each bit in the PSW register:

CY (Carry Flag, Bit 7): This flag is set when there is a carry out from the most significant bit during an addition operation, or a borrow into the most significant bit during a subtraction operation.

AC (Auxiliary Carry Flag, Bit 6): This flag is set when there is a carry out from the lower nibble (bit 3) to the higher nibble (bit 4) during an addition operation. It is used for Binary Coded Decimal (BCD) arithmetic operations.

F0 (User-defined Flag, Bit 5): This is a general-purpose user flag that can be set or cleared by the programmer.

Table 2.1: SFR's Byte Address and Bit Address

	NAME	FUNCTION	BYTE ADDRESS	BIT ADDRESS
Used for holding data and status during Programming	A*	Accumulator	E0H	E7H to E0H
	B*	Arithmetic	F0H	F7H to F0H
	PSW*	Program Status Word	D0H	D7H to D0H
	SP	Stack Pointer	81H	NA
Used in instructions topoint to memory	DPL	Address External Memory	82H	NA
	DPH	Address External Memory	83H	NA
	P0*	I/O Port latch	80H	87H to 80H
Used by the respectiveI/O Ports	P1*	I/O Port latch	90H	97H to 90H
	P2*	I/O Port latch	A0H	A7H to A0H
	P3*	I/O Port latch	B0H	B7H to B0H
Used by the Serial Port	SCON*	Serial Port Control	98H	9FH to 98H
	SBUF	Serial Port Data Buffer	99H	NA
	TCON*	Timer/Counter Control	88H	8FH to 88H
Used for Timer Control	TMOD	Timer/Counter Mode Control	89H	NA
	TL0	Timer 0 Low Byte	8AH	NA
	TL1	Timer 1 Low Byte	8BH	NA
	TH0	Timer 0 High Byte	8CH	NA
	TH1	Timer 1 High Byte	8DH	NA
Used for Interrupt Control	IE*	Interrupt Enable	A8H	AFH to A8H
	IP*	Interrupt Priority	B8H	BFH to B8H
Used for Power Control	PCON	Power Control	87H	NA

*Means the SFR is Bit Addressable |

RS1 (Register Bank Select 1, Bit 4) and RS0 (Register Bank Select 0, Bit 3): These bits are used to select one of the four register banks in the 8051 microcontroller. The register bank selection is as follows:

RS1 RS0 = 00: Bank 0 (addresses 00H to 07H)

RS1 RS0 = 01: Bank 1 (addresses 08H to 0FH)

RS1 RS0 = 10: Bank 2 (addresses 10H to 17H)

RS1 RS0 = 11: Bank 3 (addresses 18H to 1FH)

OV (Overflow Flag, Bit 2): This flag is set when there is a signed arithmetic overflow, meaning the result of an addition or subtraction is too large to be represented in the signed 8-bit format.

(Unused, Bit 1): This bit is not used and is typically read as 0.

P (Parity Flag, Bit 0): This flag is set or cleared based on the parity (even or odd) of the number of 1s in the accumulator. If the number of 1s in the accumulator is even, the parity flag is set to 1; if odd, it is cleared to 0.

The PSW register is crucial for the operation of the 8051 microcontroller as it provides essential status information that can affect the execution of the program.

2.4 Clock and Reset Circuit

The 8051 features an on-chip oscillator but requires an external clock to operate. Typically, a quartz crystal oscillator is connected to the XTAL1 (pin 19) and XTAL2 (pin 18) inputs. This quartz crystal oscillator also requires two capacitors, each with a value of 30 pF, with one terminal of each capacitor connected to ground, as shown in Figure 2.6. It's important to note that the 8051 family supports a range of clock frequencies. The speed of the 8051 refers to the maximum oscillator frequency connected to XTAL. For instance, a 12-MHz chip must be paired with a crystal of 12 MHz or lower. Similarly, a 20-MHz microcontroller requires a crystal frequency of no more than 20 MHz. When the 8051 is connected to a crystal oscillator and powered on, the frequency can be observed at the XTAL2 pin using an oscilloscope. If a frequency source other than a crystal oscillator, such as a TTL oscillator, is used, it should be connected to XTAL1 while XTAL2 remains unconnected, as illustrated in Figure 2.7.

Machine Cycle: A machine cycle refers to the time for a group of related activities, such as accessing the memory. One machine cycle for the 8051 chip consists of several clock cycles. The original 8051 was designed to have 12 clock cycles per machine cycle. Thus, depending upon the frequency of the crystal connected to it, duration of a machine cycle may vary even for this original version of the 8051.

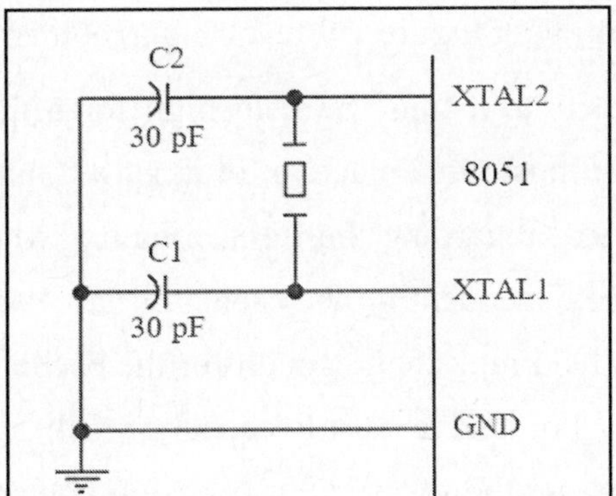

Figure 2.6: XTAL Connection to 8051 [Mazidi, 2013]

A certain number of machine cycles are needed to execute a complete instruction. The data sheet of the 8051 chip lists the number of machine cycles needed for each instruction. As noted earlier, there are many different manufacturers of 8051. With the advancement in VLSI technology, these variants support different maximum clock frequencies.

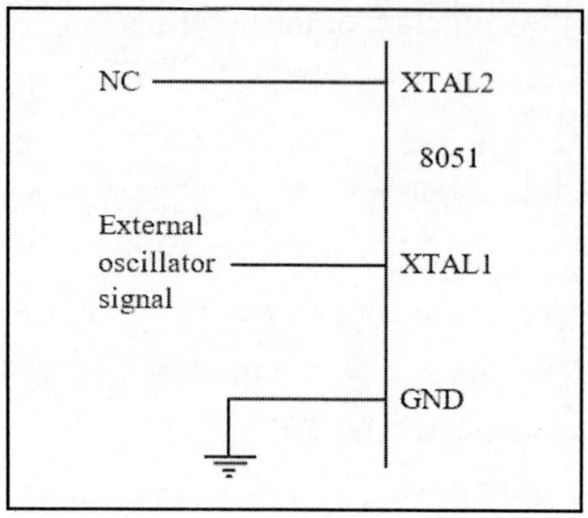

Figure 2.7: XTAL Connection to an External Clock Source [Mazidi, 2013]

The number of clock cycles per machine cycle and the number of machine cycles required for an instruction can vary among different implementations of the 8051. For instance, in the original 8051 chip, a MOV instruction requires 1 machine cycle, which consists of 12 clock cycles. In contrast, the same MOV instruction in the DS89C4x0 requires 2 machine cycles, with each machine cycle needing only one clock cycle.

Pin 9 is the RESET pin, which is an active high input (normally low). Applying a high pulse to this pin resets the microcontroller, terminating all ongoing activities. This process is commonly known as a power-on reset. Activating a power-on reset will cause all register values to be lost and set the program counter (PC) to 0000H. Figures 2.8 and 2.9 illustrate two methods of connecting the RST pin to the power-on reset circuitry, with Figure 2.9 featuring a momentary switch for the reset circuit.

For the RESET input to be effective, it must be held high for a minimum duration of 2 machine cycles. This means the high pulse must remain active for at least 2 machine cycles before returning to low. According to the Intel manual regarding the reset circuitry, when power is applied, the circuit holds the RST pin high for a time dependent on the capacitor value and its charging rate. To ensure a valid reset, the RST pin must be held high long enough for the oscillator to start up plus two machine cycles. While an 8.2K-ohm resistor and a 10-μF capacitor will suffice in most cases, it is still important to consult the data sheet for the specific 8051 version you are using.

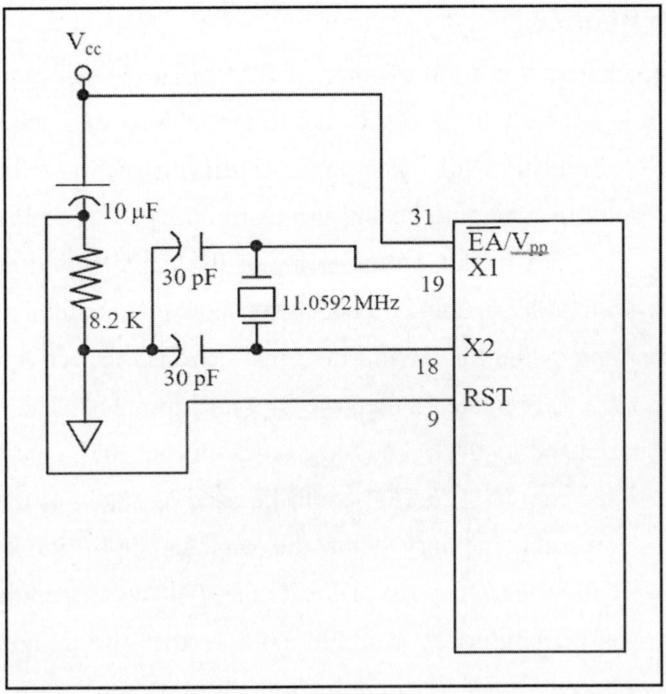

Figure 2.8: Power-On RESET Circuit [Mazidi, 2013]

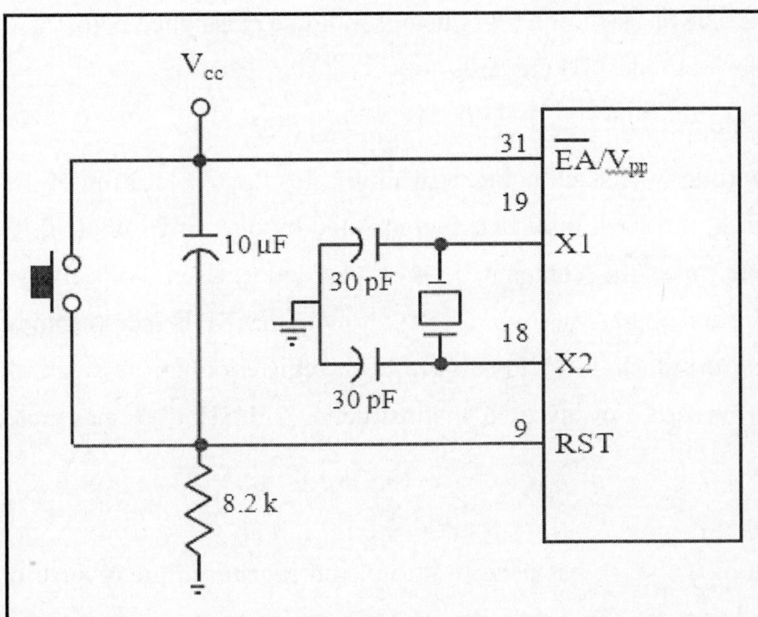

Figure 2.9: Power-On RESET with Momentary Switch [Mazidi, 2013]

2.5 Stack and Stack Pointer

In any computer system, stack is a portion of internal RAM that is used by the CPU to store some temporary information. It is typically used to save the return address of a subprogram call. The 8051 CPU saves the content of PC register while executing a CALL instruction to branch to a subprogram. At the end of the subprogram, there should be a return instruction, RET, that retrieves the value from stack and put it into PC to return to the calling point of the main program. Same is the case for interrupt handlers. Apart from address, some other register contents could also be saved in stack and retrieved back. These are done by the PUSH and POP instructions, respectively. To keep track of the stack, the 8051 CPU has a special register, called the SP (stack pointer). This is an 8-bit register. On reset, the SP register is initialized to 07H. Thus, the stack in the 8051 commences from the RAM location 08H. RAM locations from 08H to 1FH could be used as stack, as the RAM locations 20H-2FH are reserved for bit-addressable memory. Thus, the stack can be of size 24 bytes. In case a stack of size more than 24 bytes is needed, the RAM locations 30H to 7FH could be used with the SP initialized accordingly. Another important point to note is that the default stack locations 08H onwards clash with the portion of RAM used by the registers R0-R7 in Bank-1, as well. The programmer needs to take care of this while writing the code. If the program intends to use the registers in Bank 1, as well as stack, the SP register should be reassigned beforehand to create stack in some different area, for example 30H onwards.

Pushing onto the stack

In the 8051 microcontroller, the stack pointer (SP) indicates the top location of the stack. When data is pushed onto the stack, the stack pointer is incremented by one. In Example 2.1, each execution of the PUSH instruction saves the contents of the specified register onto the stack, with the SP incrementing by 1 for each operation. It's important to note that SP is incremented only once for each byte of data stored on the stack. Additionally, to push registers onto the stack, their corresponding RAM addresses must be used. For instance, the instruction "PUSH 1" pushes the contents of register R1 onto the stack.

Popping from the stack

Popping the contents of the stack back into a designated register is the reverse process of pushing. With each POP instruction, the top byte of the stack is copied to the register specified, and the stack pointer (SP) is decremented by one. This operation effectively removes the data from the stack, allowing the next byte down to become the new top of the stack.

Initial Value of SP on Reset

When the 8051 microcontroller is reset, the Stack Pointer (SP) is initialized to the value 07H. This means that the SP is set to point to memory location 07H.

Understanding the Stack Pointer

The Stack Pointer (SP) is an 8-bit register used to keep track of the top of the stack. The stack is a special area in RAM used for temporary storage during program execution. It works on a Last In, First Out (LIFO) principle. From the Example 2.1 we can understand stack operations in more detail.

Example 2.2: Stack Operations After Push and Pop.

SP = 07H, First Push Operation:

When the first PUSH instruction is executed, the SP is incremented by 1.

SP = 08H

The data is then stored at the address pointed to by the SP (08H).

Second Push Operation: The SP is incremented by 1 again.

SP = 09H, The data is stored at address 09H.

Pop Operation:

When a POP instruction is executed, the data from the address pointed to by the SP is retrieved.

SP = 09H

The data from address 09H is retrieved.

The SP is then decremented by 1.

SP = 08H

2.6 Program Counter

The Program Counter (PC) is a 16-bit register that holds the address of the next instruction to be executed. It automatically increments as each instruction is fetched, allowing the program to proceed sequentially. In the event of a branch instruction, a new address is loaded into the PC. Upon reset, the PC starts at 0000H, and it automatically increments after fetching each instruction, typically by 1 or 2 depending on the instruction size. It plays a crucial role in control flow operations, being updated during jumps, calls, and interrupts to point to new instruction addresses. For instance, JUMP instructions load the PC with a specified address, while CALL and interrupts push the current PC value onto the stack before loading the new address, ensuring the correct sequence of execution and enabling efficient program control.

2.7 I/O Ports (Input/Output Ports)

The 8051 microcontroller has four 8-bit I/O ports, which can each be configured as either input or output, providing a total of 32 input/output pins for interfacing with I/O devices. Upon system reset, all ports (P0, P1, P2, and P3) are automatically configured as input ports. This means they are ready to receive data from external devices. To make a port an output port, you need to write a 0 to it. For example, if you write a 0 to port P0, it will switch from being an input port to an output port. As an output port, it can send data to external devices. If you want to change a port back to an input port, you need to write a 1 to it. For instance, if you had previously set port P0 as an output port by writing a 0 to it, you can make it an input port again by writing a 1 to it. To use any port (P0, P1, P2, or P3) as an input port, you must program it by writing a 1 to it. This step is necessary because, after the initial reset, the ports are ready as inputs but may be reconfigured to outputs during operation.

Port 0 of the 8051 microcontroller, occupying pins 32 to 39, can be utilized for both input and output operations. However, to function correctly in these dual roles, each pin must be connected externally to a 10K-ohm pull-up resistor as shown in Figure 2.10. This is necessary because Port 0 is designed with an open-drain configuration, lacking internal pull-up resistors, which means it can only pull the pin to a low state (logic 0) or leave it floating. The external 10K-ohm pull-up resistors ensure that the pins can achieve a high logic state (logic 1) when required, thereby allowing the port to correctly handle both input and output tasks.

Dual role of port 0

As illustrated in Figure 2.3, Port 0 is designated as AD0–AD7, enabling it to serve as both an address and data bus. When connecting the 8051 to external memory, Port 0 multiplexes address and data to conserve pin usage.

Port 1 consists of 8 pins (pins 1 through 8) and can be utilized for input or output. Unlike Port 0, Port 1 does not require external pull-up resistors, as it has internal pull-ups. Upon reset, Port 1 is configured as an input port. If Port 1 has been set as an output port, it must be reprogrammed by writing 1 to all its bits to revert it back to an input port.

Port 2 also comprises 8 pins (pins 21 through 28) and can function as input or output. Similar to Port 1, Port 2 has internal pull-up resistors and is configured as an input port upon reset. To change Port 2 back to input mode, it must be programmed by writing 1 to all its bits.

Port 3 of the 8051 microcontroller includes 8 pins (pins 10 through 17) and can operate as either input or output, also without the need for external pull-up resistors, just like Ports 1 and 2.

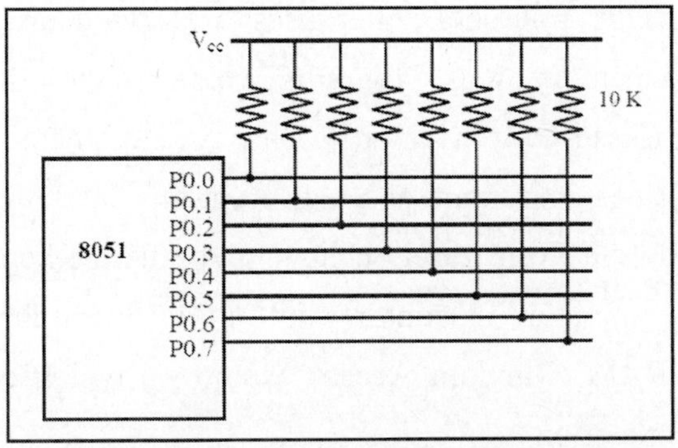

Figure 2.10: Port 0 with Pull-Up Resistors

Table 2.2: Alternate Functions of Port 3

P3 Bit	Function	Pin
P3.0	RxD	10
P3.1	TxD	11
P3.2	INT0	12
P3.3	INT1	13
P3.4	T0	14
P3.5	T1	15
P3.6	WR	16
P3.7	RD	17

Although it is set as an input port by default upon reset, it is frequently used for its special functions. These include providing important signals like interrupts (INT0 and INT1), serial communication (RxD and TxD), timer control (T0 and T1), and read/write controls for external memory (WR and RD). These multiple roles make Port 3 essential for handling various control tasks and peripheral communications in the microcontroller system.

2.8 Memory Structures

The memory in the 8051 microcontroller is divided into Program Memory and Data Memory. Program Memory (ROM) stores the program code being executed, while Data Memory (RAM) is used for temporarily storing intermediate results and variables. Figure 2.11 shows the basic memory structure for 8051. It can access up to 64 KB program memory (ROM) and 64 KB data memory (RAM). The 8051 has 4 Kbytes of internal program memory and 128 bytes of internal data memory. So, we can say that 8051 operates with 4 different memories: Internal ROM, External ROM, Internal

RAM, External RAM. The 8051 microcontroller uses a Harvard architecture, meaning it keeps programs and data in separate memory areas. Programs, which are the instructions the microcontroller follows, are stored in ROM (Read-Only Memory). This type of memory retains its contents even when the power is off, which is important because programs in devices like washing machines, remote controllers, and microwave ovens rarely change and must be kept permanently. On the other hand, data, such as current temperature or cooking time in an oven, changes frequently during use. Therefore, data is stored in RAM (Random Access Memory), which can be easily written to and modified during the device's operation.

2.8.1 Program Memory of 8051

In the 8051 microcontroller, when the EA pin is connected to Vcc, the microcontroller fetches program instructions from the internal ROM for addresses 0000H to 0FFFH, and from external ROM/EPROM for addresses 1000H to FFFFH. If the EA pin is grounded, the microcontroller fetches all program instructions from the external ROM/EPROM, and internal ROM is discarded. The PSEN signal is used to enable the external ROM/EPROM, allowing the microcontroller to read the program instructions stored there.

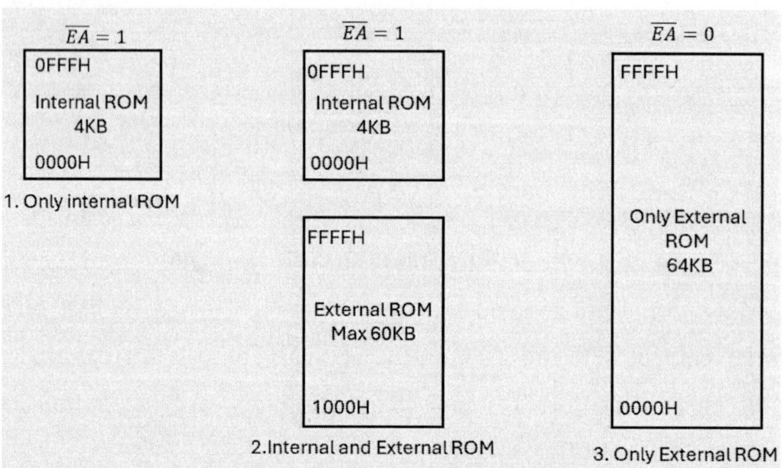

Figure 2.11: Program Memory of 8051

2.8.2 Data Memory of 8051

The 8051 microcontroller's data memory is structured into internal RAM, special function registers (SFRs), and optional external RAM. The internal RAM is 128 bytes (or 256 bytes in some variants), with the lower 128 bytes divided into four register banks (00H-1FH), a bit-addressable area (20H-2FH), and general-purpose RAM (30H-7FH). SFRs, located from 80H to FFH, control various hardware functions like I/O ports, timers, and serial communication. The stack, used for storing return addresses and local variables, resides in internal RAM. External RAM, accessible via the MOVX instruction, can extend up to 64KB, allowing for more extensive data storage beyond the internal capacity. We can discard the internal ROM but we cannot discard internal RAM.

> Example 2.2: Determine the address range of external ROM if 8KB of external ROM is interfaced with the 8051, when $\overline{EA} = 0$.
> Solution:
> Starting address: 0x0000.
> Size of external RAM: 8KB = 8x1024 bytes= 8192 bytes.
> The ending address = Starting address + Size of RAM - 1.
> Ending address = 0x0000 + 8192 - 1 =8191= 0x1FFF.

2.9 Timing Diagrams and Execution Cycles

The CPU needs a certain number of clock cycles to execute each instruction, referred to as machine cycles (MC) in the 8051 family. The original 8051 design used 12 clock periods per machine cycle, but in many newer 8051 models, the number of clocks per machine cycle has been reduced.

A machine cycle in the 8051 microcontroller consists of a sequence of six states (S1 to S6), with each state comprising two clock pulses (oscillator periods), resulting in a total of 12 clock cycles (or 12 T-states).

The duration of a machine cycle depends on the clock frequency. For an 8051 running at a typical clock frequency of 12 MHz, each clock cycle is 1/12 MHz or approximately 0.083 microseconds. Therefore, one machine cycle would be 12 x 0.083 = 1 microsecond.

Most single-byte instructions are executed in one machine cycle (12 clock cycles). Some instructions require multiple machine cycles to complete. For example, a two-byte MOVX instruction takes two machine cycles (24 clock cycles), and certain other complex instructions may take up to four machine cycles (48 clock cycles).

> Example 2.3 Crystal frequency 11.0592 MHz of 8051-based systems. Find the period of the machine cycle.
> Solution: For the 8051 microcontroller, the machine cycle period is determined by dividing the crystal frequency by 12.
> Machine Cycle frequency = 11.0592/12 = 0.9216MHz
> Machine Cycle Period = 1/Machine Cycle Frequency = 1.085 microsecond
> (a) 11.0592 MHz

The execution cycle of an instruction in the 8051 involves fetching the instruction from memory, decoding it, and executing it. The number of machine cycles required varies with the complexity of the instruction.

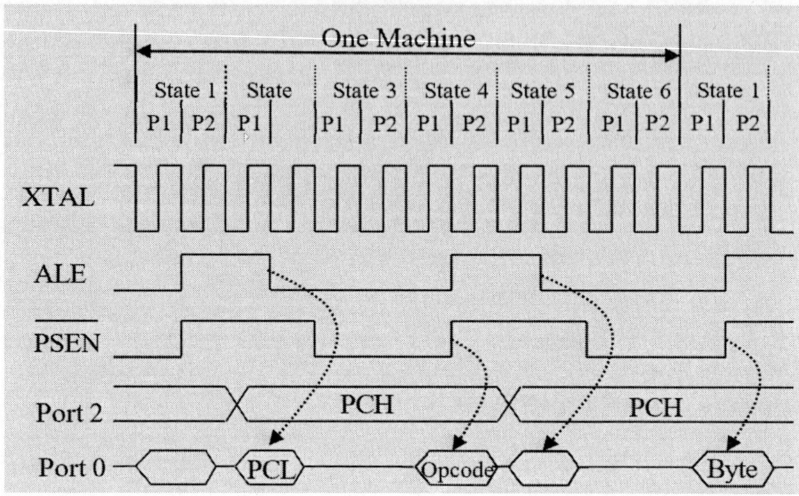

Figure 2.12: Timing Diagram for External Program Memory Access

Fig 2.12 shows a timing diagram corresponding to a read operation from the external program memory. It reads two bytes from the memory. The whole operation takes one machine cycle with the content of the first byte being available at pulse 2 of State 4. The other operand is available at pulse 2 of State 1 in the next machine cycle. That next machine cycle can use this data for any intended operation, such as, moving to some register. In each memory access, Port 2 holds the content of the higher-order address bus. Port 0 functions as the multiplexed address-data bus that holds the lower order address bus content, A0-A7 at the beginning. The falling edge of the ALE signal indicates the time at which the lower-address bus content is stable and could be used to latch the address in the external latch. The line $\overline{PSEN}$ is used as strobe for the external program memory access. The rising edge of $\overline{PSEN}$ is used as strobe for the external program memory access. The rising edge indicates the time at which valid data from the external memory is available in the data bus (that is, Port 0).

UNIT SUMMARY

This unit covers the internal block diagram and essential components of microcontroller architecture. The CPU executes instructions, while the ALU performs calculations. Data flows through the address, data, and control buses, supported by working registers and Special Function Registers (SFRs) for data handling. The Clock and RESET circuits synchronize operations and initialize the system. The Stack and Stack Pointer manage temporary data storage, and the Program Counter tracks instruction sequences. I/O ports enable external interfacing. The memory structure includes Data and Program Memory for separate data and code storage, with timing diagrams illustrating execution cycles for precise processing.

EXERCISES

Multiple Choice Questions (1 to 12)

1. If the crystal connected to the Intel 8051 chip is of frequency 15MHz, length of its machine cycle is

   (A) 1.4 µs (B) 0.8 µs

   (C) 1.0 µs (D) 1.6 µs

2. If RS0 = 1 and RS1 = 0 in the PSW register, the register bank address range in 8051 is

   (A) 00H-07H (B) 08H-0FH

   (C) 10H-17H (D) 18H-1FH

3. In 8051, to make the address range 18H-1FH as the present register bank, the bits RS0 and RS1 in PSW register set to be

   (A) RS0 = 1, RS1 = 1 (B) RS0 = 1, RS1 = 0

   (C) RS0 = 0, RS1 = 1 (D) RS0 = 0, RS1 = 0

4. Which of the following is NOT a valid status word bit in 8051?

   (A) P (B) S

   (C) CY (D) AC

5. When RESET the microcontroller, the value of SP in 8051 is

   (A) 07H (B) 00H

   (C) 0FH (D) 1FH

6. What is the maximum size of the external data memory that can be interfaced with the 8051 microcontroller ?

   (A) 64 KB (B) 128 KB

   (C) 256 KB (D) 512 KB

7. What is the address range of the internal RAM in the 8051 microcontroller?

   (A) 00H to 7FH (B) 00H to FFH

   (C) 00H to 3FH (D) 00H to EFH

8. What is the purpose of the DPTR (Data Pointer) register in the 8051 microcontroller?

   (A) To store temporary data

   (B) To point to the address of the next instruction

   (C) To point to data in external memory

   (D) To store the status of the program

9. If the Stack Pointer (SP) is set to 07H, where will the first pushed value be stored in the 8051 microcontroller?

   (A) 07H (B) 08H

   (C) 09H (D) 0AH

10. What happens to the 8051 microcontroller when a reset is applied?

    (A) It continues executing the current instruction

    (B) It stops all operations and goes into low power mode

    (C) It restarts the execution from address 0000H

    (D) It enters a debugging mode

11. What is the purpose of the clock oscillator in the 8051 microcontroller?

    (A) To control the power supply

    (B) To synchronize the internal operations of the microcontroller

    (C) To manage the input/output operations

    (D) To store program data

12. Which component in the reset circuit ensures that the reset signal is applied for a sufficient duration to reset the 8051 microcontroller properly?

    (A) Resistor (B) Capacitor

    (C) Inductor (D) Diode

Short Answer Questions (13 to 16)

13. Describe the reset mechanism in the 8051 microcontroller. What happens during a reset operation?

14. Explain the concept of machine cycles and instruction cycles in the 8051 microcontroller.

15. Determine the address range of external ROM if 16KB of external ROM is interfaced with the 8051, when $\overline{EA} = 1$.

16. Differentiate between data memory and program memory in the 8051 microcontroller. How is each type of memory accessed?

Long Answer Questions

17. Describe the internal block diagram of the 8051 microcontroller and explain the role of each block.
18. What operations can the ALU of the 8051 microcontroller perform, and how does it interact with other components of the CPU?
19. List some of the key Special Function Registers (SFRs) in the 8051 microcontroller and explain their functions.
20. How does the clock circuit of the 8051 microcontroller work, and Why is it important for the operation of the microcontroller?
21. Given the crystal frequencies for three different 8051-based systems, calculate the machine cycle period for each case: (A) 16 MHz and (B) 20 MHz.

MCQ Answer

1. (B) 2. (C) 3. (A) 4. (B) 5. (A) 6. (A) 7. (A) 8. (C) 9. (B) 10. (C) 11. (B) 12. (B)

KNOW MORE

The 8051, Intel's first microcontroller, was the brainchild of Robert Noyce, Gordon Moore, and Andy Grove, with its instruction set crafted by John H. Wharton. As the first CPU-on-a-chip to offer bit manipulation, the 8051 introduced several groundbreaking features, including the use of Register Banks. This innovation, later adopted by advanced processors like ARM, facilitates efficient context switching—the process of shifting from one executing process to another. During context switching, typically, all CPU registers must be saved before suspending the current process to begin another. This is especially important for handling interrupts, where preserving the current state is crucial for resuming processing later. However, with Register Banks, if the interrupt routine utilizes a different set of registers, saving and restoring the original registers become unnecessary, significantly speeding up the context switching process.

REFERENCES AND SUGGESTED READINGS

1. Muhammad Ali Mazidi, Janice G. Mazidi, Rolin D. McKinlay 8051 Microcontroller, The: A Systems Approach: Pearson New International Edition 1st Edition, 2013
2. Microcontrollers and Applications by Prof. Santanu Chattopadhyay, AICTE e-kumbh.

QR Code for further reading:

NPTEL Microcontroller

Intel 8051 manual

3 Instruction Set and Programming

UNIT SPECIFICS

Through this unit we have discussed the following aspects:

- *Addressing modes*
- *8051 Instruction set*
- *Assembly language programming*
- *C language programming*
- *Assemblers and compilers*
- *Programming and debugging tools.*

The practical applications of the topics are discussed to stimulate curiosity and creativity while enhancing problem-solving skills. In addition to numerous multiple-choice questions and short and long answer questions categorized by lower and higher-order Bloom's taxonomy, the unit includes assignments featuring various numerical problems, as well as a list of references and suggested readings for further practice. Notably, QR codes are provided in different sections for readers to scan and access additional relevant information on various topics of interest.

Following the practical content, there is a "Know More" section designed to provide supplementary information that benefits the readers. This section highlights the initial activity, includes interesting facts and analogies, and outlines the historical development of the subject, emphasizing key observations and findings. It also features timelines detailing the evolution of the relevant topics up to the present day, along with real-life and industrial applications of the subject matter across various aspects. Additionally, it addresses case studies related to environmental, sustainability, social, and ethical issues where applicable, and concludes with topics aimed at fostering inquisitiveness and curiosity within the unit.

RATIONALE

This unit begins with addressing modes to provide a fundamental understanding of how a processor accesses data, followed by the 8051-instruction set. This foundational knowledge enables students to engage in assembly language programming, offering hands-on experience with low-level hardware interaction. With a grasp of assembly, the unit progresses to C language programming, introducing higher-level, structured coding practices essential for complex and portable software development. Subsequently, learning about assemblers and compilers explains the translation of code into machine instructions, crucial for effective programming. Finally, the course covers programming and debugging tools, equipping students with the necessary utilities for efficient code development, troubleshooting, and optimization. This logical progression ensures a comprehensive understanding of both low-level and high-level programming in embedded systems.

PRE-REQUISITES

Unit 1st, 2nd of the book.

UNIT OUTCOMES

List of outcomes of this unit is as follows:

U3-O1: Understand the addressing modes of the 8051.

U3-O2: Demonstrate the skills in Assembly Language Programming of microcontroller.

U3-O3: Implement basic C programs to perform microcontroller-based tasks.

U3-O4: Programming timers and counters of 8051.

U3-O5: Compile and debug programs using advanced programming tools.

Unit-3 Outcomes	*EXPECTED MAPPING WITH COURSEO UTCOMES (1-Weak Correlation;2-Medium Correlation;3-Strong Correlation)*				
	CO-1	*CO-2*	*CO-3*	*CO-4*	*CO-5*
U3-O1	3	2	2	1	1
U3-O2	3	3	2	2	1
U3-O3	2	3	3	1	1
U3-O4	2	3	2	3	1
U3-O5	1	2	2	1	3

3.1 Introduction

The 8051 processor has a variety of instructions, totaling 111, which come in sizes of 1-byte, 2-bytes, and 3-bytes. Specifically, there are 49 single-byte instructions, 45 two-byte instructions, and 17 three-byte instructions. Every version of the 8051 uses the same instruction set, which is optimized for 8-bit operations. Each instruction includes an opcode, or mnemonic, that tells the CPU what action to perform, which might involve using zero, one, or two operands. These actions can include moving data between registers and memory, performing arithmetic and logical operations, controlling I/O devices, and manipulating data at the byte or bit level. The processor offers flexibility in specifying where operands come from, such as registers, memory locations, or immediate values, which are known as addressing modes. Even though modern compilers allow programmers to write code in high-level languages and skip assembly programming, understanding the 8051's instruction set is crucial for debugging at the machine code level, since machine code directly corresponds to assembly instructions. Most Integrated Development Environments (IDEs) have disassembler tools that can convert machine code back into assembly language, helping designers troubleshoot and understand their systems more deeply.

3.2 Assembly Language

An assembly language program is composed of multiple lines of instructions, each of which typically consists of four main components: an optional label, a mandatory mnemonic, operands, and an optional comment. The general format of an assembly instruction is:

[label:] mnemonic [operands] [; comment]

Components of an Assembly Instruction:

Label (optional):

Purpose: Acts as a marker or reference point within the program.

Usage: Commonly used as targets for jump or branch instructions.

Example: In the instruction HERE: MOV A, R0 ; A gets content of R0, HERE is the label.

Mnemonic (Opcode) (mandatory):

Purpose: Represents the operation to be performed by the CPU.

Function: Opcode Defines what action the CPU should take, such as moving data, performing arithmetic operations, or controlling the flow of the program.

Example: In the instruction HERE: MOV A, R0 ; A gets content of R0, MOV is the mnemonic or opcode indicating a move operation.

Operands (variable):

Purpose: Specifies the data or the locations of data to be operated on by the mnemonic.

Types: Can include registers, memory addresses, immediate values, etc.

Example: In MOV A, R0, A and R0 are operands. This means the content of register R0 is moved to register A.

Comment (optional):

Purpose: Provides human-readable explanations or notes about instruction.

Usage: Comments are ignored by the assembler and are typically used to make the code more understandable.

Example: MOV A, R0 ; A gets content of R0,

In the above example, "A gets content of R0" is the comment.

3.2.1 Additional Components of an Assembly Language Program

Beyond the basic instructions, an assembly language program may include:

Assembler Directives:

Purpose: Provides instructions to the assembler on how to process the code but does not generate machine code themselves.

Function: Can include instructions for setting up constants, defining data segments, including files, or setting the start address for execution.

Examples:

ORG 0H (sets the origin to address 0)

EQU (defines a constant)

INCLUDE (includes another file)

Storage Declarations:

Purpose: Define storage space for variables or constants.

Function: Allocate memory and possibly initialize data.

Examples:

DB (Define Byte, used to allocate a byte of storage)

DW (Define Word, used to allocate a word of storage)

DS (Define Storage, used to reserve a specified amount of storage space)

3.3 Addressing Modes

The addressing modes supported by a processor offer different methods for the programmer to specify the operands of an instruction. The 8051 CPU provides several options for identifying operands within an instruction, allowing the CPU to access data in various ways. The data could reside in a register, in memory, or be supplied as an immediate value. These different methods of accessing data are referred to as addressing modes. The specific addressing modes available in a microprocessor are established during its design and cannot be altered by the programmer. The 8051 features a total of seven distinct addressing modes, which are as follows:

1. Immediate
2. Register
3. Direct
4. Register indirect
5. Indexed
6. Bit inherent addressing
7. Bit direct addressing

In the following, each of these addressing modes have been discussed in detail, with suitable examples.

3.3.1 Immediate Addressing Mode

In immediate addressing mode, the source operand is a constant value. When the instruction is written, the operand appears right after the opcode and is preceded by the sign "#". This mode is used to load values directly into any register, including the DPTR register.

```
MOV R0,#20H ;load 25H into A
MOV A,#60 ;load the decimal value 60 into R4
MOV DPTR,#4521H ;DPTR=4512H
```

Although the DPTR register is 16 bits, it can also be accessed as two 8-bit registers: DPH for the high byte and DPL for the low byte

3.3.2 Register Addressing Mode

In register addressing mode, the operands are in the CPU registers. This mode is efficient because it allows quick access to the data. Below are some examples of register addressing mode in the 8051-assembly language, along with comments to explain each instruction.

```
MOV A, R1  ; Move the content of register R1 to A
MOV R2, A  ; Move the content of the accumulator A to R2
```

Note: It's important to note that the source and destination registers must be the same size. For example, writing "MOV DPTR, A" will result in an error because the source is an 8-bit register and the destination is a 16-bit register. Note that we can move data between the accumulator and Rn (where n = 0 to 7), but moving data directly between Rn registers is not allowed. For example, the instruction "MOV R4, R6" is invalid.

3.3.3 Direct Addressing Mode

In direct addressing mode, the instruction includes the address of the operand, which is stored at a specific memory location. This mode can be used to specify only on-chip RAM locations (Internal RAM) as operands.

The 8051 microcontroller has 128 bytes of RAM, assigned addresses from 00 to 7FH. Here's a summary of how these 128 bytes are allocated:

1. RAM locations 00–1FH are used for the register banks and stack.
2. RAM locations 20–2FH are reserved as bit-addressable space for storing single-bit data (discussed in Chapter 2).
3. RAM locations 30–7FH are available for storing byte-sized data.

All 128 bytes of RAM in the 8051 can be accessed using direct addressing mode, but it's most commonly used for RAM locations between 30H and 7FH. This preference arises because register bank locations (0–1FH) are accessed directly by the register names R0–R7, eliminating the need for direct addressing for these locations.

In direct addressing mode, data is stored in a specific RAM memory address, which is included directly in the instruction. This differs from immediate addressing mode, where the actual data (operand) is specified in the instruction itself. The "#" symbol distinguishes immediate addressing mode, while direct addressing lacks this symbol. See the examples below and note that direct addressing does not use the "#" sign.

```
MOV R0,50H ;Load the content of RAM location 50H in R0
MOV 50H,A ;Load the content of A in RAM location 50H
```

As previously mentioned, RAM locations 0 to 7 are allocated to bank 0 registers, labeled R0 to R7. These registers can be accessed in two ways, as demonstrated below.

```
MOV A,3 ;is the same as
MOV A,R3 ;which means copy R3 into A
```

Among the registers discussed, R0–R7 are part of the 128 bytes of RAM memory. In contrast, registers such as A, B, PSW (Program Status Word), and DPTR (Data Pointer) fall into a separate category known as SFRs (Special Function Registers) in the 8051 microcontroller. SFRs are crucial for managing various microcontroller functions and are frequently used in programming.

SFRs can be accessed by their names, which is more intuitive, or by their specific addresses. For example, in the 8051 microcontroller:

- Register A is located at address E0H.
- Register B is located at address F0H.

Accessing SFRs by their names (like A, B, PSW, DPTR) simplifies programming tasks, whereas accessing them by their addresses provides direct control over their memory locations. These SFRs play crucial roles in managing data, status flags, and memory addressing within the microcontroller's operation.

```
MOV E0H, #48H ; Equivalent to MOV A, #48H - loads the value 48H
into register A (A = 48H)
MOV F0H, #22H ; Equivalent to MOV B, #22H - loads the value 22H
into register B (B = 22H)
```

3.3.4 Register Indirect Addressing Mode

In register indirect addressing mode, a register acts as a pointer to access data. In the 8051 microcontroller, only registers R0 and R1 can serve this purpose for accessing data stored in RAM. Registers R2 to R7 cannot be used to hold the address of an operand in RAM when using register indirect addressing mode. When R0 or R1 are used as pointers to RAM addresses, they must be prefixed with the "@" sign in instructions. This signifies that the content of the register (R0 or R1) should be treated as an address pointing to the actual data in RAM.

```
MOV A, @R0       ; Moves the contents of the RAM location pointed
to by R0 into register A
MOV @R1, B       ; Moves the contents of register B into the RAM
location pointed to by R1
MOVX A, @DPTR    ; Moves data from the external RAM address pointed
to by DPTR (a 16-bit register) into register A
```

3.3.5 Index Addressing Mode

Indexed addressing mode in microcontrollers like the 8051 is specifically used to access data stored in code memory (internal or external ROM) through an index register. This mode is commonly applied to retrieve values from look-up tables stored in the 8051's program ROM. The instruction MOVC A, @A+DPTR is designed for this purpose, combining the 16-bit DPTR register with the accumulator (A) to form the address of the desired data in ROM. Here, MOVC (where "C" stands for code) is used because the data is located in program memory. The instruction adds the value in A to the DPTR register to calculate the 16-bit address of the data in ROM.

In embedded systems, Read-Only Memory (ROM) is typically used for storing static data—data that remains constant during normal device operation. This contrasts with dynamic data, which can be modified at runtime and is stored in RAM.

```
MOV DPTR, #2001H ; Load the base address 2001H
MOV A, #02H ; Load the index value into the accumulator MOVC A,
@A+DPTR ; Read the byte from (DPTR + A)
```

3.3.6 Bit inherent addressing

Bit inherent addressing uses predefined instructions that inherently operate on specific bits, usually within the accumulator or program status word (PSW). Typically used for bit-level operations that do not require specifying an address, such as testing or manipulating specific control bits. In **bit inherent addressing**, the instruction implicitly refers to a specific bit or condition, and you don't specify the bit address manually. The instruction is "inherent" to the processor operation, and the specific bit it operates on is predefined by the instruction itself.

```
SETB C ; Set the carry flag (C = 1)
CLR C ; Clear the carry flag (C = 0)
CPL C ; Complement the carry flag (C = NOT C)
```

3.3.7 Bit direct addressing

In the 8051 microcontroller, bit direct addressing is used to perform operations directly on specific bits of certain registers or memory locations. This addressing mode is unique to the 8051 due to its ability to directly manipulate individual bits, making it efficient for control-oriented tasks such as setting or clearing flags.

Key Points of Bit direct Addressing:

1. Direct Bit Manipulation: Allows direct access to and manipulation of individual bits in special function registers (SFRs) and bit-addressable RAM.
2. In the 8051 microcontroller, many SFRs are bit-addressable, allowing individual bits to be accessed and modified independently. This feature enables precise control over specific functions within the microcontroller without impacting the other bits in the same register.
3. Instructions: 8051 provides specific instructions for bit manipulation.

```
SETB P1.0; Sets bit 0 of Port 1 to 1.
SETB TR0; Sets the TR0 bit in the TCON register (starts Timer 0).
CLR P1.0; Clears bit 0 of Port 1 (sets it to 0).
```

3.4 8051 Instruction Set

The 8051 microcontroller has a comprehensive instruction set, consisting of 255 instructions in total. These instructions are designed to perform a variety of operations, including data transfer, arithmetic operations, logical operations, control transfer, and bit manipulation.

3.4.1 Data Transfer Instructions

The 8051 microcontroller provides a variety of data transfer instructions that allow for the movement of data between different registers, memory locations, and external memory. The opcodes in this category include MOV, MOVC, MOVX, PUSH, POP, XCH, and XCHD. Each of these will be explained in detail below.

1. **MOV**: This copies a byte from the source location to the destination only for internal RAM.

   MOV *dest-byte*, *source-byte*

Depending upon the addressing mode used to specify the destination and the source, several subvariants are possible.

(a) Register A (Accumulator) as destination: Here, any of the available addressing modes can be used to specify the source, as shown in Table 3.1.

Table 3.1: MOV with A as destination

Addressing Mode	Format	Example	Contents of A after the execution of each instruction
Immediate	MOV A, #data	MOV A, #25H	A = 25H

Addressing Mode	Format	Example	Contents of A after the execution of each instruction
Register	MOV A, Rn	MOV A, R3	A = Content of R3
Direct	MOV A, direct	MOV A, 45H	A = RAM[45H]
Indirect	MOV A, @Ri (i = 0 or 1)	MOV A, @R1	A = RAM[(R1)]
Note: *"MOV A, A" not allowed*			

(b) Register A (Accumulator) as source: In this case the destination operand can only be from either of the following modes – register, direct or register indirect. Some examples have been shown in Table 3.2.

Table 3.2: MOV with A as source

Addressing Mode	Format	Example	Contents of Register after the execution of each instruction
Register	MOV Rn, A	MOV R2, A	R2 = Content of A
Direct	MOV direct, A	MOV 43H, A	RAM[43H] = A
Indirect	MOV @Ri, A (i = 0 or 1)	MOV @R1, A	RAM[(R1)] = A

(c) Bank register as destination. Any of the registers R0-R7 in the current bank could be used as the destination. The source operand may be an immediate one, the Accumulator or a memory address. The cases have been shown in Table 3.3.

Table 3.3: MOV with bank register as destination

Addressing Mode	Format	Example	Contents of Register after the execution of each instruction
Register	MOV Rn, A	MOV R3, A	R3 = Content of A
Immediate	MOV Rn, #data	MOV R4, #46H	R4 = 46H
Direct	MOV Rn, direct	MOV R0, 44H	R0 = RAM[44H]

(d) Direct memory address as destination. With the destination operand in direct addressing mode, the source may be of any other mode including direct addressing. Table 3.4 shows the cases individually.

Table 3.4: MOV with direct memory address as destination

Addressing Mode	Format	Example	Contents of Register after the execution of each instruction
Register	MOV direct, Rn	MOV 40H, R2	RAM[40H] = R2
Immediate	MOV direct, #data	MOV 40H, #20H	RAM[40H] = 20H
Direct	MOV direct, direct	MOV 1, 5	RAM[1] = RAM[5]
Indirect	MOV direct, @Ri (i = 0 or 1)	MOV 40H, @R0	RAM[40H] = RAM[(R0)]

(e) Indirect memory address as destination. The registers R0 and R1 could be used as pointer for the destination address of MOV instruction. Table 3.5 shows the alternatives for the source operand.

Table 3.5: MOV with indirect memory address as destination

Addressing Mode	Format	Example	Contents of RAM location after the execution of each instruction
Register	MOV @Ri, A	MOV @R0, A	RAM[(R0)] = Content of A
Immediate	MOV @Ri, #data	MOV @R0, #20H	RAM[(R0)] = 20H
Direct	MOV @Ri, direct (i = 0 or 1)	MOV @R0, 5	RAM[(R0)] = RAM[5]

(f) Bit operands. MOV instruction can also be used to copy one bit to another. Following are a few examples. The addressing mode of the operands is bit direct addressing.

```
MOV C, PSW.0      ; Bit-0 (Parity bit) copied to Carry bit (PSW.7)
MOV P1.5, C       ; Carry copied to Port 1, bit 5
```

(g) 16-bit data movement. The MOV instruction works for 16-bit data as well. One of the very important 16-bit registers in the 8051 CPU is DPTR which can be used by the programmer to access external memory. The DPTR register can be initialized as follows.

```
MOV DPTR, #159AH      ; DPTR gets 159AH
```

2. **MOVC:** This instruction moves a byte from the on-chip ROM/External ROM to the A register, often used for accessing lookup tables in programs. There are two versions of this instruction, depending on whether the 16-bit base address of the table is held in the DPTR or PC register. The offset of the data element to be accessed is stored in the A register. The data from the ROM is then copied into A.

(a)

```
MOVC A, @A+DPTR; load data present at A+DPTR
```

DPTR as base register.

To use this instruction, the DPTR should be initialized to the base value.

(b) *PC as base register.* Sometimes, instead of keeping the table away from the program code, the programmer may find it more logical to keep it immediately following the code. As code is accessed via the Program Counter (PC), in such cases, it may be advantageous to use the PC as the base. The offset is as usual contained in A. The format for the instruction is "MOVC A, @A+PC".

Example 3.1: The first ten prime numbers (indexed as 0, 1, ... 9) are 2, 3, 5, 7, 11, 13, 17, 19, 23, 29. If these are stored in the ROM starting at location 200H and the register R3 contains the index of the prime we are looking for, the following code fragment using the instruction "MOVC A, @A +DPTR" could be used to get the prime in A register.

```
MOV  DPTR, #200H  ; Load DPTR with the base address of primes in ROM (200H)
MOV  A, R3        ; Move the index (contained in R3) into the accumulator (A)
MOVC A, @A + DPTR ; Retrieve the prime number at (DPTR + A) from ROM into
APRIME    DB 2, 3, 5, 7, 11, 13, 17, 19, 23, 29 ; look up table stored in ROM
```

3. **MOVX:** The instruction can be used to transfer data between the external memory (RAM) and A register. Both 16- and 8-bit addresses can be mentioned for the external memory (RAM). For 16-bit addresses, the DPTR register is used, while the registers R0 and R1 can be used to provide 8-bit address.

(a) Address by DPTR. The following instructions could be used for this purpose.

```
MOVX A, @DPTR ; A loaded by byte pointed to by DPTR
MOVX @DPTR, A ; External memory location pointed to by DPTR gets
A
```

(b) *Address by R0, R1.* The following instructions could be used to specify an 8-bit address for the external memory access.

```
MOVX A, @Ri; i = 0, 1. A gets the external memory byte
pointed to by Ri
MOVX @Ri, A; i = 0, 1. External memory location pointed to
by Ri gets
```

4. **PUSH and POP:** The PUSH instruction is used to copy one byte operand to the on-chip RAM location pointed to by the *stack pointer* (*SP*). The SP register is incremented by 1. The operand can be specified using only the direct addressing mode. Typical example of PUSH is as follows, which stores the content of A register (memory address E0H) to stack memory location 33H, assuming that the current value of SP is 32. The SP register is incremented to 33H.

```
PUSH E0H
;Instructions, such as, "PUSH A", "PUSH @R0", "PUSH R2" are
invalid.
```

On the other hand, the POP instruction copies the content from top of stack (pointed to by SP) to the direct operand address mentioned in the instruction. For example, with SP having the value 33H, the instruction "POP 0E0H" will copy the of RAM location 33H to A register. The stack pointer SP will be decremented to 32H.

5. **XCH and XCHD:** The XCH instruction swaps the content of A register with a source byte mentioned as an operand. The generic instruction is of the format "XCH *<byte>*". The addressing modes supported for the operand along with examples have been noted in Table 3.6. The XCHD (exchange digit) is like the XCH with the exception that only the lower nibbles (lower order 4 bits) of the source byte and A register get exchanged. The higher order nibbles remain unchanged. For example, if A = 45H and R1 = 7AH, "XCHD A, R1" will convert A to 4AH and R1 to 75H.

Addressing Mode	**Format**	**Example**	**Contents of Register after the execution of each instruction**
Register	XCH A, Rn XCHD A, Rn	XCH A, R1 XCHD A, R1	Contents of R1 and A exchanged Lower nibbles of R1 and A exchanged
Indirect	XCH A, @Ri	XCH A, @R0	Contents of RAM[(R0)] and A exchanged
Direct	XCH A, direct	XCH A, 40H	Contents of RAM[40H] and A exchanged

Table 3.6: XCH and XCHD instructions

3.4.2 Arithmetic instructions

The 8051 microcontroller supports a variety of arithmetic instructions like ADD, ADDC, DA, SUBB, INC, DEC, MUL, DIV. Here's a detailed overview of arithmetic instructions for the 8051 microcontroller:

1. **ADD:** Adds the contents of the accumulator (A) with the source operand.

ADD A, <source byte>

The source byte can be specified using different addressing modes. Table 3.7 shows various cases with examples. Arithmetic operations on the 8051 microcontroller affect the carry (CY), auxiliary carry (AC), and overflow (OV) status flags in PSW register. In unsigned operations, which have operands and results between 00H and FFH (0 to 255 in decimal), the CY flag becomes 1 if the result exceeds FFH, indicating a carry out of the most significant bit.

Table 3.7: ADD with different addressing modes

Addressing Mode	**Format**	**Example**	**Contents of A after the execution of each instruction**
Register	ADD A, Rn	ADD A, R2	A = A + R2
Immediate	ADD A, #data	ADD A, #21H	A = A + 21H
Direct	ADD A, direct	ADD A, 4	A = A + RAM[4]
Indirect	ADD A, @Ri (i=0 or 1)	ADD A, @R0	A = A + RAM[(R0)]

For signed operations, where valid operands and results range from -128 to +127, the OV flag becomes 1 if the result falls outside this range, indicating an overflow. The AC flag is used to indicate a carry out from the lower nibble (the 4 least significant bits) in both addition and subtraction operations, important for BCD arithmetic.

2. ADDC: The ADDC instruction in the 8051 microcontroller is used for addition with carry. This instruction adds the contents of the accumulator (A), a specified source operand, and the carry flag (CY).

ADDC A, <source byte>

After executing the instruction, the content of A register gets modified to A + <source byte> + CY.

3. DA: The DA (Decimal Adjust) instruction in the 8051 microcontroller is used to adjust the accumulator (A) after a binary-coded decimal (BCD) addition operation. This instruction ensures that the result of an addition operation is a valid BCD number. The format of the instruction is DA A

When a decimal number is converted to BCD (Binary-Coded Decimal), each digit is represented as a 4-bit binary number. For instance, 45 in decimal is 01000101 in BCD, with 4 as 0100 and 5 as 0101. Adding two BCD numbers like 45 (01000101) and 35 (00110101) directly using the ADD instruction in 8051 results in 01111010, which is not a valid BCD number. To correct this, the "DA A" instruction is used, adjusting the result to a valid BCD. For example, 01111010 becomes 10000000, representing the decimal number 80 in BCD.

4. SUBB: The SUBB (Subtract with Borrow) instruction in the 8051 microcontroller is used to subtract the source operand and the current state of the carry flag (CY) from the accumulator (A). Here's a detailed explanation:

SUBB A, <source byte>

A = A - <source> - CY

It may be noted that there is no simple SUB instruction without carry. Thus, while doing subtraction, it is implied that the carry flag be cleared beforehand. For example, the following code fragment subtracts 29H from the accumulator.

```
CLR C
SUBB A, #29H
```

Steps for SUBB Instruction Execution:

Take 2's Complement of the Source Byte:

If the source operand is a register, immediate value, or memory location, the microcontroller computes its 2's complement. This step prepares the source operand for subtraction.

Add 2's Complement to Accumulator (A):

The accumulator (A) already contains the first operand of the subtraction. The microcontroller then adds the 2's complement of the source operand to the accumulator. This addition is essentially a subtraction in two's complement arithmetic.

Invert Carry Flag (CY):

Before executing the addition in step 2, the microcontroller inverts the carry flag (CY). This inversion changes a borrow into an addition of 1 during the subtraction process, aligning with two's complement subtraction rules.

5. MUL: This is the multiplication instruction. It multiplies register A with register B. Since A and B are 8-bit registers, the result is 16-bit wide. The 16-bit result is obtained by multiplying the contents of registers A and B. The low byte of the result is stored in register A, and the high byte in register B. The instruction is of the following format.

MUL AB

For example, if A =10010 and B = 20010, after "MUL AB", the result is 2000010 = 4E20H. The A register will now have 20H and B register 4EH. The MUL instruction affects the carry (CY) and the overflow (OV) flags. The CY flag is always reset and the OV flag is set to 1 if the result is more than 255.

6. DIV: This instruction performs the operation of dividing the byte present in accumulator by the byte in B register. The instruction is of the format noted next.

DIV AB

It should be ensured that the B register content is nonzero, else the result will be undefined. After division, the quotient is made available in register A and remainder in B. For example, if A = 4510 and B = 710, after executing "DIV AB", the contents of A and B registers will be 610 and 310, respectively. Execution of DIV clears the CY flag. The OV flag is set if the instruction attempts to divide by zero, else reset.

3.4.3 Logical instructions

In the 8051-microcontroller assembly language, logical instructions refer to operations that manipulate bits within registers. These instructions are essential for tasks such as setting, clearing, testing, and manipulating individual bits within data bytes. The Boolean operators supported are AND, OR, XOR, complement, and rotational instructions. They are fundamental for tasks ranging from bit masking and flag manipulation to data processing and control operations in embedded systems programming.

1. AND: The AND operation is performed using the ANL (AND logical) instruction. The instruction has the following format.

ANL *<dest-byte>*, *<source-byte>*

A bit-by-bit ANDing of the dest-byte with the source-byte is performed and the result is stored in the dest-byte. Table 3.8 shows the usage of ANL instruction in different addressing modes.

In the 8051-microcontroller assembly language, the ANL instruction has special variants that specifically operate on individual bits, particularly targeting the carry flag (CY). Here's an explanation of these special variants:

ANL C, <source-bit>

Operation: Performs a bitwise AND operation between the carry flag (CY) and a specified bit (source-bit). Updates the carry flag (CY) with the result.

ANL C, /<source-bit>

Operation: Performs a bitwise AND operation between the carry flag (CY) and the inverted value of a specified bit (source-bit). Updates the carry flag (CY) with the result.

Table 3.8: ANL with different addressing modes

Addressing Mode	Format	Example	Contents of A after the execution of each instruction
Register	ANL A, Rn	ANL A, R2	A = A AND R2
Immediate	ANL A, #data	ANL A, #20H	A = A AND 20H
Direct	ANL A, direct ANL direct, A ANL direct, #data	ANL A, 5 ANL 5, A ANL 35, #42H	A = A AND RAM[5] RAM[5] = RAM[5] AND A RAM[35] = RAM[35] AND 42H
Indirect	ANL A, @Ri (i = 0 or 1)	ANL A, @R0	A = A AND RAM[(R0)]

2. OR, XOR: Similar to AND, there are instructions to carry out the bit-by-bit operations for OR and XOR. The addressing modes supported in these instructions are similar to that for the ANL instruction. The corresponding instructions are ORL and XRL. Some such examples are noted next.

```
ORL A, R2 ;     A = A OR R2
XRL A, #20H ;   A = A XOR 20H
```

3. CPL: This is an instruction to complement the content of the accumulator. The 1's complement of the content is computed. The instruction is as follows.

CPL A

There is another variant of the instruction that works with bit operand. It complements the specified bit. The instruction is of the following format.

CPL <bit>

For example, the instruction "CPL P1.5" will complement the port 1's bit number 5.

4. **Rotate instructions.** These instructions can be used to rotate the accumulator register A towards left or right. There are four different instructions performing rotations – RR, RL, RRC and RLC. In the following, each of these has been discussed in detail.

- **RR:** The *rotate right* (RR) instruction rotates the content of accumulator right by one bit position. All bits, starting with

MSB, are shifted right with the LSB fed back to the MSB. It has been shown in Fig 3.1. The format of the instruction is as follows.

RR A

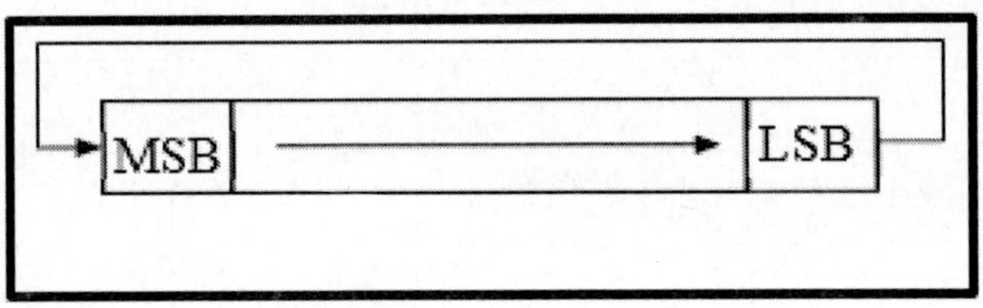

Fig 3.1: RR Instruction

> If A = 1010 1101, apply RR A.
> In this example, the original value in the Accumulator `A` was `1010 1101`. After executing `RR A`, the value becomes `1101 0110`.

- **RL**: It stands for rotate left (RL). The content of the accumulator is rotated left. The bits are shifted left from LSB towards MSB. The MSB is fed back to the LSB. The operation has been shown in Fig 3.2. The format of the instruction is as follows.

RL A

Fig 3.2: RL Instruction

If A = 1010 1101, apply RL A.

In this example, the original value in the Accumulator A was 1010 1101. After executing RL A, the value becomes 0101 1011.

- **RRC:** The instruction *rotate right through carry* (RRC) is similar to RR with the exception that the carry flag (CY) behaves as an extension to the least significant side of the accumulator. The bits from MSB towards the LSB are shifted to the right by one bit position. The LSB gets shifted to CY while the CY is rotated back to the MSB of A. The operation has been illustrated in Fig 3.3. The format of the instruction is as follows.

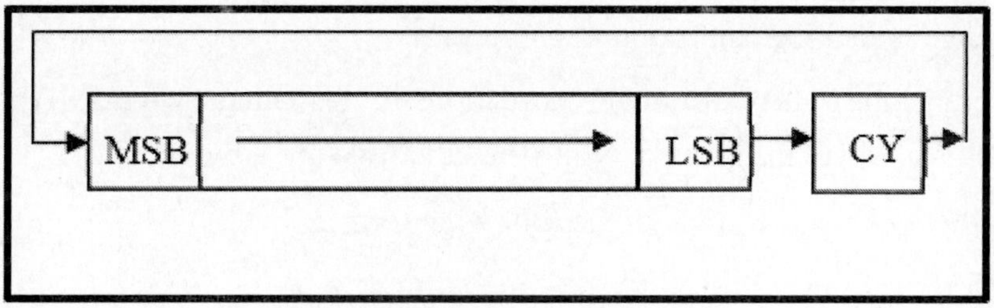

Fig 3.3: RRC Instruction

RRC A

If A = 1010 1101, apply RRC A when CY = 0.

In this example, the LSB (1) is moved into the Carry flag, making CY = 1, and the original Carry flag value (0) is moved into the MSB of A, resulting in 0101 0110.

- **RLC:** The instruction *rotate left through carry* (RLC) is just the reverse of RRC. The carry flag (CY) extends the A register in the

MSB side. The execution of the instruction is as follows. The bits from LSB towards the MSB get shifted to the left, the MSB is shifted to CY, while the CY is rotated back to the LSB. The execution of RLC has been shown in Fig 3.4. The instruction has the following format.

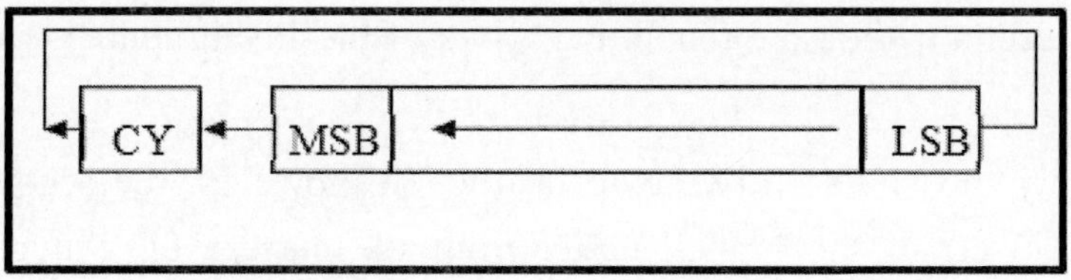

Fig 3.4: RLC Instruction

RLC A

> If A = 1010 1101, apply RLC A when CY = 0.
> In this example, the MSB (1) is moved into the Carry flag, making CY = 1, and the original Carry flag value (0) is moved into the LSB of A, resulting in 0101 1010.

3.4.4 Branch & Subroutine Instruction

Branch instructions in the 8051 microcontroller are used to alter the flow of program execution. These instructions can conditionally or unconditionally change the program counter (PC) to a different address, effectively "jumping" to another part of the program. . In the following, discussion has been carried out by grouping the relevant instructions into three categories – unconditional branching, conditional branching, subprogram call/return.

1. Unconditional branching. There are three instructions in this category – LJMP, AJMP and SJMP. Out of these, LJMP is a 3-byte instruction, while the other two are 2 byte wide.

- **LJMP**: The *long jump* instruction is of the following format.

LJMP *<16-bit addresss>*

As the address part specifies 16 bits, Jumps to the specified 16-bit address anywhere in the 64KB program memory space.

- **AJMP**: The absolute jump is a 2-byte instruction with the following syntax.

AJMP *<11-bit addresss>*

As the PC is 16-bit wide, the 11-bit address part is used to replace only the lower-order 11 bits of the PC. The higher-order 5 bits remain unaltered. Thus, the branch target must be within the 2k range of the current PC location. The AJMP (Absolute Jump) instruction on the 8051 microcontroller is indeed a 2-byte instruction, but it uses a combination of bits from both the opcode and the address byte to form an 11-bit address.

Here's how it works:

Opcode: The AJMP instruction's opcode is 1 byte (8 bits). The opcode for AJMP also includes part of the 11-bit address. Specifically, it includes the 3 most significant bits (MSBs) of the 11-bit address.

Address Byte: The second byte is the remaining 8 bits of the 11-bit address (the 8 least significant bits, or LSBs).

- **SJMP**: The short jump is also a two-byte instruction, however, the second byte provides the distance (called offset) of the branch target from the current PC value. The format of the instruction is as follows.

SJMP *<8-bit offset>*

After fetching the SJMP instruction, the content of PC is equal to the address of the next memory location. To execute SJMP, the offset part is added to the PC. Now, if the offset is a positive number, it implies a forward jump. If the offset is negative, it is a backward jump. As the offset is an 8-bit value, the target must be within a distance of -128 bytes to +127 bytes. This type of limited branching is also known as *relative branch.* While translating an SJMP instruction to machine code, the assembler computes this distance and keeps as the second byte of the translated instruction. For example, consider the following code fragment.

```
SJMP LABEL   ; Jump to LABEL (short jump within range)
LJMP 1000H    ; Jump to address 1000H
AJMP 0F0H   ; Jump to address 0F0H within the current 2KB
page
```

2. Conditional Branching. These instructions modify the PC value with the jump target if the specified condition is met. All conditional branches are relative to the PC, similar to SJMP. The following are the variants available.

- **J**<*condition*>: Several instructions belong to this category in which the identification of the *condition* makes the full mnemonic. Table 3.9 shows the instructions with their meanings.

Table 3.9: J<condition> instructions

Instruction	**Meaning**	**Example**
JZ <target>	Jump if A = 0	JZ L1
JNZ <target>	Jump if A $\neq$ 0	JNZ L1
JC <target>	Jump if CY = 1	JC L2
JNC <target>	Jump if CY = 0	JNC L2
JB <bit>, <target>	Jump if <bit> = 1	JB P1.3, L1
JNB <bit>, <target>	Jump if <bit> = 0,	JNB ACC.0, L1
JBC <bit>, <target>	Jump if <bit> = 1, clear bit	JBC ACC.4, L1

Out of all the instructions noted in Table 3.7, the JBC is a special one which also clears the bit to zero.

- **CJNE**: This instruction, *compare and jump if not equal*, compares between a source byte and a destination byte. The carry flag (CY) gets set to 1 if the destination is less than the source and reset otherwise. The format of the instruction is as follows.

CJNE *<dest-byte>*, *<source-byte>*, *<target>*

Table 3.10 shows the different addressing mode combinations supported by CJNE to specify the destination and the source bytes.

Table 3.10: CJNE instructions

Addressing Mode	**Format**	**Example**	**Function**
Immediate	CJNE A, #data, target	CJNE A, #45, L1	Jump to L1 if A $\neq$ 45
Direct	CJNE A, direct, target	CJNE A, 42H, L1	Jump to L1 if A $\neq$ RAM[42H]
Register	CJNE Rn, #data, target	CJNE R1, #45, L1	Jump to L1 if R1 $\neq$ 45
Indirect	CJNE @Ri, #data, target	CJNE @R1, #45, L1	Jump to L1 if RAM[(R1)] $\neq$ 45

- **DJNZ**: The instruction, decrement and jump if not zero, decrements a specified byte and if the result is nonzero, control branches to the mentioned target address. A specialty of the instruction is that, none of the status flags are affected. The format of the instruction is as follows.

DJNZ *<byte>*, *<target>*

Table 3.11 shows the addressing mode combinations that are permissible for specifying the DJNZ instruction.

Table 3.11: DJNZ instructions

Addressing Mode	**Format**	**Example**	**Operation**
Direct	DJNZ direct, target	DJNZ 42H, L1	Decrement RAM[42H], if result is nonzero, jump to L1
Register	DJNZ Rn, target	DJNZ R1, L1	Decrement R1, if result is nonzero, jump to L1

3. Subprogram Call/Return. A subprogram is a part of the program code dedicated to a specific subtask. The overall computation performed by a main program may have similar sub computations needed at different points. For example, while interfacing a display unit with successive patterns sent to the display, it is necessary to have some delay between two successive patterns. Thus, a separate delay routine may be created for this purpose as a subprogram and called from different places in the main program.

   Similar to the unconditional branch instructions, the 8051 supports two subprogram call instructions, namely LCALL and ACALL. A basic difference between the branch and the call instructions is that unlike branch, after the subprogram has been executed, control returns to the instruction immediately following the call instruction. For this, the return address is saved onto the stack. Any subprogram ends with a RET instruction which causes the PC to be loaded with the address available at the top of the stack. A subroutine in 8051 assembly language is a sequence of instructions that performs a specific task and can be called from other parts of the program. These instructions also called subroutine instructions.

- **LCALL**: It is a three-byte instruction with the following format.

  LCALL *<16-bit address>*

  Assuming that the LCALL instruction starts at memory location 1000H, the next instruction will be at 1003H. If the SP is at 32H, the return address 1003H is stored in RAM locations 33H and 34H. The new SP value becomes 34H. The 16-bit address specified in the instruction is copied into the PC and thus the control jumps to the subprogram.

- **ACALL:** Similar to AJMP, ACALL is a two-byte instruction of the format as follows.

  ACALL *<11-bit address>*

  The 11 least-significant bits of PC is replaced with the 11-bit address to jump to the subprogram. The 16-bit return address is saved onto the stack and SP is incremented by two. As in AJMP, ACALL restricts the target to be within 2k address range from the current PC.

- **RET and RETI**: Both RET and RETI are single byte instructions, consisting of only the mnemonic. The RET instruction is used as the last instruction of a subprogram that makes the execution to be restarted from the instruction following the last LCALL/ACALL instruction. Contents from the top two bytes are popped from the stack and loaded into the PC register. The SP is decremented by two. The RETI instruction is used in the subprograms corresponding to interrupt service routines. On occurrence of an interrupt, similar to subprogram call, the control branches to a subprogram, decided beforehand. Before that, the return address is saved onto stack, similar to LCALL/ACALL. As in RET, RETI also restores the content of PC from the stack. Apart from that, RETI also restores the interrupt logic to accept any additional interrupts. If any interrupt has been pending before RETI, corresponding service routine is taken up for execution only after executing one instruction at the return address.

3.4.5 Bit manipulation instruction

The 8051 microcontroller has a set of instructions specifically designed for bit manipulation, which allows you to set, clear, complement, and test individual bits.

- **CLR:** The instruction can be used to clear the accumulator or a bit. There are two formats of this instruction as noted next.

  CLR A ; Clears the accumulator, no status flags affected CLR <bit> ; Clears the specified bit

- **SETB** <bit> : Set Bit

  This instruction sets (makes 1) the specified bit.

  Example: SETB P1.0 sets the 0th bit of port 1.

- **CPL** <bit> : Complement Bit

  This instruction complements (inverts) the specified bit.

  Example: CPL P1.0 changes the 0th bit of port 1 from 1 to 0 or from 0 to 1.

- **ANL C, <bit>:** AND Bit with Carry

  This instruction performs a logical AND between the specified bit and the carry flag.

  Example: ANL C, P1.0 performs C = C AND P1.0.

- **ORL C, <bit>**: OR Bit with Carry

  This instruction performs a logical OR between the specified bit and the carry flag.

  Example: ORL C, P1.0 performs C = C OR P1.0.

- **MOV C, <bit>**: Move Bit to Carry

  This instruction moves the specified bit to the carry flag.

  Example: MOV C, P1.0 moves the 0th bit of port 1 to the carry flag.

- **MOV <bit>, C**: Move Carry to Bit

  This instruction moves the carry flag to the specified bit.

  Example: MOV P1.0, C moves the carry flag to the 0th bit of port 1

3.4.6 Other Miscellaneous Instructions

In the last few sections, various classes of instructions have been detailed. Apart from that, there exists some more instructions in the 8051 with specific functionalities. In the following, such instructions have been discussed.

- **NOP:** This is the *No Operation* instruction. The execution of this instruction has no effect on any of CPU registers or memory locations. Only the program counter is incremented to continue executing the next instruction. The instruction is used to introduce small delay in the execution process of the program. The instruction has the format noted next.

  NOP

- **SWAP:** This is the swap instruction that can be used to swap the nibbles of the accumulator register A. In the process, the bits D3-D0 of A gets exchanged with the bits D7-D4. Format of the instruction is as follows.

  SWAPA

  For example, the instruction "SWAP A" with A = 45H changes A to 54H

3.5 Assembly language programs

Assembly language programming is a low-level programming language that provides a direct correspondence between the instructions in the language and the architecture's machine code instructions. Here are the details of assembly language programming, its benefits, and some common use cases.

What is Assembly Language?

- **Low-Level Language:** Assembly language is one step above machine code and allows programmers to write instructions in a more readable format.
- **Hardware Specific:** It is specific to a particular processor or family of processors, as it directly interacts with the hardware.
- **Mnemonic Codes:** Uses mnemonic codes and symbols instead of binary code, making it easier to write and understand.
- **Assembler:** An assembler translates the assembly language code into machine code.

Benefits of Assembly Language Programming:

1. **High Performance:** Assembly language allows precise control over the hardware, enabling optimizations that can lead to very high performance, especially for critical sections of code.

2. **Efficiency:** Programs written in assembly language can be more efficient in terms of execution speed and memory usage, which is crucial for embedded systems and resource-constrained environments.
3. **Direct Hardware Manipulation:** Assembly language provides the ability to directly manipulate hardware components, which is essential for developing device drivers, embedded systems, and low-level system utilities.
4. **Understanding and Debugging:** Writing in assembly helps programmers understand the architecture of the CPU and the functioning of the hardware. It also aids in debugging low-level issues.
5. **Real-Time Applications:** Ideal for real-time systems where precise timing and fast response are required.

Common Use Cases

1. **Embedded Systems:** Assembly language is extensively used in programming microcontrollers and embedded systems where resources are limited, and performance is critical.
2. **Operating Systems and Kernels:** Core parts of operating systems and kernels are often written in assembly to directly manage hardware resources and ensure efficient execution.
3. **Device Drivers:** Writing device drivers often requires direct hardware manipulation, making assembly language a suitable choice.
4. **Performance-Critical Applications:** Applications requiring high performance, such as game engines, graphics rendering, and real-time simulations, may use assembly for performance-critical sections.
5. **Bootloaders:** Bootloaders, which initialize system hardware and load the operating system, are typically written in assembly.

Example 3.1 Write an assembly language program to adds two numbers 0AH and 14H and stores the result on location 30H.

```
        ORG 0000H ; Origin, starting address
        LJMP START ; Jump to the start of the program
START:          MOV A, #0AH ; Load accumulator with 10
        MOV B, #14H ; Load register B with 20
ADD A, B ; Add B to A
MOV 30H, A ; Store the result in memory location 30H SJMP $ ; Infinite loop to end the program
END
```

In this assembly program for the 8051 microcontroller, the SJMP $ instruction is used to create an infinite loop at the end of the program. The $ symbol represents the current address of the program counter, so SJMP $ tells the processor to jump to the current address indefinitely, effectively halting the program's execution from progressing any further. If SJMP $ is not used in your 8051-assembly program, the behavior of the microcontroller after the last executable instruction will depend on what follows in the memory. The program counter (PC) will continue to increment and fetch the next instruction from memory. If there is any data or code beyond your intended end of the program, the microcontroller will attempt to execute it. This can lead to unpredictable behavior, errors, or crashes, as the instructions being executed may not make any sense in the context of your program.

Example 3.2 Write an assembly language program which adds contents of RAM locations 50H to 5FH , and the sum is saved in RAM locations 70H and 71H.

```
CLR A           ; Clear the accumulator (A = 0)
MOV R0, #50H    ; Set R0 as the source pointer to 50H
MOV R2, #16     ; Set the counter (R2) to 16 (number of bytes to add)
MOV R3, #0      ; Clear R3 to count carries
A_1:
   ADD A, @R0   ; Add the value at the RAM location pointed to by R0 to A
   JNC B_1      ; If there is no carry (CY=0), jump to B_1
   INC R3       ; If there was a carry, increment R3 to count it
B_1:
   INC R0       ; Increment R0 to point to the next RAM location
   DJNZ R2, A_1 ; Decrement R2 and repeat until R2 is zero
MOV 70H, A      ; Store the low byte of the sum in RAM location 70H
MOV 71H, R3 ; Store the high byte of the sum (carry count) in RAM location 71H
```

This program calculates the sum of 16 bytes starting from the memory location pointed to by register R0 (initialized to 50H) and stores the result in memory locations 70H and 71H. Initially, the accumulator (A) and R3 are cleared to zero, and R2 is set as a counter with the value 16. The loop (labeled A_1) adds the byte at the current memory location pointed to by R0 to A. If there is no carry (CY=0), it proceeds to the next instruction; otherwise, it increments R3 to count the carries. R0 is then incremented to point to the next memory location, and the loop repeats until all 16 bytes are processed. Finally, the low byte of the sum is stored in 70H, and the high byte (carries) is stored in 71H.

Example 3.3 Write an assembly language program to reads data from Port 1 and outputs it to Port 2.

```
        ORG 0000H ; Origin, starting address
        LJMP START ; Jump to the start of the program
START:  MOV A, P1 ; Move the value from Port 1 to accumulator
        MOV P2, A ; Output the value to Port 2
        SJMP START ; Repeat the loop
        END
```

Example 3.4 Write a program for the 8052 to put 55H into the upper RAM locations of 90–99H.

```
        ORG 0
        MOV R0, #90H   ; Initialize R0 to point to RAM location 90H
        MOV R2, #10    ; Set counter (R2) for 10 locations (90H to 99H)
        MOV A, #55H    ; Load the value 55H into the accumulator
LOOP:
        MOV @R0, A     ; Store the value in the current RAM location pointed to by R0
        INC R0         ; Increment R0 to point to the next RAM location
        DJNZ R2, LOOP  ; Decrement R2 and repeat until all locations are filled
```

Example 3.5 Assuming that bit P2.3 serves as an input indicating the status of a door, where a high signal signifies that the door is open, continuously monitor this bit. Whenever it transitions to a high state, generate a low-to-high pulse on port P1.5 to activate a buzzer. HERE: ; Label for the start of the loop

```
    JNB P2.3, HERE ; Jump if Not Bit (P2.3 is 0),
    CLR P1.5; Clear P1.5 (set P1.5 to 0)
    ACALL DELAY; Call the subroutine DELAY
    SETB P1.5; Set P1.5 (creating a low-to-high pulse)
    ACALL DELAY; Call the subroutine DELAY
    SJMP HERE; Jump to HERE, creating an infinite loop
```

Example 3.6 Write a program to blinks an LED connected to Port 1, Pin 0 with a delay using a simple loop.

```
ORG 0000H ; Origin, starting address
LJMP START ; Jump to start of the program
DELAY:
        MOV R2, #50 ; Set delay counter
LOOP_DELAY:
        DJNZ R2, LOOP_DELAY ; Decrement R2 and loop until it's zero
        RET ; Return from subroutine
START:
        SETB P1.0 ; Turn on LED connected to P1.0
        ACALL DELAY ; Call delay subroutine
        CLR P1.0 ; Turn off LED
        ACALL DELAY ; Call delay subroutine
        SJMP START ; Repeat indefinitely
END
```

3.6 C language programs

The 8051 microcontroller, developed by Intel, is a widely used microcontroller in embedded systems. Programming the 8051 can be done in assembly language, but using the C programming language offers several advantages, particularly when using the Keil C51 compiler.

Why Use C for 8051 Programming?

- **Readability:** C code is generally easier to read and understand compared to assembly language. High-level constructs like loops, conditionals, and functions make the code more intuitive.
- **Maintainability:** With C, it's easier to maintain and modify the code. High-level languages allow for better organization and modularity, reducing the complexity of large projects.
- **Portability:** C code is more portable across different microcontrollers with similar architectures. Assembly code, on the other hand, is specific to the hardware for which it was written.
- **Development Speed:** Writing in C typically takes less time than writing in assembly because you can express complex operations in fewer lines of code.
- **Library Support:** The C language has a wealth of libraries and functions that simplify common tasks such as string handling, mathematical computations, and I/O operations.

Example 3.7 LED blinking using C language.

```
#include <REG51.H>
sbit LED = P1^1;  // Define P1.1 as an LED
void delay(void);  // Function prototype for delay
void main(void)
{
  while (1)
  {
    LED = 1;       // Turn ON the LED
    delay();      // Call delay function
    LED = 0;       // Turn OFF the LED
    delay();      // Call delay function
  }
}
void delay(void) // Delay function implementation
{
  unsigned int i;
  for (i = 0; i < 250; i++)
  {
    // Empty loop for creating delay
  }}
```

- Include Header File: #include <REG51.H> includes the necessary definitions for the 8051 microcontroller.
- Define Bit Using sbit: sbit LED = P1^1; defines LED as the bit P1.1. This provides a meaningful name for the bit and makes the code more readable.
- Main Function: The main function contains an infinite loop that toggles the state of P1.1 (the LED).
- Turning LED ON and OFF: LED = 1; turns the LED on by setting P1.1 to high, and LED = 0; turns the LED off by setting P1.1 to low.
- Delay Function: The delay function creates a simple software delay using nested loops.

3.6.1 Data types and Time Delay in 8051 C

In C programming for the 8051 microcontroller, specific data types are used to manage various forms of data, including standard integer types and special types for manipulating bits and special function registers. Here's a detailed look at each:

1. **signed char:** The signed char data type occupies 1 byte (8 bits) of memory and can represent integer values ranging from -128 to 127. It is used to store small integers that may be either negative or positive. This type is particularly useful for tasks such as arithmetic operations where negative values might be required. For example, signed char temperature = -10; declares a variable that can store temperature values, including negative ones.

2. **unsigned char:** The unsigned char data type also occupies 1 byte (8 bits) but, unlike signed char, it only represents positive integer values ranging from 0 to 255. This type is typically used for storing small positive numbers and characters, making it ideal for counters, flags, or any data that doesn't require negative values. For instance, unsigned char counter = 200; declares a variable for a counter that won't go below zero. It's important to remember that C compilers default to using signed char unless the unsigned keyword is specified. When declaring variables, careful consideration of data size is crucial; opting for unsigned char instead of int is advisable. This is particularly important for the 8051 microcontroller, which has a limited number of registers and data RAM locations. Utilizing int instead of char can lead to a larger hex file size, as int typically occupies more memory than char. This can be inefficient given the constraints of the 8051 architecture.

3. **signed int:** Typically occupying 2 bytes (16 bits) on an 8051 system, the signed int data type can represent integer values from -32,768 to 32,767. It is used for storing larger integers that can be both negative and positive, making it suitable for a wide range of arithmetic computations. For example, signed int pressure = -500; declares a variable for pressure values that may be negative.

   unsigned int: Also typically occupying 2 bytes (16 bits) on an 8051 system, the unsigned int data type represents positive integer values ranging from 0 to 65,535. This type is used for larger positive numbers, making it ideal for variables that count or measure quantities that cannot be negative. For instance, unsigned int distance = 40000; declares a variable to store a distance measurement.

4. **sbit:** The sbit (special bit) data type is used to access individual bits within the 8051's Special Function Registers (SFRs) or other bit-addressable memory locations. This type occupies just 1

bit of memory and is crucial for low-level hardware control, such as turning an LED on or off. For example, sbit LED = P1^0; assigns the first bit of port 1 to control an LED.

5. **bit:** The bit data type, occupying 1 bit of memory, is used for declaring and accessing individual bits within bit-addressable sections of memory. It can hold values of 0 or 1, representing Boolean states. This type is useful for flags and other binary state indicators. For example, bit flag = 0; declares a Boolean flag that can be either set (1) or cleared (0).

6. **sfr:** The sfr (special function register) data type is used to declare 8-bit registers that control various hardware functions and peripherals of the 8051 microcontroller. Each sfr occupies 1 byte and is mapped to specific addresses. For instance, sfr P0 = 0x80; declares the special function register for port 0, and sfr IE = 0xA8; declares the Interrupt Enable register, allowing direct manipulation of these hardware features.

Time Delay

There are two ways to create a time delay in 8051 C:

1. Using a simple **for** loop

2. Using the 8051 timers

Here is an explanation of two methods to create a time delay in 8051 C programming.

1. **Using a simple for loop:** Creating a time delay using a simple for loop is a straightforward method where a loop is executed a certain number of times to produce a delay. This approach is based on the time it takes for the microcontroller to execute each iteration of the loop. For example, for (unsigned int i = 0; i < 30000; i++); creates a delay by looping 30,000 times. The duration of the delay depends on the clock speed of the 8051 and the efficiency of the compiler. While easy to implement, this method is not precise and can be affected by changes in the system clock or compiler optimizations.

2. **Using the 8051 timers:** Creating a time delay using the 8051 timers involves configuring one of the microcontroller's built-in timers to generate precise delays. The 8051 has two timers, Timer 0 and Timer 1, which can be configured in different modes to count clock pulses. By loading a specific value into the timer's register and starting the timer, it counts up (or down) to generate an interrupt or overflow after a certain period, which can be used to create an accurate delay. For instance, configuring Timer 0 in Mode 1 (16-bit timer) involves setting up the timer registers (TH0 and TL0), starting the timer, and waiting for the overflow flag (TF0) to be set. This method is precise and less affected by system changes, making it ideal for applications requiring accurate timing.

Example 3.8 Write a C program for the 8051 microcontroller to send the values from 00 to FF to port P2.

```
#include <reg51.h>
void main(void) { // Main function
   unsigned char value;  // Declare variable for output value
   for (value = 0; value <= 0xFF; value++) {
      P2 = value;  // Send the current value to port P2
   }
}
```

Example 3.9 Write a C program for the 8051 microcontroller to monitor bit P1.5. If P1.5 is high, send the value 55H to port P0; otherwise, send AAH to port P2.

```
#include <reg51.h>  // Include header file for 8051 microcontrolle
sbit monitorBit = P1^5;  // Define sbit for P1.5
void main() {
   while (1) {  // Infinite loop
      if (monitorBit) {  // Check if bit P1.5 is high
         P0 = 0x55;  // Send 55H to Port 0
      } else {  // If bit P1.5 is low
         P2 = 0xAA;  // Send AAH to Port 2
      }
   }
}
```

Example 3.10 Write an 8051 C program to toggle all the bits of P1 continuously.

Solution:

```
#include <reg51.h>
void delay(void); // Function prototype for delay
void main(void) {
   while (1) {
      P1 = ~P1;  // Toggle all bits of port P1
      delay();   // Call delay function for visible toggling
   }}
void delay(void) { // Delay function implementation
   unsigned int i;
   for (i = 0; i < 50000; i++) { // Empty loop for creating a delay
   }
}
```

Example 3.11 Write an 8051 C program to toggle bits of P2 continuously forever with some delay.

Solution:

```
#include <reg51.h>  // Include header file for 8051 microcontroller
void delay_loop(unsigned int time);  // Function prototype for delay using a loop
void main() {
   while (1) {      // Infinite loop
      P2 = ~P2;     // Toggle all bits of Port 2
      delay_loop(30000);  // Call delay function
   }
}
void delay_loop(unsigned int time) {
   unsigned int i;
   for (i = 0; i < time; i++);  // Simple for loop for delay
}
```

Example 3.12 A door sensor is connected to pin P1.1, while a buzzer is connected to pin P1.7. Write a C program for the 8051 microcontroller to continuously monitor the door sensor. When the sensor detects that the door is open, sound the buzzer by generating a square wave at a frequency of several hundred Hz.

Solution:

```
#include <reg51.h> // Include header file for 8051 microcontroller
sbit doorSensor = P1^1; // Define sbit for door sensor at P1.1
sbit buzzer = P1^7;     // Define sbit for buzzer at P1.7
void delay(unsigned int time); // Function prototype for delay
void main() {
  while (1) { // Infinite loop
    if (doorSensor == 1) { // Check if door sensor is triggered (door opened)
      // Generate a square wave to sound the buzzer
      unsigned int i;
      for (i = 0; i < 500; i++) { // Adjust the loop count for desired frequency
        buzzer = 1; // Turn on the buzzer
        delay(100); // Delay to create high period
        buzzer = 0; // Turn off the buzzer
        delay(100); // Delay to create low period
      }
    } else {
      buzzer = 0; // Ensure the buzzer is off when the door is closed
    }
  }
}
void delay(unsigned int time) {
  unsigned int i;
  for (i = 0; i < time; i++); // Simple for loop for delay
}
```

Example 3.13 Write an 8051 C program to send hex values for ASCII characters of 0, D, A, B, 2, 3, 4, B, C, and 6 to port P1.

Solution:

```
#include <reg51.h>
void main(void)
{
unsigned char mynum[]= "0DAB234BC6";
unsigned char z;
for(z=0;z<=10;z++)
P1=mynum[z];
}
```

3.7 Assemblers and Compilers

ASM51: ASM51 is Intel's assembler specifically designed for the 8051 microcontroller family. It translates assembly language code directly into machine code instructions that the 8051 processor can execute. ASM51 supports all standard 8051 instructions and includes features for defining macros, constants, and variables within assembly programs.

Keil A51 Assembler: Part of the Keil development tools suite, the A51 assembler is another popular choice for programming the 8051 in assembly language. It offers similar functionality to ASM51 but integrates seamlessly with the μVision IDE, providing a user-friendly environment for writing, debugging, and managing assembly projects. A51 includes advanced features for segment management, data initialization, and efficient code generation for the 8051 architecture.

Keil C51 Compiler: The Keil C51 Compiler is a robust C compiler specifically tailored for the 8051 microcontroller. Unlike assemblers that translate assembly language directly into machine code, the C51 compiler translates high-level C language code into assembly language first and then into machine code. This approach allows developers to write more abstract and readable code, speeding up development time and reducing errors. Keil C51 offers powerful optimization features, extensive library support, and integrates seamlessly with the μVision IDE for debugging and simulation.

SDCC (Small Device C Compiler): SDCC is an open-source C compiler that supports multiple microcontroller architectures, including the 8051. It provides a cost-effective and accessible option for programming the 8051 in C language, making it popular in academic and hobbyist communities. SDCC supports inline assembly, extensive optimization options, and includes a suite of development tools for writing and debugging C programs targeting the 8051.

Differences between Assembler and Compiler

Assembler: An assembler translates assembly language code directly into machine code instructions. Assembly language is a low-level programming language that closely resembles the binary machine code of the processor, making it highly efficient but less portable and more complex to write and maintain compared to higher-level languages like C.

Compiler: A compiler translates high-level programming languages like C into assembly language and then into machine code. Compilers offer advantages such as portability, abstraction, and ease of programming compared to assembly language. They enable developers to write code that can be easily adapted to different microcontroller architectures and often include optimization features to improve code efficiency and performance.

In summary, assemblers like ASM51 and Keil A51 directly convert assembly language to machine code for precise control and efficiency on the 8051, while compilers such as Keil C51 and SDCC allow developers to write in higher-level languages like C, enhancing productivity and code portability across different microcontroller platforms. Each toolset offers unique advantages tailored to specific project requirements, from low-level optimization to rapid application development.

3.8 Programming and debugging tools

Programming and debugging tools for the 8051 microcontroller include a range of software and hardware options designed to facilitate development and troubleshooting. The Keil µVision IDE integrates a powerful debugger and simulator, allowing developers to write, compile, and debug C and assembly code with ease. Raisonance Ride7 offers similar functionality, providing an intuitive interface for code development and debugging. IAR Embedded Workbench is another comprehensive toolchain that includes advanced debugging features, such as breakpoints and watch variables, enhancing error detection and performance optimization. For open-source enthusiasts, SDCC (Small Device C Compiler) pairs well with debugging tools like gdb for 8051. Hardware tools such as In-System Programmers (ISP) and JTAG debuggers enable direct interaction with the microcontroller, allowing for real-time code upload and hardware-level debugging. Popular devices include Silicon Labs' USB Debug Adapter and Segger's J-Link, which offer robust support for debugging and flashing the 8051 microcontroller. Each of these tools provides essential capabilities for efficient

8051 microcontroller development, from writing and compiling code to detailed debugging and performance analysis.

In-System Programmers (ISP) and JTAG are crucial tools for programming and debugging microcontrollers like the 8051.

In-System Programmers (ISP): ISP allows you to program a microcontroller directly in the circuit without needing to remove it from its operating environment. This feature is particularly useful for development and production environments where microcontrollers are soldered onto a PCB. With ISP, firmware updates can be done easily, improving convenience and efficiency. ISP typically uses a serial communication interface, such as UART, SPI, or I2C. Tools like Silicon Labs' USB Debug Adapter often support ISP for the 8051, enabling direct programming and debugging.

JTAG (Joint Test Action Group): JTAG is a standard for verifying designs and testing printed circuit boards after manufacture. For microcontrollers, JTAG provides powerful debugging capabilities by allowing control over the CPU and peripherals. It supports operations like setting breakpoints, single-stepping through code, and examining and modifying memory contents. JTAG interfaces can be more complex and expensive compared to ISP but offer comprehensive debugging features. Tools like Segger's J-Link and Keil ULINK are popular JTAG debuggers for the 8051, providing robust support for on-chip debugging and real-time analysis.

In summary, ISP is ideal for straightforward programming tasks and firmware updates within an embedded system, while JTAG offers in-depth debugging and testing capabilities, making it indispensable for complex development and troubleshooting scenarios.

UNIT SUMMARY

This unit introduces addressing modes, which define how the operand of an instruction is accessed. Key modes include immediate addressing, where data is specified in the instruction; register addressing, which uses CPU registers; direct addressing, where the address of the operand is given; indirect addressing, which points to the address of the operand; and relative addressing, which uses a program counter offset. Additional modes like indexed addressing, bit inherent addressing, and bit direct addressing facilitate specialized data handling.

The unit also covers the 8051-instruction set, detailing instruction timings and various types of instructions, including data transfer, arithmetic, logical, branch, subroutine, and bit manipulation instructions. It emphasizes the use of assembly language and C language programs for microcontroller programming, as well as the roles of assemblers and compilers. Finally, it highlights the importance of programming and debugging tools in the development process.

EXERCISES

Multiple Choice Question (1-18)

1. Which addressing mode uses a constant as the operand?

   a) Direct b) Register
   c) Immediate d) Indirect

2. Which instruction is used to set the carry flag in 8051?

   a) CLR C b) SETB C
   c) MOV C d) CPL C

3. What does the MOVC instruction do?

   a) Moves data from one register to another b) Moves code byte from ROM
   c) Clears the carry flag d) Sets a bit in RAM

4. What is the purpose of the RET instruction?

   a) Return from subroutine b) Return from interrupt
   c) Clear the accumulator d) Set the accumulator

5. In 8051, what is the primary difference between the MOVX and MOV instructions?

   a) MOVX is used for code memory while MOV is used for data memory
   b) MOVX is used for external data memory while MOV is used for internal data memory
   c) MOVX is used for bit operations while MOV is used for byte operations
   d) MOVX is used for register to register transfer while MOV is used for immediate addressing

6. What is the primary use of the DPTR register in 8051?

   a) Bit manipulation b) Direct addressing
   c) Indirect addressing d) Indexed addressing

7. In the 8051 microcontroller, which register pair is used for multiplication and division operations?

   a) R0 and R1 b) A and B
   c) DPTR and PC d) SP and PSW

8. What is the purpose of the DPTR (Data Pointer) register in the 8051 microcontroller?

   a) To store temporary data b) To point to the address of the next instruction
   c) To point to data in external memory d) To store the status of the program

9. Which addressing mode is used in the instruction MOV A, @R0?

a) Direct addressing b) Immediate addressing

c) Register addressing d) Indirect addressing

10. Which bit manipulation instruction is used to complement a specific bit of a byte?

a) CPL A b) CLR bit

c) CPL bit d) SETB bit

11. What is the purpose of the ACALL instruction in 8051?

a) Call an absolute address subroutine b) Call a relative address subroutine

c) Call a direct address subroutine d) Call an indirect address subroutine

12. Which instruction is used to jump to a specified address if the accumulator is zero?

a) JZ address b) JNZ address

c) JC address d) JNC address

13. Which of the following is not a valid 8051 instruction?

a) MOV A, @DPTR b) MOVX A, @DPTR

c) MOVC A, @A+DPTR d) MOV A, @R1

14. What is the function of the SJMP instruction in 8051?

a) Short jump within 128 bytes b) Long jump within 2K bytes

c) Absolute jump within 64K bytes d) Jump if zero

15. Which addressing mode is used in the instruction MOVC A, @A+DPTR?

a) Direct addressing b) Indirect addressing

c) Indexed addressing d) Immediate addressing

16. Which of the following instructions is used to load the accumulator with data from external memory in the 8051 microcontroller?

a) MOVX A, @DPTR b) MOVC A, @DPTR

c) MOV A, @DPTR d) MOVX A, #data

17. What does the XCH instruction do in the 8051 microcontroller?

a) Exchanges data between accumulator and memory

b) Exchanges data between two registers

c) Exchanges data between accumulator and register

d) Exchanges data between DPTR and memory

18. In the following code, what does the sbit keyword do?

    sbit LED = P1^0;

    a) Defines a special function register
    b) Defines a specific bit of a port
    c) Defines a standard I/O port
    d) Defines an 8-bit register

Short Answer Question (19-26)

19. Define immediate addressing mode. Provide an example.
20. What is bit addressing mode in 8051 microcontroller?
21. Define indexed addressing mode and give an example.
22. What does the ADD A, R0 instruction do?
23. What is the purpose of the SJMP instruction?
24. What happens when the RET instruction is executed?
25. Explain the difference between a carry and an overflow.
26. Write the assembly instructions to load the value 24H into register A and the value 2FH into register B, and then add these two values together.

Long Answer Question (27-30)

27. Show the status of the CY, AC, and P flags after the addition of 38H and 2FH in the following instructions.

    MOV A,#37H

    ADD A,#2FH

28. Show the stack and stack pointer for the following. Assume the default stack area and register 0 is selected.

    MOV R6,#25H

    MOV R1,#12H

    MOV R4,#0F3H

    PUSH 5

    PUSH 6

    PUSH 4

29. Write a program to add two 16-bit numbers. The numbers are 3BE7H and 3D8DH. Place the sum in R5 and R4; R6 should have the lower byte.

30. Assume internal RAM memory locations 41H–45H contain the daily temperature for five days, as shown below. Search to see if any of the values equals 65. If value 65 does exist in the table, give its location to R4; otherwise, make R4 = 0.

    41H=(76)

    42H=(79)

    43H=(69)

    44H=(65)

    45H=(62)

MCQ Answer

1. (c) 2. (b) 3. (b) 4. (a) 5. (b) 6. (c) 7. (b) 8. (c) 9. (d) 10. (c) 11. (a) 12. (a) 13. (a) 14. (a) 15. (c) 16. (a) 17. (a) 18. (b)

KNOW MORE

Since this decade, instruction set architecture (ISA) advancements have focused on energy efficiency, AI acceleration, and security. The open-source RISC-V ISA has gained popularity for its flexibility, while ARM continues to expand beyond mobile with its energy-efficient designs, as seen in Apple's M-series chips. x86 (Intel/AMD) has introduced performance improvements through AVX-512 and hybrid architectures like Intel's Alder Lake. AI workloads have driven specialized instructions and accelerators, and new security-focused instructions target vulnerabilities and encrypted computation. Quantum computing has also introduced quantum-specific ISAs, reflecting the growing trend of heterogeneous and specialized computing architectures.

REFERENCES AND SUGGESTED READINGS

1. Muhammad Ali Mazidi , Janice G. Mazidi, Rolin D. McKinlay 8051 Microcontroller, The: A Systems Approach: Pearson New International Edition 1st Edition, 2013
2. Microcontrollers and Applications by Prof. Santanu Chattopadhyay, AICTE e-kumbh.
3. MCS@-51 INSTRUCTION SET reference manual.

QR Code for further reading:

NPTEL Microprocessor & Microcontroller

Intel 8051 Instruction Set Reference

4 Memory and I/O Interfacing

UNIT SPECIFICS

Through this unit we have discussed the following aspects:

- Memory and I/O expansion buses
- Control signals, memory wait states
- Interfacing of I/O
- Interfacing of ADC, DAC
- Interfacing of Timers, Counters
- Interfacing of Memory Devices.

The practical applications of the topics are discussed to foster curiosity, creativity, and enhance problem-solving skills. In addition to providing numerous multiple-choice questions and short and long answer questions categorized by lower and higher levels of Bloom's taxonomy, the unit includes various assignments featuring numerical problems. It also offers a list of references and suggested readings for further practice.

To access additional information on various topics of interest, QR codes are included in different sections for easy scanning, providing relevant supplementary knowledge.

Following the practical content, there is a "Know More" section designed to offer supplementary information that benefits users of the book. This section emphasizes initial activities, interesting facts, analogies, and the historical development of the subject. It highlights key observations, timelines that track the evolution of the topics up to the present day, and real-life or industrial applications across various aspects. Additionally, it includes case studies related to environmental, sustainability, social, and ethical issues where applicable, along with topics that spark inquisitiveness and curiosity within the unit.

RATIONALE

Understanding and utilizing memory and I/O expansion buses, control signals, and memory wait states, along with interfacing peripheral devices such as General Purpose I/O, ADC, DAC, timers, counters, and memory devices, is crucial for developing advanced embedded systems. These elements collectively enable the extension of a microcontroller's capabilities, allowing for increased memory and peripheral integration, which enhances the system's functionality and flexibility. Proper management of these components ensures efficient data transfer, synchronization, and processing, leading to optimized performance and reliability in applications ranging from simple automation tasks to complex industrial controls.

PRE-REQUISITES

Unit 1st , 2nd ,3rd of the book.

UNIT OUTCOMES

List of outcomes of this unit is as follows:

U4-O1: Understanding of the various types of memory and I/O expansion buses, control signals, and memory wait states.

U4-O2: Exploring the role and importance of control signals and memory wait states in interfacing peripheral devices.

U4-O3: Demonstrate the process of interfacing a microcontroller with peripheral devices such as ADC, DAC, and timers.

U4-O4: Analyze the performance implications of different memory and I/O expansion strategies.

U4-O5: Illustrate the process of interfacing memory devices.

Unit-4 Outcomes	**EXPECTED MAPPING WITH COURSE OUTCOMES** (1-Weak Correlation;2-Medium Correlation;3-Strong Correlation)				
	CO-1	**CO-2**	**CO-3**	**CO-4**	**CO-5**
U4-O1	3	2	2	2	1
U4-O2	3	2	2	2	1
U4-O3	2	3	3	2	2
U4-O4	2	1	2	3	1
U4-O5	2	2	2	2	1

4.1 Introduction

This unit focuses on the essential concepts of memory and I/O expansion buses, control signals, and memory wait states, alongside the interfacing of peripheral devices such as General Purpose I/O, ADC, DAC, timers, counters, and memory devices. Understanding these elements is crucial for designing and implementing advanced embedded systems that require extended memory, additional I/O capabilities, and efficient communication with various peripherals. By mastering the use of expansion buses and control signals, managing memory wait states, and interfacing with diverse peripheral devices, students will be equipped to develop robust and flexible systems capable of handling complex tasks and integrating multiple functionalities.

4.2 Memory expansion buses

Memory and I/O expansion buses are essential for enhancing the capabilities of the 8051 microcontroller, enabling it to interface with additional memory and peripheral devices. Here is an overview of how these concepts apply to the 8051 microcontroller:

4.2.1 Memory Expansion in 8051

The 8051 microcontroller, while powerful, has limited internal memory. To overcome these limitations and enable more complex and data-intensive applications, external memory can be interfaced with the 8051. Here's a detailed explanation of how memory expansion works in the 8051 which has been discussed in unit 2.

Types of Memory in 8051

Internal Memory:

- **On-chip ROM:** 4KB used for program storage.
- **On-chip RAM:** 128 bytes used for data storage and stack operations.

External Memory:

- **External ROM:** Can be expanded up to 64KB, used for storing larger programs.
- **External RAM:** Can also be expanded up to 64KB, used for data storage.

Addressing External Memory

The 8051 uses a multiplexed address and data bus to interface with external memory, which requires a few external components and control signals to operate efficiently.

Address and Data Bus Multiplexing:

- **Port 0 (P0):** Acts as both the lower byte of the address (A0-A7) and the data bus (D0-D7).
- **Port 2 (P2):** Acts as the higher byte of the address (A8-A15).

Control Signals:

- **ALE (Address Latch Enable):** This signal is used to de-multiplex the address and data lines on Port 0. When ALE is high, the address is latched from Port 0 into an external latch (typically a 74LS373), and when ALE is low, Port 0 is used as the data bus.
- $\overline{PSEN}$ **(Program Store Enable):** This signal is used to read data from external program memory (ROM/EPROM). It is activated when the 8051 fetches code from the external memory. When 8051 executes instructions from external memory, it activates the PSEN pin by pulling it low to signal the external memory to place the contents of the addressed memory location on the data bus.
- $\overline{EA}$ **(Pin 31):** For systems based on the 8051 microcontrollers, the EA pin should be connected to VCC if the program code is stored in the microcontroller's internal ROM. To store the program code in external ROM, connect the EA pin to GND.
    1. When $\overline{EA}$ = 0, External ROM address starts from 0000H and microcontroller discards internal ROM.
    2. When $\overline{EA}$ = 1, External ROM address starts from 1000H. The internal ROM is 4 KB. 4 KB in hexadecimal is 1000H (since 4 * 1024 = 4096 in decimal, and 4096 = 1000H in hexadecimal). The internal ROM occupies addresses from 0000H to 0FFFH (0 to 4095 in decimal). The external ROM address starts from the next address after the internal ROM. Therefore, the external ROM starts from address 1000H (4096 in decimal).
- **RD (Read) and WR (Write):** These signals are used to read from and write to external data memory (RAM).

4.2.2 Port 0 and Port2 role in addressing

The 8051 microcontrollers have a 16-bit program counter (PC), allowing them to access up to 64K bytes of program memory. In these microcontrollers, port 0 and port 2 are used to provide the 16-bit address needed to access external memory. Specifically, port 0 (P0) provides the lower 8-bit addresses (A0–A7), while port 2 (P2) provides the upper 8-bit addresses (A8–A15). Additionally, port 0 also serves as the 8-bit data bus (D0–D7). This means that pins P0.0–P0.7 are used for both address and data bus, this technique known as address/data multiplexing in processor design. It is evident that, Intel employed address/data multiplexing in the 8051 to minimize number of pins.

How do we determine when P0 is used as the data bus and when it is used for the address bus? This task is managed by the ALE (Address Latch Enable) pin. ALE is an output pin on the 8051 microcontroller. To separate the addresses from the P0 port, P0 is connected to a 74LS373 latch, utilizing the ALE pin to latch the address, as illustrated in Figure 4.1 and 4.2. This process of separating addresses from P0 is referred to as address/data demultiplexing. When ALE is set to 0, the microcontroller uses P0 for the data bus. Conversely, when ALE is set to 1, P0 is used for the address bus.

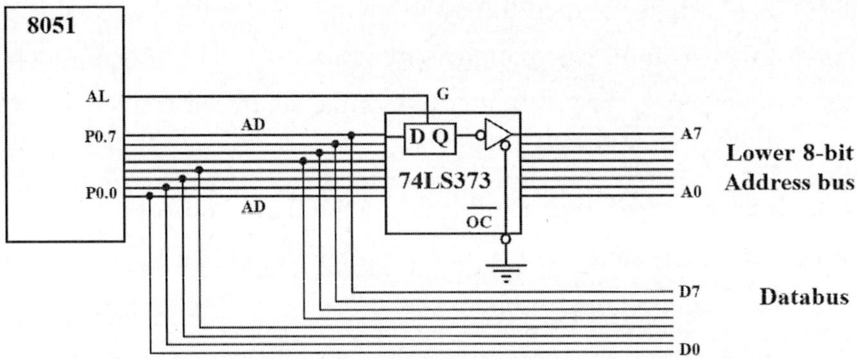

Figure 4.1: Address/Data Multiplexing [Mazidi, 2013]

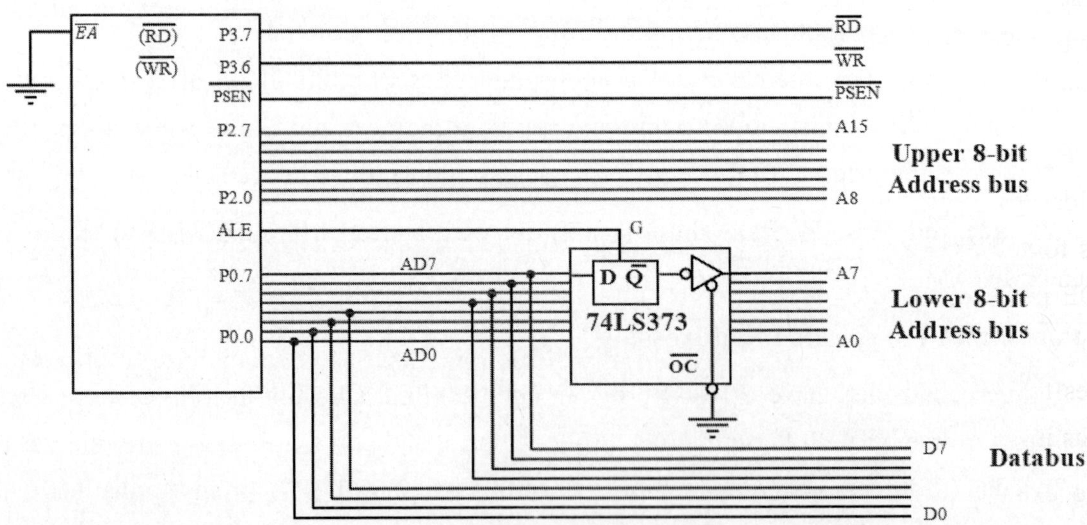

Figure 4.2: Data, Address, and Control Buses for the 8051 [Mazidi, 2013]

4.3 Interfacing 8051 microcontroller to External Program ROM

In interfacing the 8051 microcontroller with external memory, understanding the PSEN (Program Store Enable) and EA (External Access) signals is crucial. The PSEN signal is an output signal generated by the 8051 microcontroller, specifically used when the microcontroller needs to read program code from external ROM.

The PSEN pin must be connected to the OE pin and CE (Chip Enable) of the external ROM. The OE pin enables the output of the ROM, allowing data to be read by the microcontroller. When the microcontroller needs to execute an instruction stored in the external ROM, it activates the PSEN signal. This signal tells the external ROM to output the requested data (opcode) onto the data bus so the microcontroller can fetch and execute it.

EA (External Access) Pin

The EA pin determines whether the microcontroller will use its internal ROM or access external ROM for program code.

EA Connected to GND: When the EA pin is connected to ground (GND), it indicates that the microcontroller should fetch the program code from external ROM. In this mode the PSEN signal is used to read the program code from the external ROM. This setup is typical when the internal ROM capacity is insufficient, and additional memory is required.

EA Connected to VCC: When the EA pin is connected to the power supply (VCC), it indicates that the microcontroller will use its internal ROM for program storage. In this mode the PSEN signal is not activated since the program code is fetched from the on-chip ROM, eliminating the need for external memory access.

Example and Connection Diagram

Consider a system where the 8051 microcontroller is connected to external ROM. The connections are as follows: PSEN to OE & CE Connection: The PSEN pin of the microcontroller is connected to the OE pin of the external ROM. This connection allows the microcontroller to enable the ROM's output whenever it needs to read the program code. If EA is connected to GND, the microcontroller fetches the program code from the external ROM. If EA is connected to VCC, the microcontroller uses its internal ROM and does not activate the PSEN signal.

In the example shown in Figure 4.3, we want to interface 8KB of external ROM to the 8051 microcontroller. First, we need to determine how many address lines are required to interface with 8KB ROM. We can express 8KB ROM as 8Kx8 ROM, which represents a total of 8,192 memory locations (2^13). This means we need 13 address lines to interface with the 8KB ROM. As depicted in Figure 4.3, we have connected the 13 address lines of the ROM chip to the lower 13 lines of the address bus of the 8051. Additionally, we have connected the data bus of the ROM chip to the data bus of the 8051.

To interface 8Kx8 ROM with 8051 microcontroller, first need to find number of address lines and data lines required by the 8Kx8 ROM. Memory can be represented as $2^{(\text{Address Line})}$x Data Lines:

8KB = 8 x 2^{10}x Byte

= 2^{13}x8 bit

Total Address lines = 13

Data lines=8

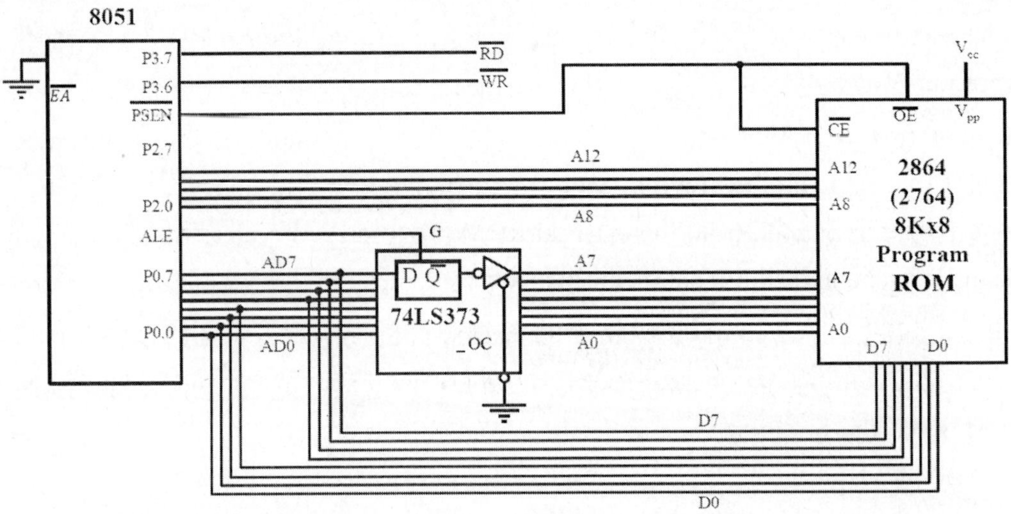

Figure 4.3: Interfacing external ROM to 8051 microcontroller [Mazidi, 2013]

4.4 Interfacing 8051 microcontroller to External Program ROM

The 8051 microcontroller can access two types of memory: one for program code and one for data. Each type can be up to 64K bytes, making a total of 128K bytes of addressable memory. The MOVC instruction is used to access the program code space, while the MOVX instruction, along with the DPTR register, is used to access the external data memory space.

The MOVC instruction in the 8051 microcontroller, where "C" stands for code, is used to indicate that data is located in the code space. The 8051 microcontroller family has two separate memory spaces: code space and data space.

Code Space: This is where the program code is stored. The 8051 can access up to 64K bytes of code space using the program counter to locate and fetch instructions.

Data Memory Space

Data Space: In addition to the code space, the 8051 also has 64K bytes of data memory space. This means the 8051 has a total addressable memory of 128K bytes, with 64K bytes reserved for program code and 64K bytes reserved for data.

Accessing Data Space: Data memory space is accessed using the DPTR (Data Pointer) register and the MOVX instruction, where "X" stands for external. This indicates that the data memory must be implemented externally.

In this section we will going to interface external ROM containing data. We need to understand the role of signals PSEN and RD. For the ROM containing the program code, PSEN is used to fetch the code. For the ROM containing data, the RD signal is used to fetch the data. To access the external data memory space, we must use the instruction MOVX as described next.

The Figure 4.4 shows how an 8KB data ROM is interfaced with the 8051 microcontroller. Since it is a ROM containing data, we do not connect the PSEN pin to the OE pin. Instead, we connect the read (RD) pin to the OE pin of the ROM. As usual, the data pins of the 8051 are connected to the data pins of the ROM. Since this is also an 8KB ROM, we need 13 address bits. The remaining bits will be used to generate the chip select signal. Since it is ROM we can only read data from it.

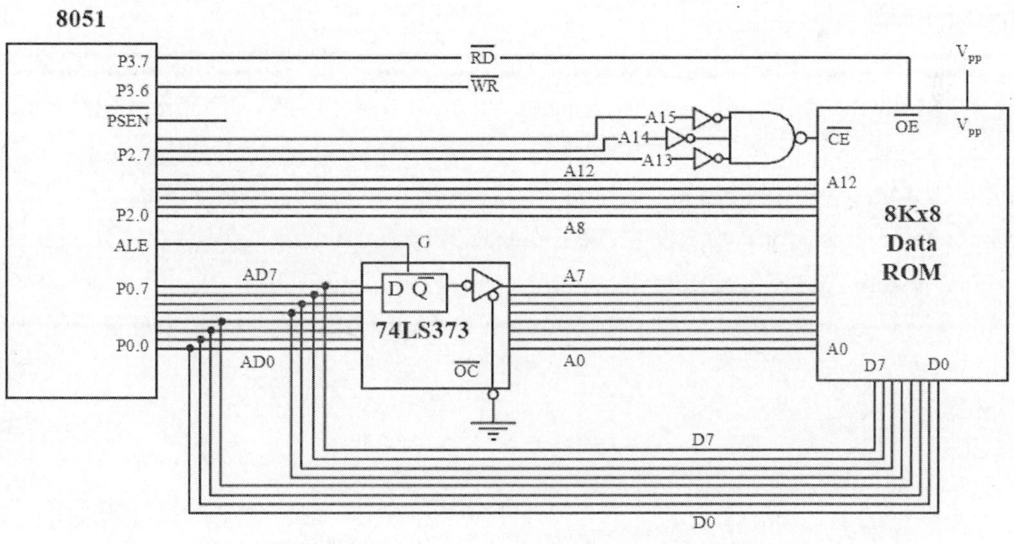

Figure 4.4: 8051 Connection to External Data ROM [Mazidi, 2013]

Example 4.1 An external ROM uses the 8051 data space to store the look-up table (starting at 1001H) for DAC data. Write a program to read 20 bytes of these data and send them to P2.

Solution:

```
MYXDATA EQU 1001H ; EQU for replace number by a symbol
COUNT EQU 20
        MOV DPTR,#MYXDATA ;pointer to external data
        MOV R2,#COUNT ;counter for number of bytes
AGAIN:          MOVX A,@DPTR ;get data byte from external mem
        MOV P2,A ; send it to P2
        INC DPTR ;next location
        DJNZ R2,AGAIN ;until all are read
```

The MYXDATA and COUNT symbols are defined as 1001H and 20 respectively. The MOV DPTR,#MYXDATA instruction initializes the Data Pointer (DPTR) to point to the external memory location 1001H, while MOV R2,#COUNT sets register R2 as a counter with an initial value of 20, indicating the number of bytes to be read. The label AGAIN marks the start of a loop. Inside the loop, the MOVX A,@DPTR instruction fetches a byte of data from the external memory pointed to by DPTR and stores it in the accumulator (A). This data is then sent to Port 2 using the MOV P2,A instruction. The INC DPTR instruction increments the DPTR to point to the next memory location. Finally, the DJNZ R2,AGAIN instruction decrements the counter R2 and jumps back to the AGAIN label if R2 is not zero, repeating the process until all 20 bytes are read and output to Port 2.

Example 4.2 Show the design of an 8051-based system with 8K bytes of program ROM and 8K bytes of data ROM.

For program ROM, the PSEN pin is used to activate both the Output Enable (OE) and Chip Enable (CE) signals. In contrast, for data ROM, the Read (RD) pin is used to activate the OE signal, while the CE signal is activated by a simple decoder, as shown in Figure 4.5

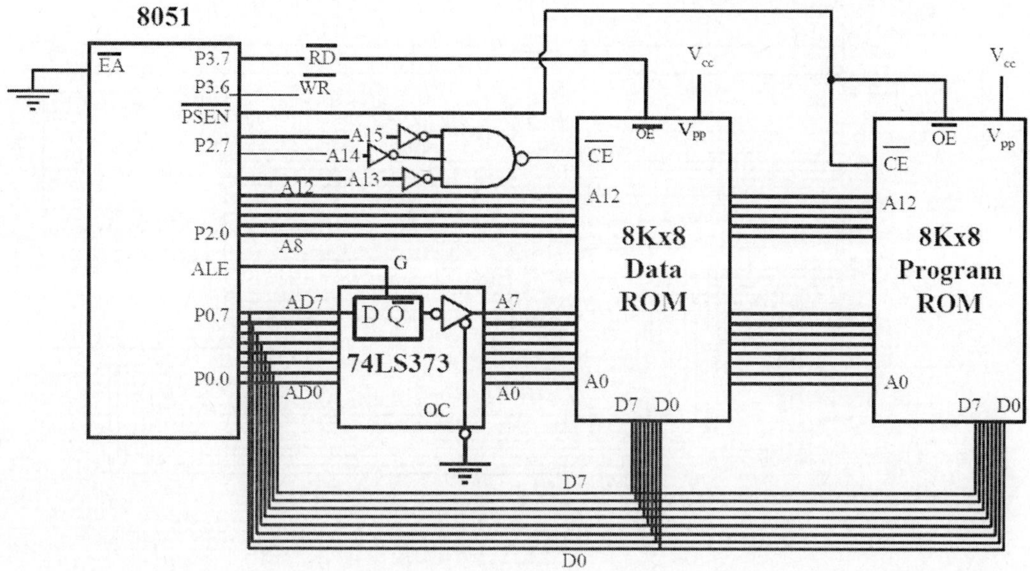

Figure 4.5: 8051 Connection to External Data ROM and External Program ROM

4.5 Interfacing 8051 microcontroller to External Data RAM

Interfacing an 8051 microcontroller to external data RAM involves connecting the microcontroller's address, data, and control pins to the corresponding pins on the RAM. The address pins select the specific memory locations in the RAM, while the data pins transfer data between the microcontroller and the RAM. The Read (RD) and Write (WR) pins of the 8051 are connected to the corresponding Output Enable (OE) and Write Enable (WE) pins of the RAM to control data reading and writing operations. Additionally, the Chip Enable (CE) pin of the RAM is activated using a chip select signal generated by decoding the higher address lines. This setup allows the 8051 to access and manipulate data stored in the external RAM effectively.

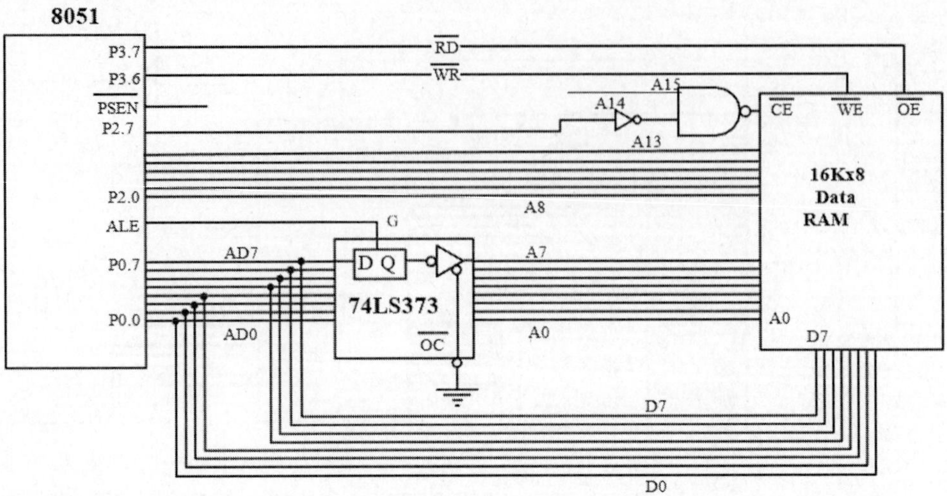

Figure 4.6: 8051 Connection to External Data RAM [Mazidi, 2013]

In the Figure 4.6 we are interfacing an 8051 microcontroller to external data RAM for 16KB data memory. First, connect the microcontroller's address and data pins to the corresponding pins on the RAM. For 16KB (16Kx8) of RAM, you need 14 address lines to select specific memory locations. The data pins are used for bidirectional data transfer between the microcontroller and the RAM. The Read (RD) and Write (WR) control pins from the 8051 are connected to the Output Enable (OE) and Write Enable (WE) pins on the RAM to manage data reading and writing operations. A chip select signal for the RAM is generated by decoding the higher address lines, which ensures the RAM is activated only when addressed by the microcontroller. This setup allows the 8051 to efficiently access and manipulate up to 16KB of external data memory.

Example 4.2 Write a program to read 100 bytes of data from P1 and save the data in external RAM starting at RAM location 4000H.

```
RAMDATA EQU 4000H
COUNT EQU 100
        MOV DPTR,#RAMDATA ;pointer to external Data RAM
        MOV R3,#COUNT ;counter
AGAIN:  MOV A,P1 ;read data from P1
        MOVX @DPTR,A ;save it external Data RAM
        ACALL DELAY ;wait before next sample
        INC DPTR ;next data location
        DJNZ R3,AGAIN ;until all are read
HERE:   SJMP HERE ;stay here when finished
```

4.6 I/O Expansion Buses

The 8051 microcontroller comes with four parallel I/O ports (P0, P1, P2, and P3), providing a total of 32 I/O lines. However, some applications require more I/O lines than what is available on the microcontroller. In such cases, I/O port expansion is necessary. This can be achieved using external hardware components like 8255 Programmable Peripheral Interface (PPI) to increase the number of I/O ports available for interfacing with various peripheral devices.

4.6.1 8051 interfacing with 8255 (Programmable Peripheral Interface)

The 8255 Programmable Peripheral Interface (PPI) is a versatile and widely-used I/O device that provides 24 additional I/O pins for microcontrollers and microprocessors. It is commonly used to expand the I/O capabilities of systems, allowing for more input and output devices to be connected and controlled.

Features of 8255

- PA0 - PA7 (8-bit port A) Can be programmed as all input or output.
- PB0 - PB7 (8-bit port B) Can be programmed as all input or output.
- PC0 – PC7 (8-bit port C) Can be all input or output

Can also be split into two parts:

CU (upper bits PC4 - PC7)

CL (lower bits PC0 – PC3) each can be used for input or output. Any of bits PC0 to PC7 can be programmed individually.

- **Control Register:** A control word written to this register configures the operational mode and direction of the ports.
- **Flexible Operating Modes:**

Mode 0: Basic input/output mode, where ports function as simple I/O ports.

Mode 1: Strobed input/output mode, useful for interfacing with devices that require handshake signals.

Mode 2: Bidirectional bus mode, allowing bidirectional handshaking data transfer on Port A.

- $\overline{RD}$ and $\overline{WR}$ These two active-low control signals are inputs to the 8255.
- The $\overline{RD}$ and $\overline{WR}$ signals from the 8051 are connected to these inputs.
- D0 – D7 are connected to the data pins of the microcontroller allowing it to send data back and forth between the controller and the 8255 chip.

- RESET An active-high signal input Used to clear the control register. When RESET is activated, all ports are initialized as input ports.
- A0, A1, and $\overline{CS}$ (chip select)

CS is active-low. While $\overline{CS}$ selects the entire chip, it is A0 and A1 that select specific ports. These 3 pins are used to access port A, B, C, or the control register.

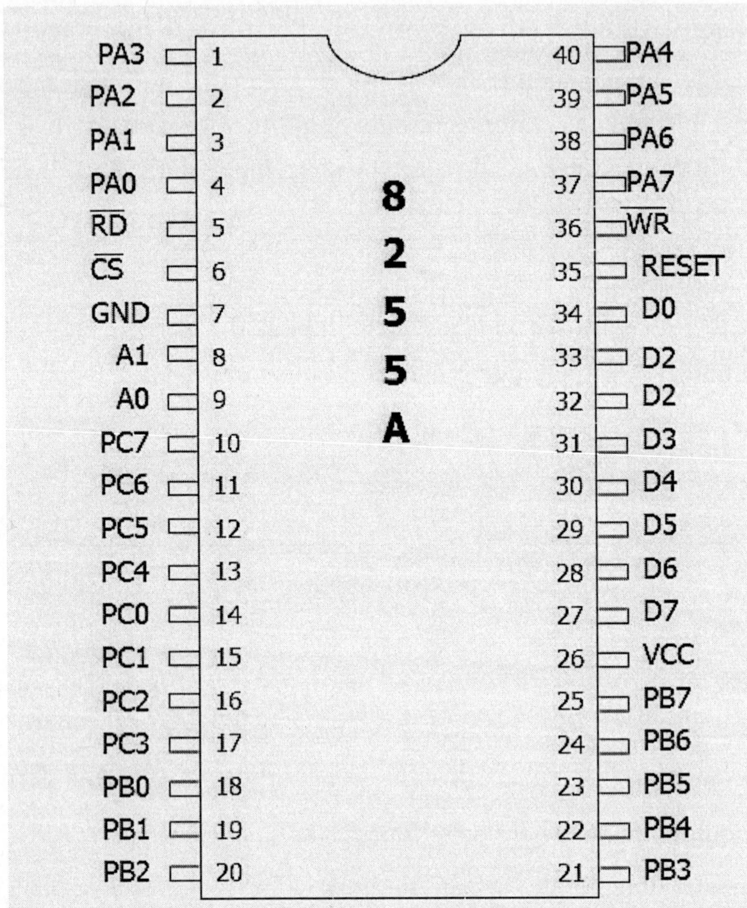

Figure 4.7: 8255 PPI pin diagram

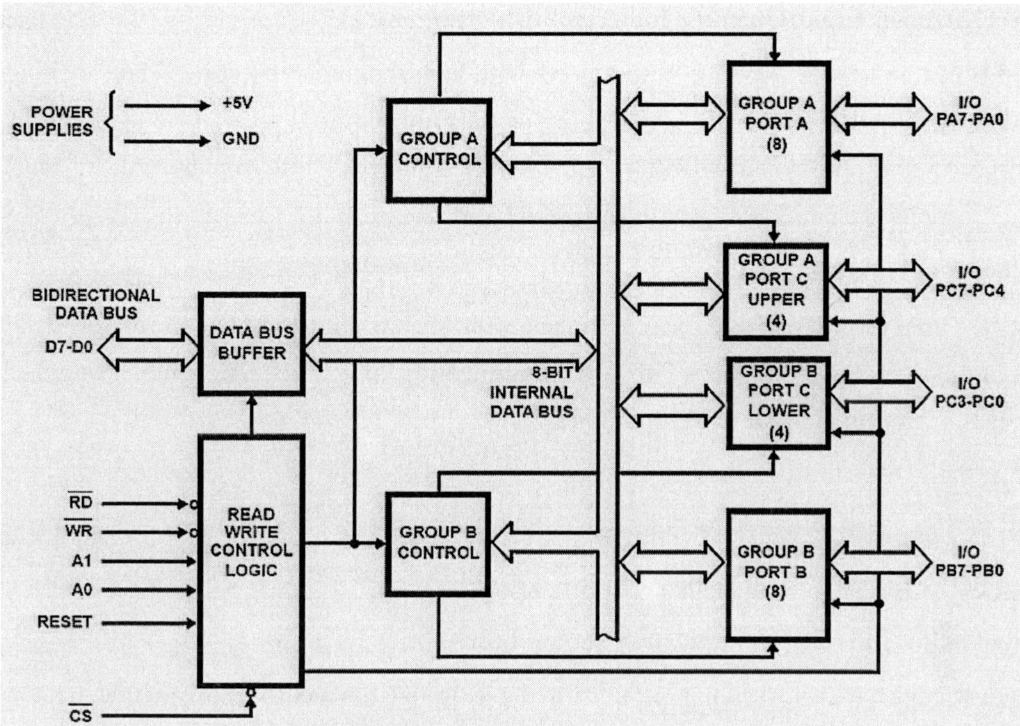

Figure 4.8: Block Diagram of 8255

Table 4.1: 8255 Port Selection

$\overline{CS}$	A1	A0	Selection
0	0	0	Port A
0	0	1	Port B
0	1	0	Port C
0	1	1	Control register
1	X	X	8255 is not selected

While ports A, B and C are used to input or output data, the control register must be programmed to select operation mode and direction of three ports. The ports of the 8255 can be programmed in any of the following modes:

1. Mode 0, simple I/O

Any of the ports A, B, CL, and CU can be programmed as input out output. All bits are out or all are in. There is no signal-bit control as in P0-P3 of 8051.

2. Mode 1, Strobed Input/Output Mode (Handshaking mode)

Port A and B can be used as input or output ports with handshaking capabilities Handshaking signals are provided by the bits of port C. Handshaking signals are required to manage the flow of data to ensure proper timing and synchronization and reliable transfer. These signals prevent data loss or miscommunication when interfacing with slower devices.

Role of Port C in Handshaking:

Port C bits are used to generate and receive the necessary handshaking signals to support data transfer on Port A and Port B. Specific bits of Port C are assigned for this purpose, depending on whether Port A or Port B is operating in input or output mode.

For Port A:

PC3, PC4, PC5 are used as handshaking lines:

PC3: Input buffer full (IBF) – indicates data is ready to be read.

PC4: Output buffer full (OBF) – indicates data has been written.

PC5: Acknowledge (ACK) – signal sent from the external device to confirm that data has been received or read.

For Port B:

PC0, PC1, PC2 are used as handshaking lines:

PC0: Input buffer full (IBF) for Port B.

PC1: Output buffer full (OBF) for Port B.

PC2: Acknowledge (ACK) for Port B.

Operation:

When Port A or B is configured as input in Mode 1, the external device sends data to the port, and a handshaking signal (e.g., STB, or Strobe) is provided via a Port C pin to indicate data is ready. The 8255 sets the corresponding handshaking bits (e.g., IBF) to indicate data has been received, and the CPU can then read the data. When Port A or B is configured as output, the 8255 uses the handshaking signals to indicate that data is ready for the external device and waits for an acknowledgment from the external device to ensure successful data transfer.

3. Mode 2, Bidirectional Data Transfer Mode

Port A can be used as a bidirectional I/O port with handshaking capabilities provided by port C. Port B can be used either in mode 0 or mode 1.

4. **BSR (bit set/reset) mode**

Bit-set/reset operation: Any individual bit of Port C can be programmed as either high (set) or low (reset) using the control word.

The S/R bit in the control word for BSR command determines whether the selected bit is to be set or reset:

S/R = 1: Set the selected bit of Port C to logic 1.

S/R = 0: Reset the selected bit of Port C to logic 0.

Control Word I/O command

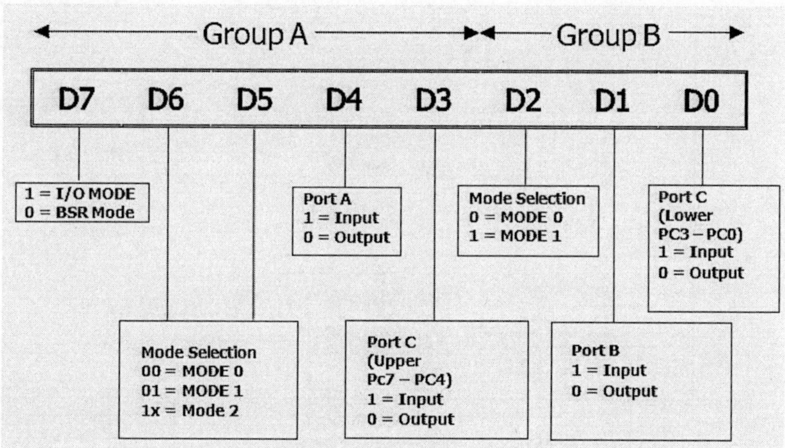

Figure 4.9: Control Word Format for I/O command

Control Word I/O command

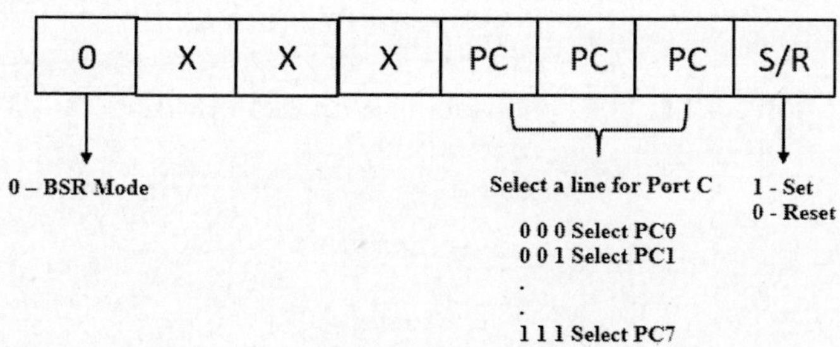

Figure 4.10: Control Word Format for BSR command

The 8255 chip can be programmed into any of the four previously mentioned modes by sending a byte, referred to as a control word by Intel, to its control register. Before this, we need to determine the port addresses assigned to ports A, B, C, and the control register, a process known as mapping the I/O ports.

Circuit Diagram Connections

Connect the power pins of 8255 (VCC and GND) to the appropriate sources. Connect the EA pin of 8051 to VCC.

Connect P3.6 (WR) and P3.7 (RD) of 8051 to the WR and RD pins of 8255, respectively.

Connect Port 0 of 8051 to the 74LS373 decoder. Connect the ALE pin of 8051 to the Enable pin (G) of 74LS373.

Connect the AD0-AD7 lines of Port 0 directly to the D0-D7 pins of 8255.

Connect the A0 and A1 pins of 8255 to the output of the 74LS373 decoder.

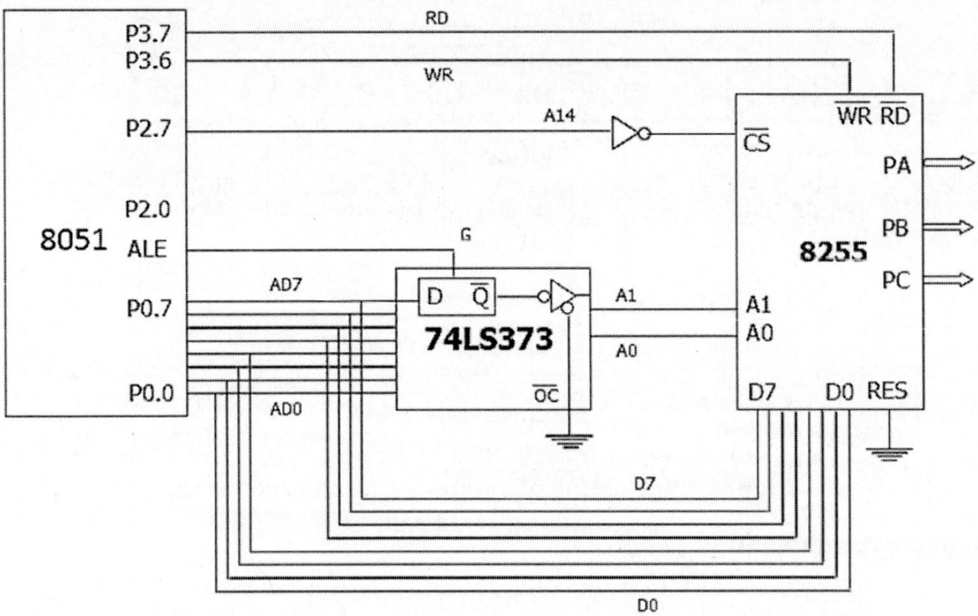

Figure 4.11: 8051 interfacing with 8255 [Mazidi, 2013]

Example 4.3 Find the control word of the 8255 for the following configurations:
(a) All the ports of A, B and C are output ports (mode 0)
(b) PA = in, PB = out, PCL = out, and PCH = out
(a) All Ports (A, B, and C) as Output Ports (Mode 0)
In Mode 0, all three ports (Port A, Port B, and Port C) can be configured as either input or output. We have to look at control word format for I/O mode shown in figure 4.9. For this configuration, where all ports are output, the control word can be derived as follows:

- **D7**: 1 (indicates I/O mode)
- **D6**: 0 (Mode 0 for Port A)
- **D5**: 0 (Mode 0 for Port A)
- **D4**: 0 (Port A is output)
- **D3**: 0 (Port C upper nibble is output)
- **D2**: 0 (Mode 0 for Port B)
- **D1**: 0 (Port B is output)
- **D0**: 0 (Port C lower nibble is output)

Thus, the control word in binary is 10000000, which converts to hexadecimal as 0x80.
(b) PA = Input, PB = Output, PCL = Output, PCH = Output
In this configuration, Port A is set as an input port, while Port B and both nibbles of Port C are set as output ports. The control word is configured as follows:

- **D7**: 1 (indicates I/O mode)
- **D6**: 0 (Mode 0 for Port A)
- **D5**: 0 (Mode 0 for Port A)
- **D4**: 1 (Port A is input)
- **D3**: 0 (Port C upper nibble is output)
- **D2**: 0 (Mode 0 for Port B)
- **D1**: 0 (Port B is output)
- **D0**: 0 (Port C lower nibble is output)

Thus, the control word in binary is 10010000, which converts to hexadecimal as 0x90.

4.7 Memory Wait States

Memory wait states in the 8051 microcontroller context refer to the additional clock cycles introduced to accommodate slower external memory and peripheral devices. These wait states are necessary when the memory access time is longer than the microcontroller's instruction cycle time. When accessing external memory or peripheral, the 8051 may need to insert wait states to allow the slower external memory or peripheral to respond.

Wait States in 8051

The 8051 has a maximum clock frequency of 12 MHz. External memory is typically slower than the on-chip memory. When fetching instructions or data from external memory, the 8051 may need to insert wait states to allow the external memory to respond before the next bus cycle begins. The number of wait states depends on the speed of the external memory relative to the 8051-clock frequency. Slower memory requires more wait states. The 8051 does not have a dedicated wait state input pin. The number of wait states is determined by the speed of the external memory.

4.8 Interfacing General Purpose I/O

Microcontrollers are predominantly utilized in control applications, where they monitor the environment or a specific system and control devices accordingly. Depending on the task at hand, the connected devices can be broadly categorized into input devices (mostly sensors) and output devices (mostly actuators). A simple example of an input device is a switch with two positions, ON and OFF, which can be interfaced with a port bit of the 8051 microcontroller to read its status through a program. Similarly, an LED can be used as an output device to display the status of a port bit, reflecting the results of a control algorithm executed by the 8051. Many input-output devices are electro-mechanical, requiring specific voltage, current, and timing considerations. For instance, the output pattern displayed on a device should be flicker-free and steady to be interpretable by human eyes. An input switch might have jittery operation, potentially causing input errors. A motor running at a certain speed needs time to stop or change direction. Thus, interfacing input/output devices with the 8051 involves two critical tasks. The first task is designing the circuit to connect the device. The hardware must convert the control program's port bit settings into the appropriate voltage, current, or other requirements of the device. The second task is creating the software for the 8051 to read input devices or control output devices. Given the limited number of I/O bits and driving capacity of the 8051 ports, additional chips or components may be needed to enhance these capabilities. In module 6 we will interface LED, LCD and keyboard, Stepper motor, DC Motor, sensor.

4.9 ADC Interfacing

Analog-to-digital converters (ADCs) are essential for data acquisition, bridging the gap between the analog world and digital computers. While digital systems use binary (discrete) values, the physical world operates in analog (continuous) signals. Examples of analog quantities include temperature, pressure (wind or liquid), humidity, and velocity. These physical quantities are converted into electrical signals (voltage or current) using transducers, also known as sensors. Sensors for various natural quantities, such as temperature, velocity, pressure, and light, generate output in the form of voltage or current. Therefore, an ADC is necessary to convert these analog signals into digital numbers that a microcontroller can read and process. ADCs come with different resolutions, typically 8, 10, 12, 16, or even 24 bits. Higher resolution ADCs offer smaller step sizes, which is the smallest change an ADC can detect. This concept is illustrated in Table 4.2. In addition to resolution, conversion time is another critical factor when evaluating an ADC. This chapter will explore several 8-bit ADC chips, focusing on both resolution and conversion time. Conversion time refers to the duration an ADC takes to convert an analog input into a digital (binary) number. ADC chips can be classified as either parallel or serial. In parallel ADCs, there are eight or more pins dedicated to outputting the binary data. In contrast, serial ADCs use only one pin for data output.

Table 4.2: Resolution versus Step Size for ADC for Vcc = 5V

n-bit	Number of Steps	Step Size (mV)
8	256	5/256 = 19.53
10	1024	5/1024 = 4.88
12	4096	5/4096 = 1.2
16	65536	5/65536 = 0.076

4.9.1 ADC0804 Interfacing

The ADC0804 is an 8-bit parallel analog-to-digital converter (ADC) from the ADC0800 series created by National Semiconductor, and it is also available from several other manufacturers. This ADC operates on a +5 V power supply and provides an 8-bit resolution. The conversion time for the ADC0804 is affected by the clock signals applied to the CLK IN pin, with a minimum conversion time of 110 µs. The following section contains the pin description for the ADC0804.

Pin Configuration:

1. **VCC (Pin 20):** Power supply pin (5V).
2. **GND (Pin 10):** Ground.
3. **Vref/2 (Pin 9):** The reference voltage input sets the baseline for the analog input range. Pin 9 serves as the input for the reference voltage. If this pin is left unconnected, the analog input voltage range for the ADC0804 will be 0 to 5V, which matches the Vcc pin. However, in many applications, the analog input voltage applied to Vin may need to fall outside the 0 to 5V range. To accommodate different analog input voltage ranges, Vref/2 can be used. For instance, if the

desired analog input range is 0 to 4V, Vref/2 should be set to 2V. Table 4.3 provides the Vin ranges corresponding to various Vref/2 inputs. When the pin is left open, Vref/2 measures 2.5V when Vcc is 5V. The step size, or resolution, is defined as the smallest change that can be detected by the ADC

Table 4.3: Resolution versus Step Size for ADC for Vcc = 5V

$V_{ref}/2$ (V)	V_{in} (V)	Step Size (mV)
Not connected*	0 to 5	5/256 = 19.53
2.0	0 to 4	4/255 = 15.62
1.5	0 to 3	3/256 = 11.71
1.28	0 to 2.56	2.56/256 = 10

4. **Vin (+) and Vin (−):** These are the differential analog inputs where Vin = Vin (+) − Vin (−). Often the Vin (−) pin is connected to ground and the Vin (+) pin is used as the analog input to be converted to digital.
5. **CLK IN (Pin 4) & CLK R:** The CLK IN pin is an input that connects to an external clock source when an external clock is used for timing. However, the ADC0804 features an internal clock generator. To take advantage of the internal clock generator (also referred to as self-clocking), the CLK IN and CLK R pins are connected to a capacitor and a resistor, as shown in Figure 4.11. In this setup, the clock frequency is determined by the following equation:

$$f = \frac{1}{1.1RC}$$

6. **CS (Pin 1):** Chip select. Active low to enable the ADC.
7. **RD (Pin 2):** Read. Active low to read the converted data. The ADC0804 uses an active-low input signal. It converts the analog input to its binary equivalent and stores it in an internal register. To retrieve the converted data, the RD pin is used. When CS is set to 0, applying a high-to-low pulse to the RD pin causes the 8-bit digital output to appear on the D0–D7 data pins. The RD pin is also known as output enable (OE).
8. **INTR (Interrupt Pin):** This is an active-low output pin. It remains high under normal conditions, but when the conversion is complete, it transitions to a low state to indicate to the CPU that the converted data is ready for retrieval. Once the INTR pin goes low, set CS to 0 and generate a high-to-low pulse on the RD pin to read the data from the ADC0804 chip

9. **WR (Pin 3):** This is an active-low input that signals the ADC0804 to initiate the conversion process. When CS is set to 0 and WR transitions from low to high, the ADC0804 begins converting the analog input value (Vin) into an 8-bit digital number. The conversion time is influenced by the values of CLK IN and CLK R, as explained below. Once the conversion is finished, the ADC0804 pulls the INTR pin low.
10. **D0-D7 (Pins 11-18):** Data output pins. Provide the 8-bit digital output. D0–D7 (with D7 as the MSB) are the digital data output pins of the ADC0804, a parallel ADC chip. These pins are tri-state buffered, and the converted data can only be accessed when CS is set to 0 and RD is brought low. To calculate the output voltage, use the following formula:

$$Dout = \frac{Vin}{Step\ Size}$$

where Dout = digital data output (in decimal), Vin = analog input voltage, and step size (resolution) is the smallest change, which is (2 × Vref/2)/256 for ADC0804.
11. **Analog ground and digital ground:** These pins function as ground connections for both analog and digital signals. The analog ground is connected to the ground of the analog input (Vin), while the digital ground is linked to the ground of the Vcc pin. By having separate ground pins, the analog Vin signal is isolated from the transient voltages produced by the digital switching of the output pins D0–D7. This separation enhances the accuracy of the digital data output.

Based on this discussion, the following steps should be followed to perform data conversion using the ADC0804 chip also depicted in Figure 4.12:

- Set CS to 0 and send a low to high pulse to the WR pin to initiate the conversion process.
- Monitor the INTR pin. When INTR goes low, the conversion is complete, and you can proceed to the next step. If INTR is high, continue polling until it goes low.
- Once INTR is low, set CS to 0 and send a high-to-low pulse to the RD pin to read the data from the ADC0804 chip, as shown in timing diagram 4.11.

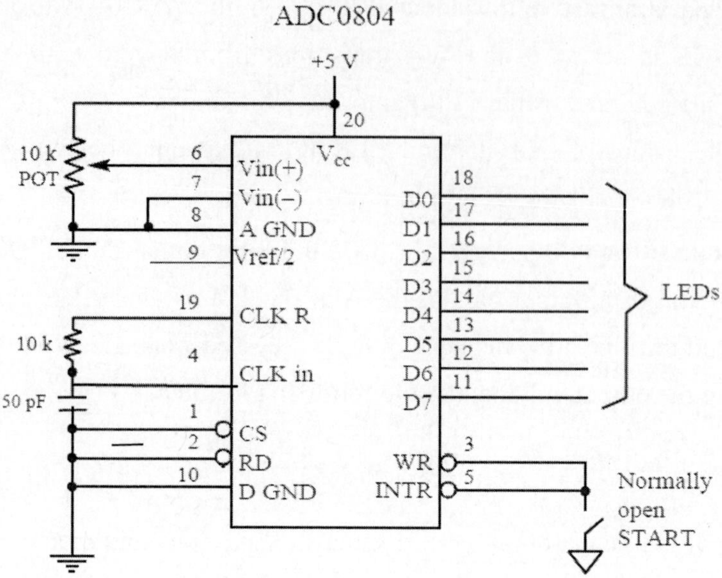

Figure 4.12: ADC0804 Chip [Mazidi, 2013]

Clock source for ADC0804

The speed at which an analog input is converted to a digital output by the ADC0804 depends on the frequency of the CLK input. According to the ADC0804 datasheets, the typical operating frequency is around 640 kHz at 5 V. Figures 4.13 and 4.14 illustrate two methods for providing the clock signal to the ADC0804. In Figure 4.14, the clock input for the ADC0804 is sourced from the microcontroller's crystal oscillator. Given that this crystal operates at a much higher frequency, D flip-flops (74LS74) are used to divide the frequency down to a suitable level. A single D flip-flop can divide the frequency by 2 when its Q output is fed back to its D input. For even higher-frequency crystals, multiple flip-flops, such as four in series, can be employed to achieve the desired clock frequency for the ADC0804.

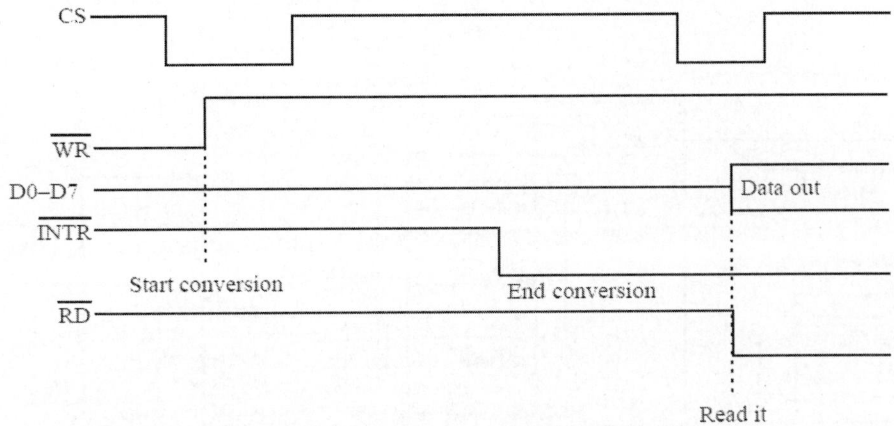

Figure 4.13 Read and Write Timing for ADC0804 [Mazidi, 2013]

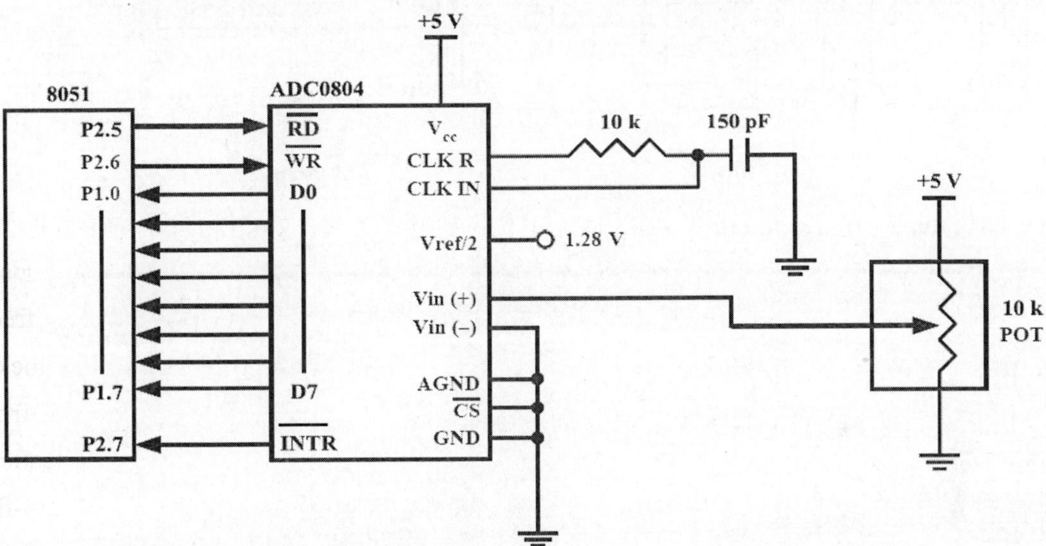

Figure 4.14: 8051 Connection to ADC0804 with Self-Clocking [Mazidi, 2013]

Programming ADC0804 in Assembly

```
; Define control bits for the ADC0804
     RD    BIT P2.5    ; Read signal
     WR    BIT P2.6    ; Write signal (start conversion)
       INTR BIT P2.7    ; End-of-conversion signal
MYDATA  EQU P1       ; P1.0-P1.7 = D0-D7 of the ADC0804
     MOV P1, #FFH      ; Set P1 as input
```

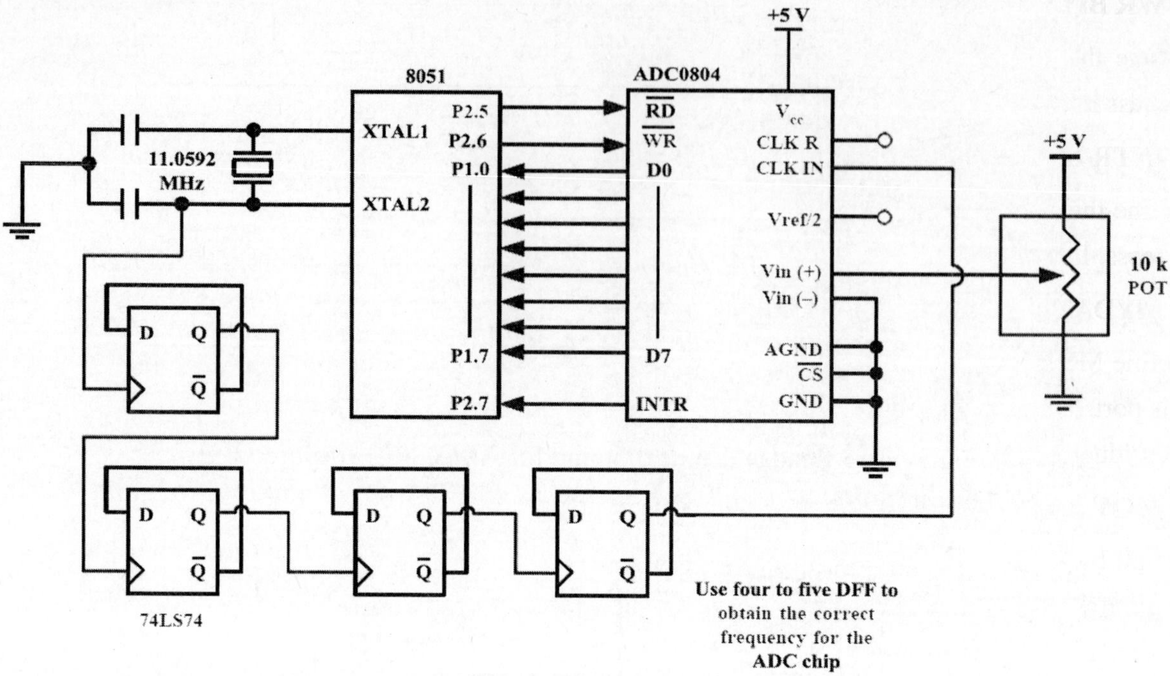

Figure 4.15: 8051 Connection to ADC0804 with Clock from XTAL2 of the 8051 [Mazidi, 2013]

```
SETB INTR            ; Set INTR high initially
BACK:
CLR WR             ; Set WR low to initiate conversion
SETB WR            ; Set WR high (low-to-high transition to start
conversion)
HERE:
JB INTR, HERE      ; Wait for the end of conversion
CLR RD             ; Conversion complete, enable RD
MOV A, MYDATA      ; Read the converted data from ADC0804
SETB RD            ; Set RD high for the next round
SJMP BACK          ; Jump back to start the process
```

Detailed Explanation:

1. RD BIT P2.5; RD

Define the RD pin as a bit-addressable location at P2.5. This pin is used to read data from the ADC0804. In the 8051 microcontroller, BIT is used to define a single-bit addressable location, allowing control of individual pins.

2. WR BIT P2.6; WR (start conversion)

Define the WR pin as a bit-addressable location at P2.6. This pin is used to start the conversion process in the ADC0804. Similarly, WR is used to initiate the conversion by sending a write pulse.

3. INTR BIT P2.7 ;end-of-conversion

Define the INTR pin as a bit-addressable location at P2.7. This pin signals the end of the conversion process. INTR is checked to determine when the ADC0804 has completed the conversion.

4. MYDATA EQU P1 ;P1.0-P1.7=D0-D7 of the ADC0804

Define MYDATA as a reference to port P1. The ADC0804's digital output (D0-D7) is connected to this port. This makes it easier to refer to the entire port as MYDATA rather than dealing with each bit individually.

5. MOV P1,#0FFH ;make P1 = input

Set all bits of port P1 to high, configuring the port as an input. MOV P1,#FFH configures all bits of port P1 as inputs, which is necessary to read the 8-bit digital data from the ADC0804.

6. SETB INTR

Set the INTR pin to high. This is typically done to ensure the initial state of INTR is high before starting the conversion.

7. BACK: CLR WR ;WR=0

Clear the WR pin to start a write pulse. CLR WR sets WR low, initiating the conversion process.

8. SETB WR ;WR=1 L-to-H to start conversion

Set the WR pin high to complete the write pulse. SETB WR returns WR to high, completing the write pulse and starting the ADC conversion.

9. HERE: JB INTR, HERE ;wait for end of conversion

Loop until the INTR pin goes low. JB INTR,HERE continuously checks the INTR pin. The loop waits until INTR goes low, indicating the conversion is complete.

10. CLR RD ;conversion finished, enable RD

Clear the RD pin to read data from the ADC0804. CLR RD sets RD low, enabling the output data pins (D0-D7) of the ADC0804 to be read.

11. MOV A,MYDATA ;read the data

Move the data from port P1 (MYDATA) into the accumulator. MOV A,MYDATA reads the 8-bit digital data from the ADC0804 and stores it in the accumulator (A).

12. SETB RD ;make RD=1 for next round

Set the RD pin high to prepare for the next conversion cycle. SETB RD returns RD to high, making it ready for the next read operation.

13. SJMP BACK

Short jump to the label BACK. SJMP BACK creates a loop by jumping back to the label BACK, allowing the process to repeat.

The 8051 C version of the above program is given below.

```
#include <reg51.h>
// Define control signals for the ADC0804
sbit RD = P2^5;        // Read signal
sbit WR = P2^6;        // Write signal (start conversion)
sbit INTR = P2^7;      // End-of-conversion signal
sfr MYDATA = P1;       // Data register for ADC0804
void ConvertAndDisplay(unsigned char value); // Function prototype
void main() {
unsigned char value;
 // Initialize port settings
  MYDATA = 0xFF;  // Set P1 as input (ADC data)
INTR = 1;       // Set INTR high to initialize
RD = 1;         // Set RD high to ensure readiness
WR = 1;         // Set WR high to ensure readiness
 while (1) {
WR = 0;     // Send a low pulse on WR to start conversion
 WR = 1;    // Set WR high (low-to-high transition starts conversion)
  // Wait for end of conversion (INTR goes low)
while (INTR == 1);
RD = 0;    // Send a low pulse on RD to read data
value = MYDATA; // Read the converted value from the ADC
ConvertAndDisplay(value); // Process and display the value
      RD = 1;    // Set RD high for the next operation
   }
}
```

```
void ConvertAndDisplay(unsigned char value)
{
unsigned char x,d1,d2,d3;
x=value/10;
d1=value%10;
d2=x%10
d3=x/10
P0=d1; //LSByte
MSDelay(250);
P0=d2;
MSDelay(250);
P0=d3; //MSByte
MSDelay(250);
}
void MSDelay(unsigned int value)
{
unsigned char x,y;
for(x=0;x<value;x++)
for(y=0;y<1275;y++);
}
```

4.10 DAC Interfacing

Interfacing a Digital-to-Analog Converter (DAC) with an 8051 microcontroller involves several key steps. The DAC converts digital data from the microcontroller into an analog voltage.

4.10.1 DAC Construction Methods

1. Binary Weighted DAC:

Principle: In a binary weighted DAC, each resistor in the network has a value that is a binary fraction of a reference resistor. The resistors are weighted in powers of two (e.g., 1R, 2R, 4R, 8R, etc.).

Precision: This method can be less precise because small changes in resistor values can lead to significant errors, especially in high-resolution DACs where a large number of resistors with closely matched values are needed.

2. R/2R Ladder DAC:

Principle: The R/2R ladder DAC uses a repeating network of resistors with only two values: R and 2R. This configuration forms a ladder-like structure with fewer resistor values compared to the binary weighted method.

Precision: The R/2R ladder DAC achieves high precision with fewer components because it relies on fewer resistor values and does not require highly accurate resistor matching. This design simplifies manufacturing and improves accuracy, which is why it's commonly used in integrated circuit (IC) DACs.

4.10.2 Resolution of DACs

Resolution: The resolution of a DAC refers to the number of discrete output levels it can produce. It is determined by the number of binary inputs (or bits) the DAC has.

8-bit DAC: For an 8-bit DAC, like the DAC0808, there are 2^8=256 discrete output levels. This means it can produce 256 different analog output voltages or currents levels.

4.10.3 DAC0808 Interfacing

Interfacing the DAC0808 with an 8051 microcontroller involves connecting the digital data lines from the microcontroller to the DAC and setting up the necessary control and reference signals.

Overview of DAC0808 Operation

1. Digital Inputs to Current Conversion:

The DAC0808 is a type of Digital-to-Analog Converter (DAC) that takes a digital input and converts it into a corresponding analog current. The digital inputs are binary numbers (ranging from 0 to 255 in the case of an 8-bit DAC). These inputs determine how much current the DAC0808 will produce at its output pin, labeled as Iout.

2. Reference Current (Iref):

The DAC0808 uses a reference current, Iref, as a baseline for its output. This reference current is set by an external resistor and is crucial for determining the output current based on the digital input.

3. Current Calculation:

The total current output (Iout) from the DAC0808 is proportional to the digital value input. The output current is calculated based on the digital input value and the reference current (Iref). Essentially, the DAC0808 translates the digital number into a specific amount of current.

$$Iout = Iref(\frac{D7}{2} + \frac{D6}{4} + \frac{D5}{8} + \frac{D4}{16} + \frac{D3}{32} + \frac{D2}{64} + \frac{D1}{128} + \frac{D0}{256})$$

In this setup, D0 is the least significant bit (LSB) and D7 is the most significant bit (MSB) for the inputs. The reference current (Iref) is applied to pin 14, typically set to 2 mA. Figure 4.15 illustrates how to generate this reference current (Iref = 2 mA). Some digital-to-analog converters (DACs) use a zener diode (such as the LM336) to counteract any power supply voltage fluctuations. Assuming Iref is 2 mA, when all the DAC inputs are high, the maximum output current will be 1.99 mA.

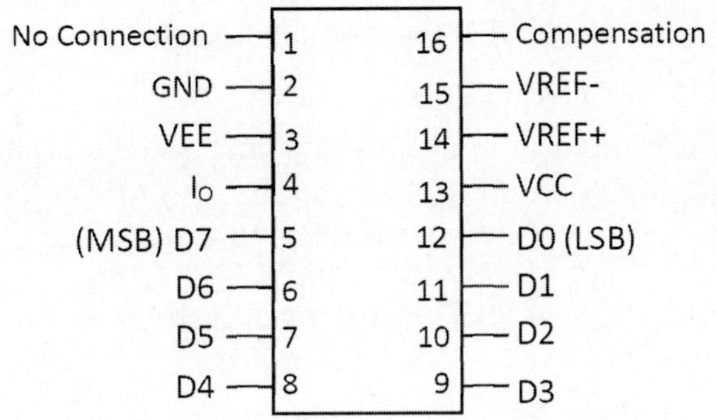

Figure 4.16: Pin Description of DAC 0808

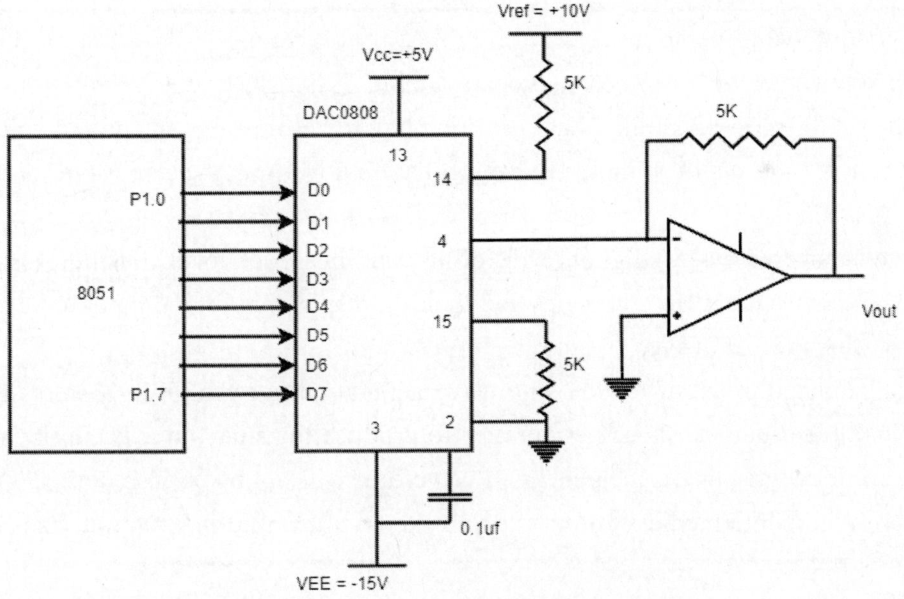

Figure 4.17: Interfacing 8051 with DAC0808

Ideally, the output pin (Iout) of the DAC0808 is connected to a resistor to convert the current to a voltage, which can then be monitored on an oscilloscope. However, in practical applications, this setup can introduce inaccuracies due to the input resistance of the load affecting the output voltage. To mitigate this, the Iout current is isolated by connecting it to an operational amplifier (op-amp), such as the 741, with a feedback resistor (Rf) of 5 kΩ. With Rf set to 5 kΩ, changing the binary input will result in corresponding changes to the output voltage.

Example 4.4 Assuming that R = 5K and Iref = 2 mA, calculate Vout for the following binary inputs: (a) 10011001 binary (99H) (b) 11001000 (C8H).

Solution: To calculate the output voltage *Vout* for the DAC0808 given the reference current *Iref*=2 mA and the resistor *R*=5 kΩ, we use the formula:

$Vout = Iout \times R$

where *Iout* is the output current determined by the binary input. The output current can be calculated using the formula:

$Iout = Iref \times (D/2^n)$

Here, *D* is the decimal equivalent of the binary input, and *nn* is the number of bits (in this case, *n*=8).

(a) Iout = 2 mA (153/256) = 1.195 mA and Vout = 1.195 mA × 5K = 5.975 V

(b) Iout = 2 mA (200/256) = 1.562 mA and Vout = 1.562 mA × 5K = 7.8125 V

Example 4.5 Sine Wave Generation.

To generate a sine wave, we first need to prepare a table of the sine values of different angles in the range 0 to 360 degrees. Assuming that corresponding to zero degree, the output voltage is 5V and that the peak voltage can be at most 10V, the equation governing the sine wave is as follows.

$Vout = 5\text{ V} + (5 \times \sin\theta)$

The 10V range is covered by 256 digital levels of inputs. Thus, each level constitutes a voltage of 25.6V. Table 4.4 shows the different angles and their corresponding digital input to be sent to the DAC for generating the sine wave.

The assembly language program for the sine wave generation is as follows. It stores the values noted in Table 4.4 and outputs those periodically to produce the sine wave. It may be noted that as the values are 30 degree apart, the generated waveform will not be very smooth. To produce a better waveform, more intermediary values are to be kept in the table and output to the DAC

Table 4.4: Table for Sine wave generation

Angle (θ)	sin θ	V_{out}	Digital value
0	0	5	128
30	0.5	7.5	192
60	0.866	9.33	238
90	1.0	10	255
120	0.866	9.33	238
150	0.5	7.5	192
180	0	5	128
210	-0.5	2.5	64
240	-0.866	0.669	17
270	-1.0	0	0
300	-0.866	0.669	17
330	-0.5	2.5	64
360	0	5	128

Assembly Language Code:

```
ORG 300H ; Set the origin for the table
TABLE: DB 128, 192, 238, 255, 238, 192 ;
DB 128, 64, 17, 0, 17, 64, 128
; Define constants
COUNT EQU 13 ; Number of entries in the table
AGAIN:
MOV DPTR, #TABLE ; Load the address of the TABLE into the Data Pointer (DPTR)
MOV R2, #COUNT ; Load the COUNT of entries into R2 (loop counter)
BACK:
CLR A ; Clear the Accumulator (A) for fresh data
MOVC A, @A + DPTR ; Move the value from the table pointed by DPTR into A
MOV P1, A ; Output the value in A to Port P1
INC DPTR ; Increment DPTR to point to the next table entry
DJNZ R2, BACK ; Decrement R2 and repeat if it's not zero
SJMP AGAIN ; Jump back to the start to repeat the process
```

```
#include <reg51.h>
// Define the Data Register for the DAC
sfr DACDATA = P1;
void main() {
   // Define an array of wave values
   unsigned char WAVEVALUE[12] = {
      128, 192, 238, 255,
      238, 192, 128, 64,
      17, 0, 17, 64
   };
   unsigned char index; // Variable for loop control
   while(1) { // Infinite loop
  for(index = 0; index < 12; index++) { // Iterate through wave values
DACDATA = WAVEVALUE[index]; //Output the wave value
      }
   }
}
```

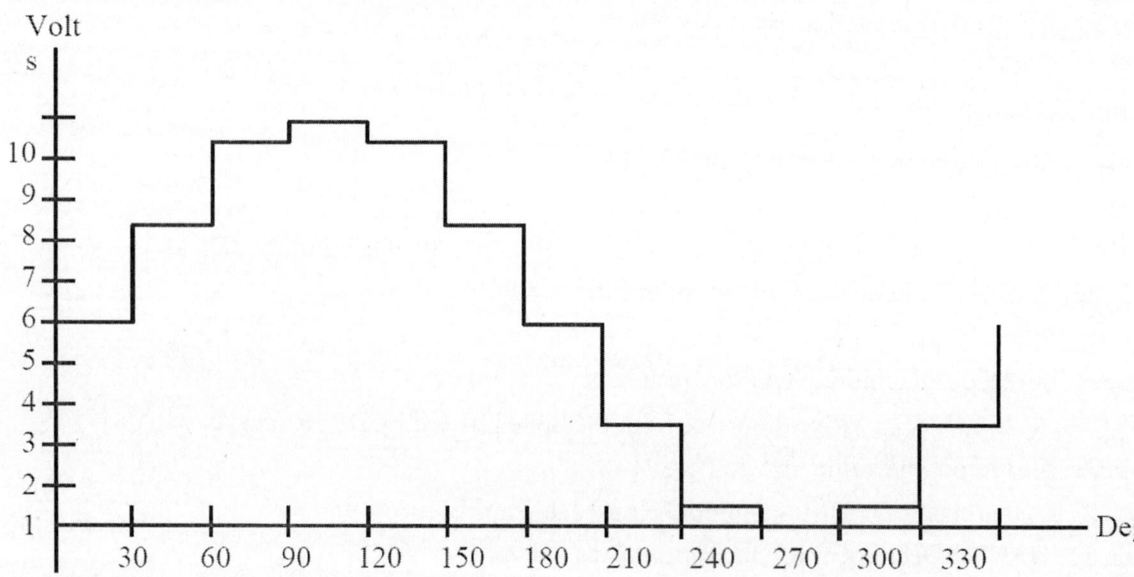

Figure 4.18: Angle versus Voltage Magnitude for Sine Wave

4.11 Timers/Counters

The 8051 microcontroller features two 16 bit timers/counters, Timer 0 and Timer 1, which can be utilized in two distinct modes: as timers for generating time delays or as counters for counting external events.

In the 8051 microcontroller, **timers** and **counters** are integral components used for different purposes. The primary difference between a timer and a counter depends on the source of the clock signal:

1. Timers:

- When configured as a timer, the 8051 uses the internal clock source. This clock source is typically derived from the crystal oscillator connected to the microcontroller (which determines the frequency of the 8051, often 12 MHz or 11.0592 MHz).
- The internal clock drives the timer, incrementing its value at regular intervals based on this frequency.
- For example, with a 12 MHz clock and assuming the timer runs in 12-clock mode (Clock frequency divided by 12), the timer increments every 1 μs (1 microsecond).
- Timers are typically used for time delays, generating time-based events, or for scheduling tasks in programs.

2. Counters:

- When configured as a counter, the 8051 uses an external clock source applied to specific pins (T0 for Timer 0 and T1 for Timer 1).
- The counter increments based on events or pulses applied externally, rather than the internal clock. These pulses could come from an external device, like a switch or sensor, where each pulse corresponds to one increment of the counter.
- Counters are useful for counting external events, such as the number of objects passing a sensor or the number of button presses.

4.11.1 Timers

Both Timer 0 and Timer 1 are 16 bits wide. They count up to FFFFH and after it rolls back to 0000H, this is called timer overflow. Given that the 8051 has an 8-bit architecture, each 16-bit timer is accessed as two separate special function registers (SFR): a low byte and a high byte.

Timer 0 & Timer 1 Registers

Timer 0 Registers

- TL0: Timer 0 Low byte
- TH0: Timer 0 High byte

Timer 1 Registers

- TL1: Timer 1 Low byte
- TH1: Timer 1 High byte

These registers are used to control the timers and hold the timer counts. When accessing the timers in the 8051, you manipulate these registers directly.

TH								TL							
D15	D14	D13	D12	D11	D10	D9	D8	D7	D6	D5	D4	D3	D2	D1	D0

Figure 4.19: Timer 0 Registers

TH								TL							
D15	D14	D13	D12	D11	D10	D9	D8	D7	D6	D5	D4	D3	D2	D1	D0

Figure 4.20: Timer 1 Registers

Timer Control Register (TCON)

The TCON (Timer Control) register in the 8051 microcontroller is a crucial component for managing the operation of the timers and the external interrupts. It is an 8-bit register that controls the functioning of the two timers (Timer 0 and Timer 1) and the external interrupt system. Here's a detailed overview of the TCON register:

TCON Register Overview

- **Address**: The TCON register is located at address **88H** in the 8051's special function register (SFR) space.
- **Bit Structure**: The TCON register consists of 8 bits, each serving specific functions related to timer control and external interrupts.

TF1	TR1	TF0	TR0	IE1	IT1	IE0	IT0

TCON Register

Functions of TCON Bits

Timer Control:

- **TR0 and TR1** These bits are used to start (set to 1) or stop (set to 0) Timer 0 and Timer 1, respectively. These bits are used to software control the Timers.
- **TF0 and TF1**
- **Function:** This bit is set by hardware when Timer 0 and Timer 1 overflows, meaning that the timer has counted from its initial value (often 0000H) to its maximum value (FFFFH in 16-bit mode or FFH in 8-bit mode).
- **Purpose:** Once TF0 and TF1 is set, it typically triggers an interrupt (if the interrupt for Timer 0 and Timer 1 is enabled), or it signals the software that the timer overflow event has occurred, allowing the programmer to take some action, such as resetting the timer or executing a specific task.
- **Reset:** After the timer overflow event occurs and the necessary action is taken, the TF0 is automatically cleared when the interrupt service routine for Timer 0 is start execution.

External Interrupt Control:

- **IE0 and IE1**: These bits indicate whether an external interrupt has occurred. They are set when the respective external interrupt is triggered.
- **IT0 and IT1**: These bits define the triggering mode for the external interrupts. Setting them to 0 configures the interrupt as a level-triggered interrupt, while setting them to 1 configures it as an edge-triggered interrupt.

In the previous examples, we have utilized the TR0 and TR1 bits to control the operation of the timers, which are part of the TCON (Timer Control) register—a bit-addressable 8-bit register. The upper four bits of this register are designated for the TF and TR bits of both Timer 0 and Timer 1, while the lower four bits are reserved for managing the interrupt bits. It is important to note that, since the TCON register is bit-addressable, instead of using instructions like "SETB TR1" and "CLR TR1," we can directly manipulate the bits using "SETB TCON.6" and "CLR TCON.6," respectively.

TMOD (timer mode) register

Both Timer 0 and Timer 1 use a single register, called TMOD, to configure their various operation modes. TMOD is an 8-bit register where the lower 4 bits are allocated for Timer 0 and the upper 4 bits for Timer 1. For each timer, the lower 2 bits determine the timer mode, while the upper 2 bits specify the operation.

GATE	$C/\overline{T}$	M1	M0	GATE	$C/\overline{T}$	M1	M0
Timer 1				Timer 0			

(MSB) (LSB)

GATE Enabled hardware control. When set, the timer/counter is enabled only when the INTx pin is high and the TRx control pin is set. When cleared, timer/counter is independent on INTx and they are enabled whenever the TRx control bit is set.

$C/\overline{T}$ Timer or counter selected $C/\overline{T}$ =1 for counter, $C/\overline{T}$ = 0 for Timer.

M1 Mode bit 1

M0 Mode bit 0

M1	M0	Mode	Operating Mode
0	0	0	13-bit timer mode 8-bit timer/counter THx with TLx as 5-bit prescaler
0	1	1	16-bit timer mode 16-bit timer/counters THx and TLx are cascaded; there is no prescaler
1	0	2	8-bit auto-reload 8-bit auto-reload timer/counter; THx holds a value that is to be reloaded into TLx each time it overflows.
1	1	3	Split timer mode

Figure 4.21: TMOD Register

C/T (clock/timer)

The C/T (Counter/Timer) bit in the TMOD (Timer Mode) register of the 8051 microcontroller is used to determine whether the timer operates as a timer for generating time delays or as a counter for counting external events. When the C/T bit is set to 0, the timer operates in timer mode, generating time delays based on the crystal frequency of the 8051 microcontroller. Here's a more detailed explanation:

Timer Mode (C/T = 0):

- When C/T = 0, the timer operates in timer mode, counting internal clock pulses generated by the crystal oscillator.
- The clock source for the timer is derived from the crystal frequency, operating at a frequency of 1/12th of the oscillator frequency.
- For example, if the crystal frequency is 11.0592 MHz, the timer clock frequency would be approximately 921.6 kHz (11.0592 MHz ÷ 12).
- The timer counts these internal clock pulses and generates time delays based on the configured mode (Mode 0, 1, 2, or 3) and the initial value loaded into the timer registers.

Counter Mode (C/T = 1):

- When C/T = 1, the timer operates in counter mode, counting external events or pulses.
- In this mode, the timer counts the falling edges of the signals applied to the corresponding timer input pin (T0 or T1).
- The maximum counting rate is limited to 1/24th of the crystal frequency due to the nature of counting external events.

By setting the C/T bit to 0, the timer operates in timer mode, allowing for precise time delay generation based on the crystal frequency of the 8051 microcontroller. This is useful for applications that require accurate timing, such as generating delays, controlling timing-critical events, or implementing time-based protocols.

GATE

The GATE bit in the TMOD (Timer Mode) register of the 8051 microcontroller serves an important function in controlling the operation of the timers. Both Timer 0 and Timer 1 have this GATE bit, and its purpose is as follows:

Software Control: The GATE bit determines how the timers can be started and stopped. When GATE is set to 0, the timers can be controlled entirely through software. This means that the timers can be started and stopped using the TR (Timer Run) bits, TR0 for Timer 0 and TR1 for Timer 1, with the instructions SETB TR0 or SETB TR1 to start the timer, and CLR TR0 or CLR TR1 to stop it.

Hardware Control: When GATE is set to 1, the operation of the timers is controlled by both software and an external hardware signal. In this configuration, the timer will only run when the corresponding TR bit is set and the external interrupt pin (INT0 or INT1) is high. This allows for more precise control, as the timer can be started or stopped based on external events.

In summary, the GATE bit provides flexibility in timer control, allowing for both software-based and hardware-based operation modes. When GATE = 0, the timer operates under software control, while GATE = 1 enables hardware control, making it possible to synchronize timer operation with external events.

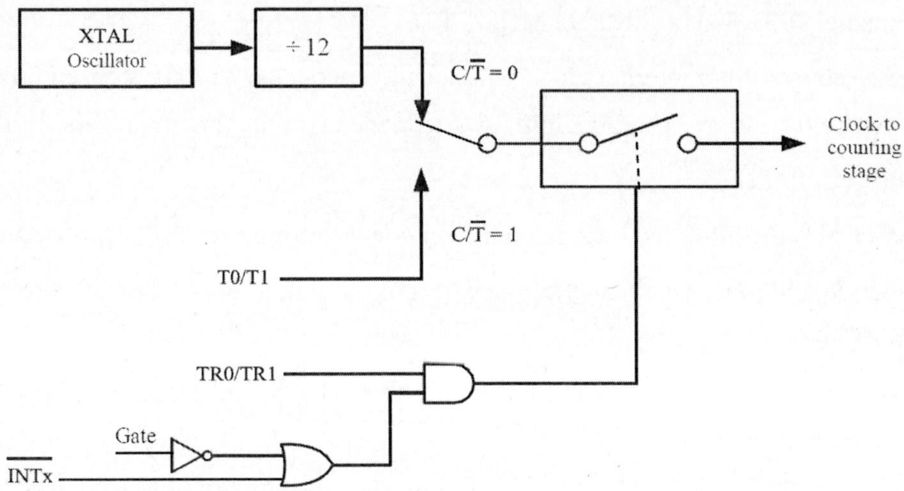

Figure 4.22 Timer/Counter logic diagram

Main Components of the Timer/Counter Logic

1. Clock Source Selection:

The timer/counter can either use The internal clock (when functioning as a timer) or an external clock input (when functioning as a counter).

This selection is made by the C/T (Counter/Timer) bit in the TMOD register:

C/T = 0: The timer uses the internal clock (derived from the microcontroller's crystal oscillator). C/T = 1: The counter uses an external signal applied to the appropriate pin (T0 for Timer 0, T1 for Timer 1).

2. Gate Control

The operation of the timer/counter can be gated (controlled) by the external interrupt pins (INT0 for Timer 0 and INT1 for Timer 1). This gating feature allows the timer/counter to only run when a specific external signal is active (high on the INTx pin).

This behavior is controlled by the GATE bit in the TMOD register.

GATE = 0: The timer/counter runs as long as the TRx bit is set, independent of the external signal.

GATE = 1: The timer/counter runs only when both the TRx bit is set and the external interrupt pin is high.

Operating Modes of Timer/Counter (M1, M0)

The M0 and M1 bits in the TMOD register are used to select the timer mode. As illustrated in Figure 4.19, there are four modes available: 0, 1, 2, and 3. Mode 0 functions as a 13-bit timer, Mode 1 operates as a 16-bit timer, and Mode 2 serves as an 8-bit timer. Our primary focus will be on Modes 1 and 2, as they are the most frequently utilized. We will detail the characteristics of these modes after discussing the other components of the TMOD register.

Mode 0: 13-bit Timer/Counter

In this mode, Timer 0 or Timer 1 operates as a 13-bit timer. The high byte (THx) is an 8-bit register, while the low byte (TLx) is a 5-bit register. The timer counts from 0 to 1FFFH. When it overflows, it resets to 0000H and sets the overflow flag (TF).

In this mode, the timer/counter is configured to operate as a 13-bit timer. It uses the TLx (low byte) register as a 5-bit prescaler and the THx (high byte) register as the main 8-bit timer/counter. The total count value is 13 bits, which means the counter can count from 0000H to 1FFFH (8191 in decimal).

Prescaler Meaning

A prescaler is a component used to divide the clock frequency by a specific factor before it reaches the timer. In Mode 0 of the 8051: The 5-bit prescaler means that the TLx register (low byte) functions as a 5-bit counter. The main purpose of the prescaler is to slow down the counting rate of the timer by counting multiple pulses before incrementing the higher byte, THx. Since TLx is 5 bits wide, it can count from 00000B to 11111B (0 to 31 in decimal). After TLx reaches its maximum value (31), it overflows and increments the THx register by 1. Thus, the prescaler acts like a divider or scaler for the clock pulses. For every 32 pulses applied to the timer (since TLx counts from 0 to 31), THx increments by 1. This effectively slows down the rate at which THx increments.

Mode 1: 16-bit Timer/Counter

This mode allows the timer to operate as a full 16-bit timer/counter. Both THx and TLx are 8-bit registers, enabling counts from 0000H to FFFFH. Upon reaching the maximum count, the timer rolls over to 0000H and sets the overflow flag (TF). This is most preferred mode to produce the delay.

Mode 2: 8-bit Timer/Counter with Auto-Reload

In this mode, Timer 0 or Timer 1 operates as an 8-bit timer. The high byte (THx) holds the value to be reloaded into the low byte (TLx) upon overflow. TLx counts from 00H to FFH, and when it overflows, it automatically reloads the value from THx.

Mode 3: Split Timer Mode

This mode is unique as it allows Timer 0 and Timer 1 to function independently. Timer 0 is split into two 8-bit timers (TL0 and TL1), while Timer 1 is disabled. This mode is less commonly used but can be useful for specific applications requiring two separate 8-bit timers.

Timer 0 in Mode 3: When Mode 3 is selected for Timer 0, TL0 is used as an 8-bit timer, and TH0 is also used as a separate 8-bit timer. Each can run independently, TL0 operates as an 8-bit timer controlled by TR0. TH0 operates as a separate 8-bit timer but is controlled by TR1.

Impact on Timer 1:

In Mode 3, the TR1 and TF1 bits (which normally control Timer 1) are repurposed to control TH0. Since the control bits and interrupt flags for Timer 1 are being used by Timer 0, Timer 1 is effectively disabled and cannot be used in this mode.

Mode 1 programming

1. It functions as a 16-bit timer, enabling the loading of values ranging from 0000H to FFFFH into the timer's TL and TH registers.
2. Once the TH and TL registers are loaded with a 16-bit initial value, the timer must be started. This is accomplished by using the instructions "SETB TR0" for Timer 0 and "SETB TR1" for Timer 1.
3. Once the timer is started, it begins counting up until it reaches its maximum value of FFFFH. When it overflows from FFFFH back to 0000, it sets a flag called TF (timer flag) to high. This flag can be monitored to determine when the timer has overflowed. To stop the timer when the flag is set, you can use the instructions "CLR TR0" for Timer 0 or "CLR TR1" for Timer 1. Each timer has its own flag: TF0 for Timer 0 and TF1 for Timer 1.
4. After the timer reaches its maximum value and overflows, you must reload the TH and TL registers with the original value and reset the TF flag to 0 in order to repeat the timing process.

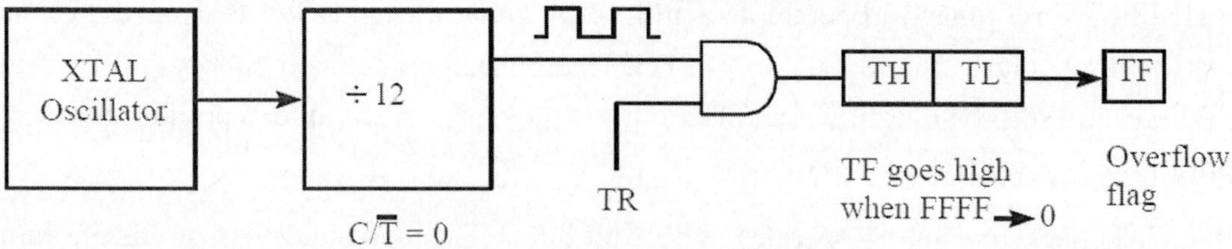

Figure 4.23: Timer working

Steps to program in mode 1

1. Load the TMOD Register:

Purpose: The TMOD register is used to select the timer mode and specify which timer to use. Each timer has 4 bits in the TMOD register.

The lower 4 bits are for Timer 0, and the upper 4 bits are for Timer 1.

Bits 0 and 1 (M0 and M1) select the mode of the timer (Mode 0, 1, 2, or 3).

Bit 2 (C/T) selects whether the timer is a timer or counter.

Bit 3 (GATE) controls whether the timer is enabled by an external signal.

Example: MOV TMOD, #01H ; Select Timer 0 in Mode 1 (16-bit timer)

2. Load Initial Count Values into TL and TH:

Purpose: Set the initial value from which the timer will start counting.

The timer counts from the loaded value up to FFFFH. The initial count value determines the time delay. You need to calculate the initial values based on the desired delay.

Example: MOV TH0, #HIGH_BYTE ; Load the high byte of the initial count

MOV TL0, #LOW_BYTE ; Load the low byte of the initial count

3. Start the Timer:

Purpose: Begin the timer counting. This is done by setting the TR (Timer Run) bit in the TCON register.

Example: SETB TR0; Start Timer 0

4. Monitor the Timer Flag (TF):

Purpose: Wait for the timer to overflow and set the TF flag. Use the JNB (Jump if Not Bit) instruction to repeatedly check the TF flag. Exit the loop when the TF flag is set, indicating the timer has overflowed.

Example: WAIT_LOOP:

JNB TF0, WAIT_LOOP; Wait until TF0 is set

5. Stop the Timer:

Purpose: Stop the timer to prevent it from continuing to count. This is done by clearing the TR bit in the TCON register.

Example: CLR TR0; Stop Timer 0

6. Clear the TF Flag:

Purpose: Prepare for the next round of timing by resetting the TF flag. Clear the TF flag to ensure it is not set from the previous timing cycle.

Example: CLR TF0; Clear TF0 for the next round

7. Reload TH and TL and Repeat:

Purpose: Reload the initial count values to start the timing process again. Repeat the process by loading the initial values into TL and TH and starting the timer again.

Example: MOV TH0, #HIGH_BYTE; Reload the high byte of the initial count

MOV TL0, #LOW_BYTE; Reload the low byte of the initial count

SETB TR0; Restart Timer 0

```
ORG 0H          ; Origin, start at address 0
MAIN:
MOV TMOD, #01H        ; Select Timer 0, Mode 1
MOV TH0, #HIGH_BYTE  ; Load high byte of initial count
MOV TL0, #LOW_BYTE   ; Load low byte of initial count
SETB TR0             ; Start Timer 0
WAIT_LOOP:
JNB TF0, WAIT_LOOP   ; Wait for TF0 to be set (timer overflow)
CLR TR0              ; Stop Timer 0
CLR TF0              ; Clear TF0 for the next round
MOV TH0, #HIGH_BYTE  ; Reload high byte of initial count
MOV TL0, #LOW_BYTE   ; Reload low byte of initial count
SETB TR0             ; Restart Timer 0
SJMP MAIN            ; Repeat the process
```

Example 4.6 Indicate which mode and which timer are selected for each of the following:

(a) MOV TMOD,#01H (b) MOV TMOD,#20H (c) MOV TMOD,#12H.

Solution: We convert the values from hex to binary. From Figure 3, we have:

(a) TMOD = 00000001, mode 1 of Timer 0 is selected.

(b) TMOD = 00100000, mode 2 of Timer 1 is selected.

(c) TMOD = 00010010, mode 2 of Timer 0, and mode 1 of Timer 1 are selected.

Example 4.7 Find the timer's clock frequency and its period for various 8051-based systems, with the following crystal frequencies.

(a) 12 MHz

(b) 16 MHz

(c) 11.0592 MHz

Solution: (a) $1/12 \times 12$ MHz = 1 MHz and T = 1/1 MHz = 1 μs

(b) $1/12 \times 16$ MHz = 1.333 MHz and T = 1/1.333 MHz = .75 μs

(c) $1/12 \times 11.0592$ MHz = 921.6 kHz;

T = 1/921.6 kHz = 1.085 μs

Note that 8051 timers use 1/12 of XTAL frequency, regardless of machine cycle

Example 4.8 Generate a 50% duty cycle square wave (equal high and low durations) on bit P1.4 using Timer 0 to control the time delay.

```
MOV TMOD, #01        ; Set Timer 0 to Mode 1 (16-bit mode)
MAIN_LOOP:
   MOV TL0, #0F2H   ; Load low byte of timer with F2H
   MOV TH0, #0FFH   ; Load high byte of timer with FFH
   CPL P1.4         ; Toggle P1.4 to create square wave
   ACALL DELAY      ; Call delay subroutine
   SJMP MAIN_LOOP   ; Repeat process continuously
; Delay subroutine using Timer 0
DELAY:
   SETB TR0         ; Start Timer 0
WAIT_FOR_OVERFLOW:
   JNB TF0, WAIT_FOR_OVERFLOW ; Wait until Timer 0 overflows
   CLR TR0          ; Stop Timer 0
   CLR TF0          ; Clear Timer 0 overflow flag
   RET              ; Return from subroutine
```

The TMOD register is configured to use Timer 0 in Mode 1. The initial value FFF2H is loaded into the Timer 0 registers TH0 and TL0. Pin P1.4 is toggled to create a pulse, and the DELAY subroutine is called. Within the subroutine, Timer 0 is started with the SETB TR0 instruction, and it begins counting up with each clock cycle provided by the crystal oscillator. As Timer 0 counts from FFF2H to FFFFH, it increments through intermediate values such as FFF3, FFF4, and so on. Upon reaching

FFFFH, the next clock pulse causes it to roll over to 0000, setting the Timer 0 overflow flag (TF0 = 1). The JNB instruction detects this flag, and execution continues. The timer is then stopped with the CLR TR0 instruction, the DELAY subroutine ends, and the process repeats, toggling P1.4 and generating a time delay in a continuous loop.

4.11.2 Counters

In the previous section, we discussed using the 8051's timer/counter to generate time delays. These timers can also function as counters, recording events occurring outside the 8051. This section covers using the timer/counter as an event counter. When used as a counter, all programming principles from the timer section apply, except for the frequency source. For timers, the 8051's crystal provides the frequency source. As a counter, an external pulse increments the TH and TL registers. Despite this difference, the TMOD and TH, TL registers remain the same, with identical names and functionalities. The timer modes also remain unchanged.

C/T bit in TMOD register

As discussed previously, the C/T bit in the TMOD register determines the clock source for the timer. When C/T = 0, the timer receives pulses from the crystal oscillator. Conversely, when C/T = 1, the timer operates as a counter, receiving pulses from an external source. With C/T = 1, the counter increments with pulses fed from pins 14 and 15, designated as T0 (Timer 0 input) and T1 (Timer 1 input), respectively. These pins are part of port 3. For Timer 0, when C/T = 1, pin P3.4 provides the clock pulse, causing the counter to increment with each pulse. Similarly, for Timer 1, when C/T = 1, the counter increments with each pulse from pin P3.5.

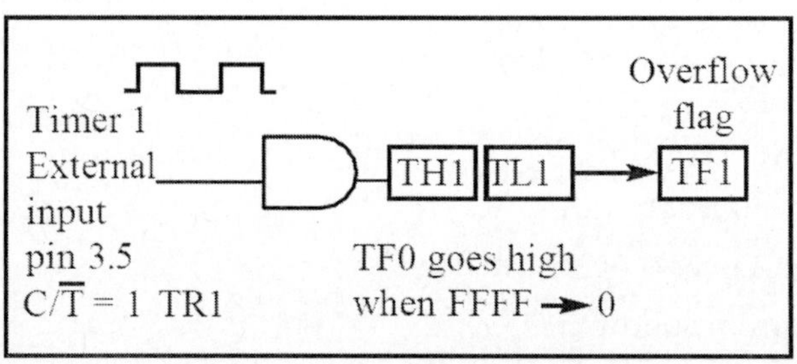

Figure 4.24: Counter working

Example 4.9 Write a program to configure Counter 1 in Mode 2 to count pulses and display the current value of TL1 on Port 2 (P2). Clock pulses are provided to the T1 pin.

Solution:

```
MOV TMOD, #01100000B ; Configure Counter 1 in Mode 2, C/T=1 for external pulses
MOV TH1, #0          ; Clear TH1 to start from zero
SETB P3.5            ; Set T1 as input for external pulses
AGAIN:
   SETB TR1          ; Start Counter 1
COUNT_LOOP:
   MOV A, TL1        ; Copy the current count from TL1
   MOV P2, A         ; Display the count on Port 2
   JNB TF1, COUNT_LOOP ;Loop until the overflow flag TF1 is set
   CLR TR1           ; Stop Counter 1
   CLR TF1           ; Clear the overflow flag TF1
   SJMP AGAIN        ; Repeat the process
```

The given code configures and uses Timer 1 of the 8051 microcontroller as an event counter in Mode 2 (8-bit auto-reload mode). The TMOD register is set to 01100000B, configuring Timer 1 to counter mode (C/T = 1) and Mode 2. TH1 is cleared to 0. Pin P3.5 is set as the input for Timer 1, receiving external pulses. The main loop begins with SETB TR1 to start the counter. The current count value in TL1 is copied to the accumulator (A) and displayed on Port 2 (P2). The program continuously checks if the Timer 1 overflow flag (TF1) is set. If not, it loops back to read and display the count. When TF1 is set, indicating the counter has overflowed, the counter is stopped with CLR TR1, TF1 is cleared, and the process repeats by jumping back to the start of the main loop. This loop continuously displays the count of external pulses on Port 2.

UNIT SUMMARY

This unit focuses on memory and I/O expansion buses, which are essential for connecting additional memory and peripheral devices to a microcontroller. It discusses the role of control signals in managing communication between the CPU and these external components, as well as the concept of memory wait states, which occur when the CPU must pause while waiting for data from slower memory devices. The unit also covers the interfacing of peripheral devices, including General Purpose I/O ports for digital input and output, Analog-to-Digital Converters (ADC) for converting analog signals to digital, and Digital-to-Analog Converters (DAC) for the reverse process.

Additionally, it explores the integration of timers and counters for event timing and counting applications, along with memory devices for data storage, emphasizing the importance of these components in expanding the functionality of microcontroller systems.

EXERCISES

Multiple Choice Questions (1 to 10)

1. What is the purpose of the ALE (Address Latch Enable) signal in the 8051?

   a) To latch the lower 8 bits of the address onto Port 0

   b) To enable the external program memory

   c) To enable the external data memory

   d) To enable the on-chip peripherals

2. Which of the following is NOT a control signal used for external memory interfacing in the 8051?

   a) EA (External Access)
   b) PSEN (Program Store Enable)

   c) RD (Read)
   d) WR (Write)

3. What is the purpose of the EA (External Access) pin in the 8051?

   a) To enable the on-chip program memory
   b) To enable the on-chip data memory

   c) To enable the external program memory
   d) To enable the external data memory

4. Which of the following is used to expand the I/O capabilities of the 8051?

   a) 8255 Programmable Peripheral Interface (PPI)

   b) 8259 Programmable Interrupt Controller (PIC)

   c) 8237 Direct Memory Access (DMA) Controller

   d) 8253 Programmable Interval Timer (PIT)

5. What is the purpose of the GATE bit in the TMOD (Timer Mode) register of the 8051?

   a) To enable the timer to start/stop based on an external signal

   b) To enable the timer to operate in 16-bit mode

   c) To enable the timer to operate in 8-bit auto-reload mode

   d) To enable the timer to operate in 8-bit counter mode

6. Which of the following is a disadvantage of using memory wait states in the 8051?

   a) Increased power consumption b) Reduced system performance

   c) Increased complexity of the hardware design d) Increased cost of the system

7. What is the purpose of the PSEN (Program Store Enable) signal in the 8051?

   a) To enable the on-chip program memory b) To enable the external program memory

   c) To enable the on-chip data memory d) To enable the external data memory

8. Which of the following is a feature of the ADC0808/ADC0809 analog-to-digital converter?

   a) 8-bit resolution b) 10-bit resolution

   c) 12-bit resolution d) 16-bit resolution

9. How many timers does the 8051 microcontroller have?

   a) 1 timer b) 2 timers

   c) 3 timers d) 4 timers

10. What is the purpose of the TCON (Timer Control) register in the 8051?

    a) To control the operation of the timers and external interrupts

    b) To control the operation of the ADC and DAC

    c) To control the operation of the on-chip peripherals

    d) To control the operation of the external memory

Short answer Questions (11 to 15)

11. In a particular 8051 system, the starting address is 0000H, and it contains only 16K bytes of program memory. What is the ending address for this system?
12. When the 8051 CPU is powered up, at which address does it expect to find the first opcode?
13. True or false. For any member of the 8051 family, if EA = Gnd the microcontroller fetches program code from external ROM.
14. What is the purpose of the SJMP instruction?
15. In an 8051 with 16K bytes of on-chip program ROM, explain what happens if EA = Vcc.
16. Calculate the output voltage of an 8-bit DAC with a reference voltage of 5V when the digital input is 10101100 (binary).
17. If the **TCON** register in the 8051 microcontroller has a value of **80H**, what is the status of Timer 0 and Timer 1? How does this affect their operation, and what steps are needed to start both timers?

18. If the **TMOD** register of the 8051 microcontroller is set to **89H**, what are the operating modes of Timer 0 and Timer 1? Explain how the timers are controlled and their modes of operation based on this configuration.

Long answer Questions (16 to 19)

19. Sawtooth Waveform using DAC0808.
20. Explain the steps required to interface an ADC0808 with the 8051 microcontroller and write a short code snippet to read the converted digital value.
21. Write an 8051 assembly program to count external events using Timer 1 in counter mode. Assume the external events are connected to T1 pin.
22. Explain the process of interfacing an external ROM with the 8051 microcontroller and write a program to read a byte of data from the ROM.

MCQ answer

1. (a) 2. (a) 3. (c) 4. (a) 5. (a) 6. (b) 7. (b) 8. (a) 9. (b) 10. (a)

KNOW MORE

Memory and I/O expansion buses facilitate communication between a processor and peripheral devices, enabling efficient data transfer and system scalability. Control signals orchestrate this communication by directing operations within the system, while memory wait states manage timing discrepancies between the CPU and memory or I/O devices, ensuring synchronized data access. Interfacing with peripheral devices, such as General Purpose I/O (GPIO), Analog-to-Digital Converters (ADC), Digital-to-Analog Converters (DAC), timers, counters, and memory devices, involves configuring these components to work seamlessly with the main processing unit. Emerging technologies in this area focus on improving speed, reducing latency, and enhancing the versatility of these interfaces, supporting advanced applications like IoT and real-time data processing.

REFERENCES AND SUGGESTED READINGS

1. Muhammad Ali Mazidi , Janice G. Mazidi, Rolin D. McKinlay 8051 Microcontroller, The: A Systems Approach: Pearson New International Edition 1st Edition, 2013
2. Microcontrollers and Applications by Prof. Santanu Chattopadhyay, AICTE e-kumbh.

QR Code for further reading:

NPTEL
Microprocessor &
Microcontroller

8051 Online
Reference

5 External Communication Interface

UNIT SPECIFICS

Through this unit we have discussed the following aspects:

- *Synchronous and Asynchronous Communication*
- *RS232, SPI, I2C*
- *Introduction and interfacing to protocols like Blue-tooth and Zig-bee*

The practical applications of the topics are discussed to foster curiosity, creativity, and enhance problem-solving skills. In addition to multiple-choice, short-answer, and long-answer questions categorized according to lower and higher levels of Bloom's taxonomy, assignments with various numerical problems are provided. A list of references and suggested readings is included for further practice, and QR codes are placed throughout different sections, offering access to additional relevant information.

After the related practical content, a "Know More" section is included. This section has been thoughtfully designed to offer supplementary information that benefits readers. It highlights key activities, intriguing facts, analogies, and the history of the subject's development, focusing on major observations and findings. Timelines trace the evolution of the topic from its inception to the present day, and its real-life or industrial applications in various contexts are explored. The section also includes case studies on environmental, sustainability, social, and ethical issues where applicable, as well as topics intended to spark inquisitiveness and curiosity within the unit.

RATIONALE

This unit begins with understanding synchronous and asynchronous communication, along with protocols like RS232, SPI, and I2C, is essential for comprehending how data is transferred and managed in digital systems, forming the foundation for effective design and troubleshooting. Learning about Bluetooth and Zigbee broadens this knowledge to include wireless communication, vital for modern applications. These protocols are ubiquitous in embedded systems, impacting everything from consumer electronics to industrial automation.

PRE-REQUISITES

Previous chapters of this book.

UNIT OUTCOMES

List of outcomes of this unit is as follows:

U5-O1: Illustrate the key characteristics and differences between synchronous and asynchronous communication.

U5-O2: Demonstrate the configuration of a microcontroller for synchronous and asynchronous communication.

U5-O3: Define the RS232 communication standard and its basic components.

U5-O4: Define the SPI & I2C protocol and its main components.

U5-O5: Define Bluetooth and Zigbee protocols and their primary uses.

Unit-5 Outcomes	*EXPECTED MAPPING WITH COURSE OUTCOMES (1-Weak Correlation;2-Medium Correlation;3-Strong Correlation)*				
	CO-1	*CO-2*	*CO-3*	*CO-4*	*CO-5*
U5-O1	2	2	1	3	2
U5-O2	2	3	2	3	1
U5-O3	2	2	1	2	1
U5-O4	2	3	2	3	2
U5-O5	2	2	1	2	3

5.1 Introduction

Computers transfer data using two main methods: parallel and serial. In parallel data transfers, multiple lines often eight or more are used to transmit data to a nearby device, typically within a few feet. This method, seen in devices like printers and hard disks, employs cables with multiple wire strips. Although parallel communication allows for rapid data transfer by sending multiple bits simultaneously, it is limited by distance. For communication over longer distances, serial data transfer is utilized. In serial communication, data is sent one bit at a time, unlike parallel communication, which transmits data in larger chunks, such as a byte at a time. This chapter explores the serial and parallel communication, Synchronous and Asynchronous Communication. Introduction and interfacing to protocols like RS232, SPI, I2C and Blue-tooth and Zig-bee.

5.2 Serial and Parallel Data Communication

When a microprocessor communicates with external devices, it typically sends data in byte-sized chunks. For instance, in scenarios like interfacing with printers, data is transferred directly from the microprocessor's 8-bit data bus to the printer's 8-bit data bus. This method is called parallel communication. It is practical for short distances but becomes problematic over longer cables due to signal degradation and distortion. Additionally, the use of an 8-bit data path can be costly. To address these issues, serial communication is employed for transferring data over long distances, from hundreds of feet to millions of miles. Unlike parallel communication, which requires multiple data lines, serial communication uses a single data line, significantly reducing costs and enabling long-distance communication, such as transmitting data between computers located in different cities over telephone lines. Figure 5.1 shows Serial vs Parallel data communication.

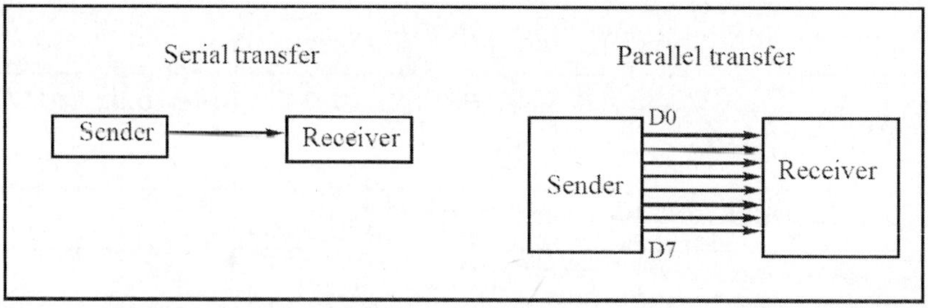

Figure 5.1: Serial & Parallel Data Communication

For serial data communication to function, data must be converted from bytes to serial bits using a parallel-in-serial-out shift register before being transmitted over a single data line. At the receiving end, a serial-in-parallel-out shift register collects the serial data and reconstructs it into a byte. When data needs to be sent over a telephone line, it must be transformed from binary 0s and 1s into audio tones, which are sinusoidal signals. This conversion is accomplished by a device called a modem, which stands for "modulator/demodulator." For short distances, digital signals can be transferred directly over a simple wire without the need for modulation, as seen with IBM PC keyboards communicating with the motherboard. However, for long-distance communication via telephone lines, a modem is required to modulate the data (convert 0s and 1s to audio tones) or converts digital signal to analog signal. The demodulate works just opposite to it it (convert audio tones back to 0s and 1s) or analog signal to digital.

5.3 Synchronous & Asynchronous Communication

- **Synchronous Serial Communication**: Data bits are transmitted in a continuous stream, synchronized by a clock signal shared between the sender and receiver as shown in Figure 5.2.

This method transfers a block of data (characters) at a time. This method ensures that both devices are in sync, allowing for high-speed data transfer. Common protocols include SPI (Serial Peripheral Interface) and I2C (Inter-Integrated Circuit).

- **Asynchronous Serial Communication:** Data is transmitted in discrete packets, with each packet containing a start bit, data bits, an optional parity bit, and one or more stop bits. This method transfers a single byte at a time. The timing of data transmission is not synchronized by a clock signal, but instead, both devices agree on a baud rate. UART (Universal Asynchronous Receiver/Transmitter) is a typical example used in many serial communication applications.

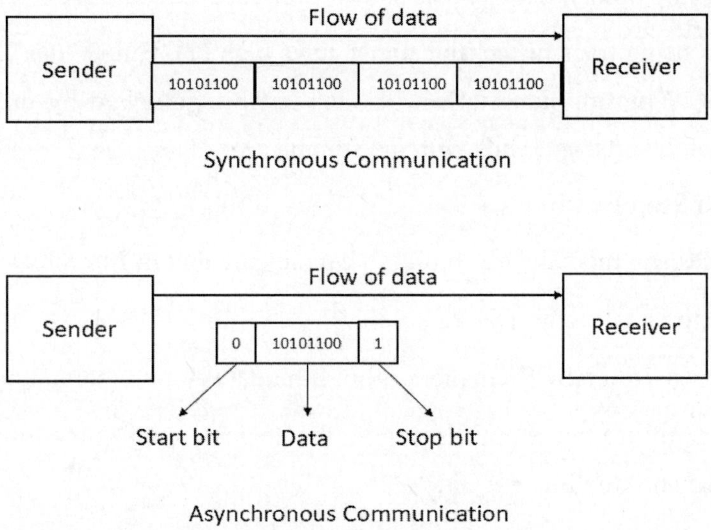

Figure 5.2: Synchronous & Asynchronous communication

5.3.1 Half- and full-duplex transmission

In data transmission, if data can be both transmitted and received, it is called duplex transmission, unlike simplex transmission (e.g., printers) where the computer only sends data. Duplex transmissions can be either half or full duplex. In half duplex, data transfer occurs one way at a time, whereas in full duplex, data can be transferred simultaneously in both directions. Full duplex requires two wire conductors for the data lines (in addition to the signal ground), one for transmission and one for reception.

5.3.2 Asynchronous serial communication and data framing

In serial data transfer, the data received is a stream of 0s and 1s, which can be confusing without a set of rules, or a protocol, to define how the data is organized, how many bits make up a character, and when the data starts and stops.

Asynchronous Serial Data Communication:

- Commonly used for character-oriented transmissions.
- Each character is framed with a start bit at the beginning and a stop bit at the end. This is called "framing."
- The start bit is always 0 (low), and the stop bit is always 1 (high). The stop bit can be one or two bits long.
- For example, the ASCII character "A" (binary 0100 0001) is sent with a start bit (0) at the beginning and a stop bit (1) at the end as shown in Figure 5.2.
- When no data is being transmitted, the signal stays high (1), called "mark." The low signal (0) is called "space." Transmission starts with the start bit, followed by the least significant bit (LSB), the rest of the bits, and ends with the stop bit.

Character Width and Stop Bits:

- Peripheral devices and modems can be set to handle data that is 7 or 8 bits wide.
- The number of stop bits can be 1 or 2.
- Older systems used 7-bit ASCII characters, but 8-bit data is more common now.
- Older devices might use two stop bits to give the device enough time to process data. Modern PCs typically use one stop bit.

Overhead in Data Transmission:

- Each character has a total of 10 bits: 8 bits for the ASCII character, 1 start bit, and 1 stop bit.
- This means there are 2 extra bits for each 8-bit character, resulting in a 20% overhead in the data transmission.

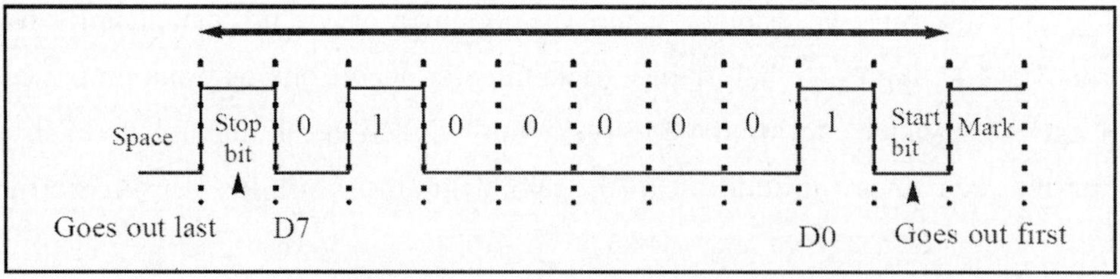

Figure 5.3: Framing ASCII "A" (41H)

In some systems, a parity bit is added to the character byte in the data frame to ensure data integrity. This means that each character (whether 7-bit or 8-bit) includes a single parity bit along with the start and stop bits. The parity bit can be set for odd or even parity.

- **Odd Parity:** The total number of 1s in the data bits plus the parity bit is odd.
- **Even Parity:** The total number of 1s in the data bits plus the parity bit is even.

For example, the ASCII character "A" (binary 0100 0001) would have a parity bit of 0 in an even-parity system. UART chips can be programmed to use odd parity, even parity, or no parity.

5.3.3 Data transfer rate

The rate at which data is transferred in serial communication is measured in bits per second (bps). Another term often used is baud rate. However, bps and baud rate are not always the same.

- **bps (Bits Per Second):** Refers to the actual number of bits transmitted per second.
- **Baud Rate:** Refers to the number of signal changes or symbols sent per second.

For example, if a modem sends data where each signal change represents multiple bits, the bps rate can be higher than the baud rate.

In practical use, the baud rate and bps are often treated as the same because, for many systems, each signal change represents one bit.

5.4 RS232 Protocol

RS232 is a standard for serial communication established by the Electronics Industries Association (EIA) in 1960, with subsequent revisions known as RS232A, RS232B, and RS232C. It is widely used for serial input/output interfacing in PCs and various equipment. The standard defines voltage levels that are not compatible with modern TTL logic; specifically, a logical 1 is represented by -3 to -25 volts, and a logical 0 by +3 to +25 volts, with the range between -3 and +3 volts being undefined. To interface RS232 with microcontrollers, which use TTL logic levels, voltage converters like the MAX232 IC are used. The MAX232 converts TTL logic levels to RS232 voltage levels and vice versa, ensuring compatibility and proper communication between different devices.

Usage:

Widespread Adoption: RS232 is the most widely used standard for serial input/output communication.

Applications: Extensively used in personal computers (PCs) and various types of equipment, including printers, modems, and other peripheral devices.

Compatibility Issues:

Historical Context: RS232 was established before the development of the Transistor-Transistor Logic (TTL) family, leading to compatibility issues with modern systems.

Voltage Levels:

Logical 1: Represented by a voltage range of -3 to -25 volts.

Logical 0: Represented by a voltage range of +3 to +25 volts.

Undefined Range: Voltages between -3 and +3 volts are considered undefined.

Incompatibility: RS232 voltage levels are not directly compatible with the 0 to 5-volt range used by TTL logic in modern microcontroller systems.

Interfacing with Microcontrollers:

Need for Conversion: To connect RS232 devices to microcontroller systems, voltage level conversion is necessary to ensure compatibility.

MAX232 IC:

Function: The MAX232 integrated circuit (IC) is widely used to convert TTL logic levels to RS232 voltage levels and vice versa.

Role: Known as a line driver, it facilitates communication between devices by handling voltage conversions.

Operation: The MAX232 converts the higher voltage levels of RS232 to the lower voltage levels of TTL (and vice versa), enabling seamless communication between devices.

5.4.1 RS232 Pin

A DB-9 connector, also known as a DE-9 connector, is a common type of electrical connector that is used for serial communications. It features nine pins and is commonly associated with RS-232 serial communication ports. A null modem connection is a method used to directly connect two Data Terminal Equipment (DTE) devices, such as two computers, without the need for Data Communication Equipment (DCE) like modems or routers. This type of connection is often used for direct serial communication between two devices.

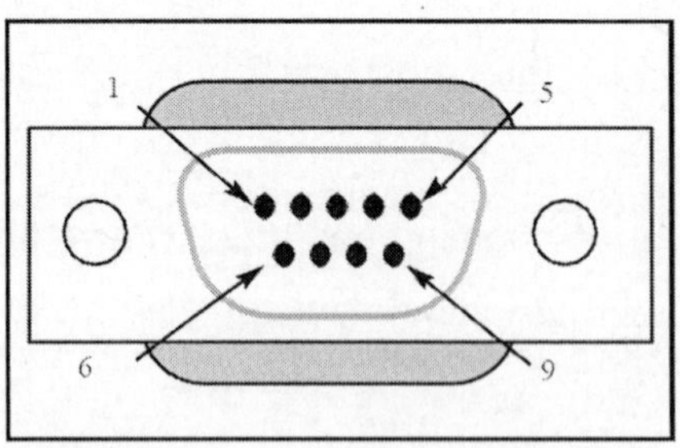

Figure 5.4: DB-9 9-Pin Connector [Mazidi, 2013]

Here's a typical pinout for a DB-9 connector used in RS-232 serial communication:

1. **Carrier Detect ($\overline{CD}$):** Used by modems to signal the presence of a carrier.
2. **Receive Data (RD):** Carries data from the connected device to the computer.
3. **Transmit Data (TD):** Carries data from the computer to the connected device.
4. **Data Terminal Ready (DTR):** Signals that the computer is ready to communicate.
5. **Ground (GND):** Common ground for all signals.
6. **Data Set Ready ($\overline{DSR}$):** Signals that the connected device is ready to communicate.
7. **Request to Send ($\overline{RTS}$):** Used to prepare the connected device for data transmission.
8. **Clear to Send ($\overline{CTS}$):** Used to indicate that the connected device is ready to accept data.
9. **Ring Indicator (RI):** Used by modems to signal an incoming call.

5.4.2 8051 Interfacing to RS232

This section details the physical connections between the 8051 microcontroller and RS232 connectors. As mentioned in previous section, the RS232 standard is not TTL-compatible. Therefore, a line driver like the MAX232 chip is required to convert RS232 voltage levels to TTL levels, and vice versa. The 8051 microcontroller has two pins specifically designated for serial data transmission and reception: TxD and RxD, which are part of port 3 (P3.0 and P3.1). Pin 11 (P3.1) is assigned to TxD, and pin 10 (P3.0) is designated as RxD. Since these pins are TTL-compatible, a line driver (Voltage Converter) is needed to convert them to RS232-compatible levels. The MAX232 chip is a commonly used line driver for this purpose.

The MAX232 chip features two sets of line drivers for data transmission and reception, as illustrated in Figure 5.4. The line drivers designated for TxD are labeled T1 and T2, while those for RxD are labeled R1 and R2.

Connection: 8051 to RS232

8051 TxD (P3.1, Pin 11) to MAX232 T1IN (Pin 11)

MAX232 T1OUT (Pin 14) to DB-9 Pin 2 (RD - Receive Data)

8051 RxD (P3.0, Pin 10) to MAX232 R1IN (Pin 13)

MAX232 R1OUT (Pin 12) to DB-9 Pin 3 (TD - Transmit Data)

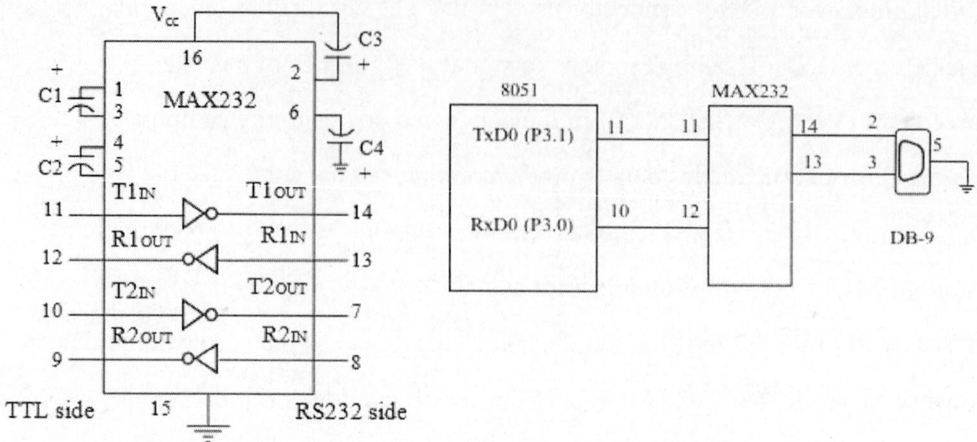

Figure 5.5: 8051 Interfacing to RS232 [Mazidi, 2013]

5.5 Serial communication registers of the 8051

In this section, we discuss the serial communication registers of the 8051 microcontroller and demonstrate how to program them for serial data transmission and reception. Given the widespread use of IBM PC/compatible computers for communication with 8051-based systems, we will focus on the serial communications between the 8051 and a PC's COM port. To ensure error-free data transfer between the PC and the 8051 system, it is crucial to match the baud rate of the 8051 system with that of the PC's COM port. These baud rates can be reviewed in the Windows HyperTerminal program by selecting the Communication Settings option.

Baud rate in the 8051:

The baud rate refers to the rate at which data is transmitted over a serial communication link. It is defined as the number of signal or symbol changes that occur per second. In simpler terms, it indicates the number of bits transmitted per second (bps). For example, a baud rate of 9600 means that 9600 bits are transmitted per second.

The baud rate formula for the 8051 microcontroller in conjunction with the Timer 1 and the UART (serial port) comes from the internal structure and operation of the 8051's timers and serial communication module. Here's a step-by-step explanation of how the formula is derived:

Clock Frequency and Machine Cycle Frequency:

The 8051 microcontroller operates with an external clock frequency (XTAL), often an 11.0592 MHz crystal. The internal operations are based on the machine cycle frequency, which is the external clock frequency divided by 12.

Machine cycle frequency= $\frac{XTAL}{12}$

For an 11.0592 MHz crystal, the machine cycle frequency is:

Machine cycle frequency = $\frac{11{,}059{,}200\,Hz}{12}$ = 921,600 Hz

UART Clock frequency:

The UART in the 8051 provides a clock frequency to Timer 1 by dividing the machine cycle frequency by 32.

UART frequency= $\frac{921.6\,k\,Hz}{32}$ = 28800 Hz

Timer 1 in Mode 2 (8-bit Auto-reload Mode):

Timer 1 is configured in mode 2, which counts from the value loaded in TH1 to 255 and then reloads. The baud rate is determined by the frequency of timer overflows:

Baud rate= $\frac{UART\ Frequency}{256-TH1}$

Since the UART frequency is 28,800 Hz

Baud rate= $\frac{28800}{256-TH1}$

SBUF Register

The SBUF register in the 8051 microcontroller is integral to serial communication, serving as the interface for data transmission and reception via the TxD and RxD lines. Here's a more detailed explanation and examples of how SBUF is used:

SBUF Register Overview

- **Transmission (TxD):** When a byte of data is written to SBUF, it is automatically framed with start and stop bits and then transmitted serially through the TxD pin.
- **Reception (RxD):** When data is received serially via the RxD pin, the 8051 microcontroller deframes it by removing the start and stop bits, and the resulting byte is stored in SBUF.

Transmitting Data

- The above instruction places the ASCII value of 'D' (0x44) into the SBUF register.
- The 8051 microcontroller will then frame this byte with start and stop bits and transmit it via the TxD pin.

```
MOV SBUF,#'D' ;load SBUF=44H, ASCII for 'D'
```

Receiving Data

- When data is received serially via the RxD (Receive Data) pin, the UART hardware in the 8051 collects the bits and detects the start bit, data bits, and stop bit.
- The UART deframes the received byte by removing the start and stop bits.
- When a byte is received through the RxD pin, it is stored in SBUF.
- The above instruction transfers the byte from SBUF to the accumulator (A).

```
MOV A,SBUF ;copy SBUF into accumulator
```

SCON (serial control) register

The SCON register is an 8-bit register used to configure the start bit, stop bit, and data bits for data framing, as well as other serial communication settings. It is 8 bit register. Following is the detail description of every bit:

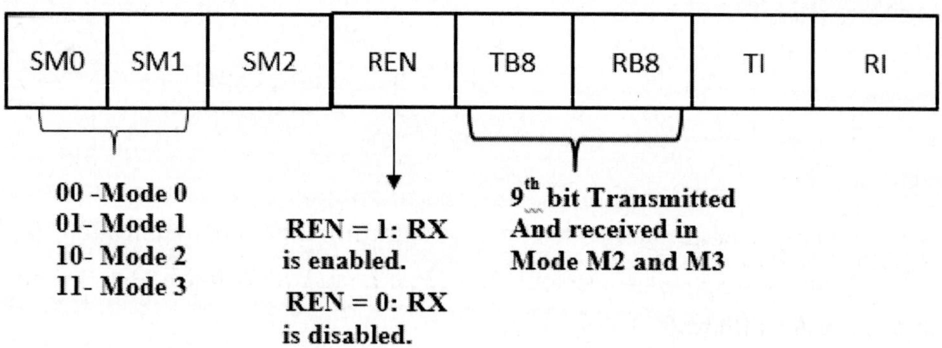

Bits 7 and 6 (SM0 and SM1): These bits set the serial communication mode.

Mode 0: Serial mode 0, 8-bit.

Mode 1: Serial mode 1, 8-bit UART with variable baud rate. It has one start bit, 8 data bits and, one stop bit.

Mode 2: Serial mode 2, 9-bit UART with Fixed Baud Rate. It has one start bit, 8 data bits, one programmable 9th bit and, one stop bit.

Mode 3: Serial mode 3, 9-bit UART variable baud rate. It has one start bit, 8 data bits, one programmable 9th bit and, one stop bit.

For our purposes, we are focusing on serial mode 1, which is one of the four serial modes. In serial mode 1, the SCON register is configured for 8-bit data framing with 1 start bit and 1 stop bit, making it compatible with the COM ports on IBM/compatible PCs. This mode also features a variable baud rate, which is controlled by Timer 1 of the 8051 microcontroller. In serial mode 1, each character is transmitted using a total of 10 bits: 1 start bit, 8 data bits, and 1 stop bit.

Bit 5 (SM2): This bit is used in Mode 1, Mode 2 and Mode 3. It enables multiprocessor communication in Mode 2 and Mode 3.

Mode 1 (8-bit UART with Variable Baud Rate):

Mode 1 uses an 8-bit data frame with 1 start bit and 1 stop bit. There is no dedicated 9th bit. SM2 in Mode 1 is used to control the behavior of the RI (Receive Interrupt) flag when receiving data. When SM2 is set to 1, the 8051 will only set the RI flag if a valid stop bit (logic level 1) is detected at the end of the 8-bit data frame. This means that SM2 = 1 can help ensure that the received data frame is valid and that the stop bit is correctly detected. If SM2 is 0, the RI flag will be set regardless of the state of the stop bit, meaning the microcontroller will accept any received frame, even if the stop bit is incorrect.

Mode 2 and Mode 3:

In Mode 2, SM2 can also be used for multiprocessor communication and error detection. When SM2 is set to 1, the microcontroller will only set the RI flag (indicating data reception) if the 9th bit (RB8) of the received frame is 1. If RB8 is 0, the data byte is ignored.

This helps to identify address bytes in a multiprocessor setup. If SM2 is 0, the microcontroller will accept all bytes. This is similar to how Mode 1 uses SM2, allowing the microcontroller to selectively process certain incoming frames.

Bit 4 (REN): This bit enables or disables the reception of serial data.

REN = 1: Reception is enabled.

REN = 0: Reception is disabled.

The REN (Receive Enable) bit is located at bit D4 in the SCON register, and it is also referred to as SCON.4 since the SCON register is bit-addressable. When the REN bit is set high, it enables the 8051 microcontroller to receive data on the RxD pin. Therefore, to allow both data transmission and reception, REN must be set to 1. Conversely, setting REN to 0 disables the receiver. To manipulate this bit, you can use the instructions “SETB SCON.4” to set REN to 1 and “CLR SCON.4” to clear REN to 0. These instructions leverage the bit-addressable nature of the SCON register. The REN bit is crucial for controlling serial data reception and is a key feature of the SCON register.

Bit 3 (TB8): This bit is used in Mode 2 and Mode 3 for transmitting the 9th bit of data.

Bit 2 (RB8): This bit is used in Mode 2 and Mode 3 to receive the 9th bit of data.

Bit 1 (TI): The TI (Transmit Interrupt) bit is bit D1 in the SCON register and serves as a critical flag. When the 8051 has completed the transmission of an 8-bit character, it sets the TI flag to signal that it is ready to transmit another byte. The TI bit is set at the start of the stop bit. We will explore its role in more detail when discussing programming examples related to data transmission.

Bit 0 (RI): The RI (Receive Interrupt) bit is bit D0 in the SCON register and is another crucial flag. When the 8051 receives serial data through the RxD pin, it removes the start and stop bits and stores the byte in the SBUF register. It then sets the RI flag to signal that a byte has been received and needs to be processed before it is overwritten. We will discuss its application in serial data reception in upcoming programming examples.

5.6 Programming the 8051 for serial data transfer

Here's a step-by-step explanation for programming the 8051 to transfer data serially.

1. Configure Timer Mode:

Load the TMOD register with the value 20H to set Timer 1 in Mode 2 (8-bit auto-reload mode). This mode is used to generate the baud rate for serial communication.

2. Set Baud Rate:

Load the TH1 register with the appropriate value to configure the baud rate for serial data transfer. This value depends on the crystal frequency (e.g., XTAL = 11.0592 MHz) and the desired baud rate.

3. Configure Serial Mode:

Load the SCON register with the value 50H to configure the 8051 for Serial Mode 1. In this mode, each data frame consists of 8 data bits, with 1 start bit and 1 stop bit.

4. Start Timer 1:

Set the TR1 bit to 1 to start Timer 1, which will generate the baud rate clock for serial communication.

5. Clear Transmit Interrupt Flag:

Clear the TI (Transmit Interrupt) flag using the CLR TI instruction. This prepares the TI flag for indicating the completion of the next data byte transmission.

6. Load Data to Transmit:

Write the character byte that you wish to transfer into the SBUF (Serial Buffer) register. This initiates the transmission of the byte.

7. Monitor Transmit Interrupt Flag:

Use the JNB TI, xx instruction to monitor the TI flag. This instruction waits until TI is set, indicating that the current character has been completely transmitted.

8. Prepare for Next Character:

Once TI is set, indicating the previous character has been fully transmitted, clear the TI flag again (using CLR TI), and repeat the process from Step 6 to transmit the next character.

Exmple 5.1 Write a program for the 8051 to transfer letter “B” serially at 9600 baud, continuously.

```
            MOV TMOD,#20H ;Timer 1, mode 2(auto-reload)
            MOV TH1,#FDH ;9600 baud rate
            MOV SCON,#50H ;8-bit, 1 stop, REN enabled
            SETB TR1 ;start Timer 1
AGAIN:      MOV SBUF,#"B" ;letter "A" to be transferred
HERE: JNB TI,HERE ;wait for the last bit
            CLR TI ;clear TI for next char
            SJMP AGAIN ;keep sending A
```

Calculation for TH1: We have derived the formula for baud rate calculation,

$$\text{Baud rate}=\frac{28800}{256-TH1}$$

$$9600=\frac{28800}{256-TH1}$$

TH1 = 253 = FDH

SCON register value:

Explanation of 50H (Binary: 01010000):

SM0 (Bit 7): 0

Mode selection: The combination of SM0 and SM1 selects the serial mode.

In this case, SM0 = 0 and SM1 = 1, which selects Mode 1 (8-bit UART, variable baud rate).

SM1 (Bit 6): 1

This is combined with SM0 to choose Mode 1 (8-bit data, 1 start bit, 1 stop bit, and variable baud rate). This mode is often used for standard serial communication.

SM2 (Bit 5): 0

Multiprocessor communication is not needed, so SM2 is set to 0.

REN (Bit 4): 1
REN (Receive Enable) is set to 1 to allow the microcontroller to receive data via serial communication. Even though your program only sends data, keeping this enabled is common practice.
TB8 (Bit 3): 0
Not used in 8-bit mode (only used in 9-bit communication). Set to 0.
RB8 (Bit 2): 0
Not used in 8-bit mode. Set to 0.
TI (Bit 1): 0
Initially cleared. This bit is set by hardware when a byte is transmitted, and it is cleared by software after handling the interrupt.
RI (Bit 0): 0
Initially cleared. This bit is set by hardware when a byte is received and is cleared by software after handling the interrupt.

5.6.1 Programming the 8051 to receive data serially

Here's a rephrased version of the steps for initializing and operating serial communication using an 8051 microcontroller:

1. Load the TMOD register with the value 20H to configure Timer 1 in mode 2 (8-bit auto-reload) for setting the baud rate.
2. Load TH1 with a value to set the desired baud rate, assuming the crystal frequency (XTAL) is 11.0592 MHz.
3. Set the SCON register to 50H to configure serial mode 1, which frames 8-bit data with start and stop bits and enables the receiver.
4. Set TR1 to 1 to start Timer 1.
5. Clear the RI flag using the instruction CLR RI.
6. Monitor the RI flag with the JNB RI,xx instruction to check if a complete character has been received.
7. When the RI flag is set, the received byte is in SBUF. Move its contents to a safe location.
8. Repeat from Step 5 to receive the next character.

Example 5.2 Write a program for the 8051 to receive data bytes serially and output them to Port 2. Set the baud rate to 2400 with 8-bit data and 1 stop bit.

```
MOV TMOD, #20H    ; Configure Timer 1 in mode 2 (auto-reload)
MOV TH1, #244     ; Load TH1 for 2400 baud rate
MOV SCON, #50H    ; Set serial mode: 8-bit data, 1 stop bit, REN enabled
SETB TR1          ; Start Timer 1
MAIN_LOOP:
JNB RI, MAIN_LOOP ; Wait for a byte to be received
MOV A, SBUF       ; Move the received byte from SBUF to accumulator
MOV P2, A         ; Send the data to Port 2
CLR RI            ; Clear RI flag to prepare for the next byte
SJMP MAIN_LOOP    ; Repeat to receive and display the next byte
```

8051 UART

5.7 Serial Peripheral Interface (SPI Protocol)

The Serial Peripheral Interface (SPI) is a communication protocol used for data transfer between multiple devices, arranged in a master-slave configuration. In this setup, the master device controls the communication, while the slave devices receive instructions from the master. The most common SPI configuration involves one master and multiple slaves. SPI is a synchronous communication protocol that allows for simultaneous transmission and reception of data at high transfer rates, making it ideal for board-level communication over short distances.

SPI is particularly advantageous for multi-device communication due to its high data transfer rates and the ability to send and receive data concurrently. However, SPI requires more signal lines or wires compared to other communication protocols. Additionally, there is no standardized message protocol for SPI communication, meaning each device may have its own data message formatting convention.

The SPI bus, originally developed by Motorola Corp. (now Freescale), has become a widely used standard among many semiconductor manufacturers. Unlike traditional buses, which require eight or more pins, SPI devices use only two pins for data transfer: SDI (data in) and SDO (data out). This reduction in the number of data pins significantly minimizes package size and power consumption, making SPI ideal for space-constrained applications. The SPI bus also includes an SCLK (shift clock) pin to synchronize data transfer between two chips. The final pin, CE (chip enable), controls the initiation and termination of data transfer. Thus, the SPI bus is a four-wire interface comprising SDI, SDO, SCLK, and CE. In many chips, these signals are also referred to as MOSI (master out, slave in), MISO (master in, slave out), SCK (serial clock), and SS (slave select).

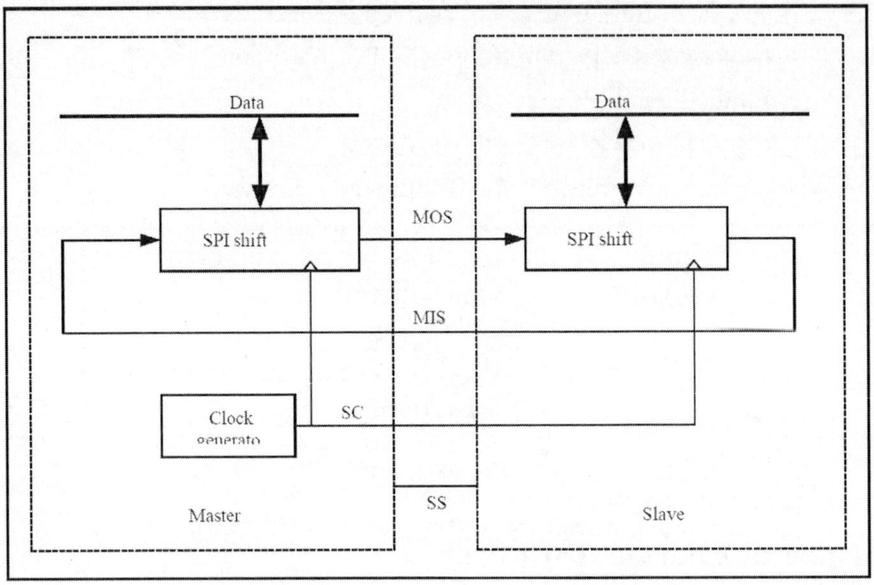

Figure 5.6: SPI Architecture

SPI (Serial Peripheral Interface) involves two shift registers: one on the master side and one on the slave side. The master also has a clock generator that synchronizes the shift registers. As shown in Figure 5.6, the master's serial-out pin (MOSI - Master Out Slave In) connects to the slave's serial-in pin, while the master's serial-in pin (MISO - Master In Slave Out) connects to the slave's serial-out pin. The clock generated by the master drives both shift registers, which can be triggered by either a falling or rising edge. In SPI, each shift register is 8 bits long, meaning that after eight clock pulses, the data in the two shift registers is exchanged. When the master wants to send a byte, it loads the byte into its shift register and generates eight clock pulses, transferring the byte to the slave's shift register. Similarly, when the master wants to receive data, the slave places the byte into its shift register, and after eight clock pulses, the master receives the byte. It's important to note that SPI is full-duplex, allowing simultaneous sending and receiving of data. When connecting a device with an SPI bus to a microcontroller, the microcontroller functions as the master while the SPI device acts as the slave. This setup means the microcontroller generates the SCLK, which is sent to the SCLK pin of the SPI device. The SPI protocol uses SCLK to synchronize data transfer, sending one bit at a time, starting with the most significant bit (MSB). During this transfer, the Chip Enable (CE) pin must remain HIGH. Information, including the address and data, is exchanged between the microcontroller and the SPI device in 8-bit segments, with the address byte immediately followed by the data byte. To differentiate between read and write operations, the D7 bit of the address byte is set to 1 for writing, and set to 0 for reading, as will be explained further.

5.8 I2C Protocol (Inter-Integrated Circuit Protocol)

Communication between microcontrollers and various peripheral devices requires a digital protocol. I2C (Inter-Integrated Circuit) is a widely used two-wire serial communication protocol, commonly employed across a range of devices from different TI product families. I2C uses a serial data line (SDA) and a serial clock line (SCL) to facilitate communication. The protocol supports multiple target devices on the same communication bus and can accommodate multiple controllers that send and receive commands and data. Data is transmitted in byte packets, with each target device identified by a unique address.

I2C communication uses just two bidirectional open-drain pins (SDA for data and SCL for clock), with each line requiring a 4.7 kΩ pull-up resistor to create a wired-AND condition. This means that if any device pulls the line low, the line stays low; it's only high when no devices pull it low. Up to 120 devices, called nodes, can share the same I2C bus as shown in Figure 5.7. Each node can function as either a master or slave, depending on the situation. The master generates the clock signal, initiates, and ends communication, while the slave responds to the master's commands. Both master and slave can send and receive data, leading to four possible modes: master transmitter, master receiver, slave transmitter, and slave receiver. However, a node can only operate in one mode at a time. I2C is a synchronous serial protocol, meaning each data bit on the SDA line is synchronized with the clock pulses on the SCL line. According to the protocol, data on the SDA line can only change when the SCL line is low, except during the START and STOP conditions, which mark the beginning and end of communication. In summary, the I2C protocol is a synchronous communication method where a master device initiates interaction with a slave device. In this master-slave setup, the master generates the clock signal, which determines the data transfer rate or clock frequency. I2C is a bidirectional serial bus, allowing the master to both write to and read from the slave. Data is transferred serially, bit by bit, using two bus lines: the serial clock (SCL) and the serial data (SDA) lines.

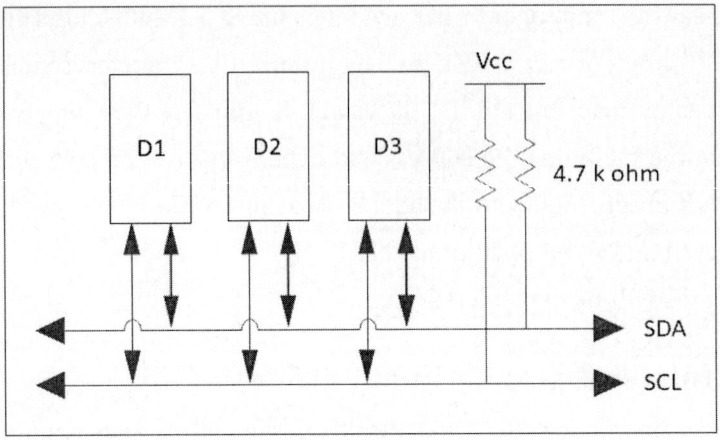

Figure 5.7: I2C bus

5.9 Introduction to Blue-tooth

Bluetooth (IEEE 802.15.1) is a standardized protocol designed for secure, short-range, low-power, and low-cost wireless data transmission over a 2.4GHz link. It's a key player in the wireless revolution, powering a wide range of consumer devices such as headsets, video game controllers, and even livestock trackers.

In the realm of embedded electronics, Bluetooth is ideal for transmitting small amounts of data wirelessly over short distances (less than 100 meters). It's a great alternative to traditional serial communication interfaces, and it can be used in various DIY projects, like creating a custom HID computer keyboard or building a wireless MP3-playing speaker with the right module.

This tutorial will provide a brief overview of the Bluetooth protocol, covering its specifications and profiles, and comparing it to other wireless communication protocols. The Bluetooth protocol operates at 2.4GHz within the same unlicensed ISM frequency band as other RF protocols like ZigBee and WiFi. What sets Bluetooth apart is its standardized set of rules and specifications that distinguish it from these other protocols.

Masters, Slaves, and Piconets

Bluetooth networks, known as piconets, operate using a master/slave model to manage data transmission. In this setup, a single master device can connect with up to seven slave devices simultaneously, while each slave device in the piconet is connected to only one master. The master manages communication within the piconet, sending data to any of its connected slaves and requesting data from them as needed. Slaves can only transmit to and receive from the master; they are not permitted to communicate directly with other slaves in the piconet.

Bluetooth Addresses and Names

Every Bluetooth device is assigned a unique 48-bit address, known as the BD_ADDR, typically displayed as a 12-digit hexadecimal value. This address is divided into two parts: the most significant 24 bits form the Organizationally Unique Identifier (OUI), which identifies the device's manufacturer. The remaining 24 bits are unique to each device, ensuring that no two Bluetooth devices share the same address. This unique address is crucial for identifying and distinguishing devices during communication.

Connection Process

Establishing a Bluetooth connection involves several steps, progressing through three main states:

1. **Inquiry:** If two Bluetooth devices are unfamiliar with each other, one device initiates an inquiry to discover nearby devices. The inquiring device sends out a request, and any device listening for such requests will respond with its address, and possibly its name and other details.
2. **Paging (Connecting):** Once the inquiry process provides the addresses of the devices, the paging process begins. This step involves establishing a connection between the devices. Both devices need to know each other's addresses, obtained during the inquiry phase, to proceed with paging.
3. **Connection:** After the paging process is complete, the devices enter the connection state. In this state, devices can operate in various modes:
    - **Active Mode:** The device is fully operational, actively transmitting or receiving data.
    - **Sniff Mode:** A power-saving mode where the device is less active, periodically waking up to listen for transmissions at set intervals (e.g., every 100ms).
    - **Hold Mode:** A temporary power-saving mode where the device sleeps for a defined period before returning to active mode. The master device can command a slave to enter hold mode.
    - **Park Mode:** The deepest power-saving mode, where a slave device becomes inactive until the master device commands it to wake up.

HC-05 Bluetooth Module Interfacing with 8051

The HC-05 is a Bluetooth module designed for wireless serial communication. It operates using UART (Universal Asynchronous Receiver/Transmitter) for data exchange.

- The HC-05 module has 6 pins and operates in two modes: Data Mode: Used for regular data transfer between devices. Command Mode: Used for configuring and changing the module's settings through AT commands.

- The module can operate at either 5V or 3.3V and includes an onboard 5V to 3.3V regulator.
- For interfacing with a microcontroller: The HC-05's TX pin operates at 3.3V, which is compatible with the 8051's RX pin, so no voltage level shifting is required for the module's transmit signal. However, the HC-05's RX pin expects a 3.3V signal, so when interfacing with the 8051's TX pin (which operates at 5V), you need to use a voltage divider or level shifter to reduce the 5V signal to 3.3V to prevent damage to the HC-05 module.

We can calculate the reduced voltage on RX pin of the HC-05 module by voltage divider rule. As you can see from the figure 5.7 we have used 1k and 2k resistor for voltage division. Assume that Vin voltage we are getting from TX pin of 8051 and V_{out} voltage we are feeding to HC-05 modules RX pin.

$$V_{out} = \frac{R2}{R1+R2} \times V_{in}$$

Where R1=1k, R2=2k, V_{in}=5V So,

$V_{out} = 3.33V$

Using the 1 kΩ and 2 kΩ resistors in a voltage divider, the output voltage (V_{out}) is approximately 3.33V. This voltage is suitable for the HC-05's RX pin, as it safely reduces the 5V signal from the 8051.

Example Application: Controlling an LED via Smartphone

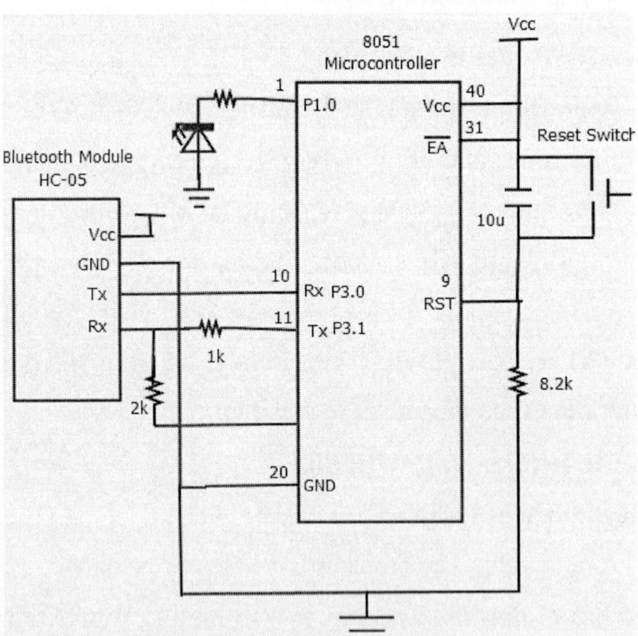

Figure 5.8: Bluetooth module HC-05 interfacing with 8051

In this example, we'll create a simple application to control an LED using a smartphone by interfacing an 8051 microcontroller with an HC-05 Bluetooth module. The 8051 will handle serial communication with the HC-05 to receive and transmit data.

Application Description

LED Control: When the number 1 is sent from the smartphone, the LED will turn ON. When the number 2 is sent, the LED will turn OFF.

Error Handling: If the data received is neither 1 nor 2, the 8051 will send a message back to the smartphone instructing the user to select a valid option.

This setup allows you to control the state of an LED from your smartphone via Bluetooth, providing a practical example of wireless control in an embedded system.

```
#include <reg51.h>
#include "UART_H_file.h"  /* Include UART library */
sbit LED = P1^0;
void main()
{
    char receivedData;
    UART_Init();       /* Initialize UART */
    P1 = 0;            /* Initialize port to 0 */
    LED = 0;           /* Ensure LED is OFF initially */

    while(1)
    {
        receivedData = UART_RxChar();  /* Receive character serially */

        if(receivedData == '1')
        {
            LED = 1;                 /* Turn ON LED */
            UART_SendString("LED_ON");  /* Send status message */
        }
        else if(receivedData == '2')
        {
            LED = 0;                 /* Turn OFF LED */
            UART_SendString("LED_OFF"); /* Send status message */
        }
        else
        {
            UART_SendString("Select a proper option");  /* Error message */
        }
    }
}
```

5.10 Introduction to Zig-bee

Zigbee is a wireless communication protocol designed for low-power, low-data-rate, and short-range applications. It operates on the IEEE 802.15.4 standard and is widely used in applications like home automation, industrial controls, and sensor networks.

Key Features of Zigbee:

- **Low Power Consumption:** Ideal for battery-operated devices due to its energy-efficient design.
- **Mesh Networking:** Zigbee supports mesh networks, allowing devices to communicate with each other and extend the range of the network.
- **Scalability:** Supports large networks with up to 65,000 devices.
- **Secure Communication:** Provides security features like encryption to protect data.
- Zigbee operates in the 2.4 GHz ISM band, similar to Bluetooth and Wi-Fi, but it is optimized for simpler, less power-intensive tasks.

Zigbee wireless mesh networks, known for their redundant, self-configuring, and self-healing capabilities, are ideal for a variety of applications:

- **Energy Management and Efficiency:** Enables greater control and monitoring of energy usage, allowing customers to make informed choices, receive better service, efficiently manage resources, and reduce environmental impact.
- **Home Automation:** Facilitates flexible control of lighting, heating, cooling, security, and entertainment systems from any location within the home.
- **Building Automation:** Centralizes and integrates the management of lighting, heating, cooling, and security systems for improved efficiency.
- **Industrial Automation:** Enhances the reliability and extension of existing manufacturing and process control systems.

The ZigBee Network

ZigBee networks consist of three types of devices:

- **Coordinator:** This device initiates and manages the network. It stores critical information about the network, acts as the Trust Center, and serves as the repository for security keys.
- **Router:** Routers extend the network's coverage area, dynamically route around obstacles, and provide backup routes in case of network congestion or device failure. They can connect to both the coordinator and other routers, as well as support child devices.

- **End Devices:** These devices can send and receive messages but cannot perform routing operations. They must connect to either the coordinator or a router and do not support child devices.

The ZigBee Protocol Stack

ZigBee sits on top of the IEEE 802.15.4 PHY and MAC layers. The top layer of the ZigBee protocol stack includes the Application Framework, ZigBee Device Object (ZDO), and Application Support (APS) Sublayer.

- **Application (APL) Layer:** The top layer in the ZigBee protocol stack consists of the Application Framework, ZigBee Device Object (ZDO), and Application Support (APS) Sublayer.
- **Application Framework:** This framework provides guidelines for creating profiles on the ZigBee stack, ensuring consistency. It defines standard data types, descriptors for service discovery, data frame formats, and a key-value pair system for rapidly developing simple, attribute-based profiles.
- **Application Objects:** These are software components that control the ZigBee device at each endpoint. A ZigBee node can support up to 240 application objects, each associated with endpoints numbered from 1 to 240, with endpoint 0 reserved for the ZDO.
- **ZigBee Device Object (ZDO):** The ZDO determines the device's role in the network (such as coordinator, router, or end device), manages binding and discovery requests, and establishes secure relationships between network devices. It also offers a comprehensive set of management commands through the ZigBee Device Profile, and is always associated with endpoint 0.
- **ZDO Management Plane:** This component facilitates communication between the APS and NWK layers and the ZDO. It allows the ZDO to handle requests for network access and security from applications, using ZigBee Device Profile (ZDP) messages.
- **Application Support (APS) Sublayer:** The APS sublayer provides data services to applications and ZigBee device profiles, and also manages binding links and maintains the binding table.
- **Security Service Provider (SSP):** The SSP provides security mechanisms for layers that require encryption, particularly the NWK and APS layers. It is initialized and configured through the ZDO.

- **Network (NWK) Layer:** This layer manages network addresses and routing, interacts with the MAC layer to perform tasks such as network initiation (by the coordinator), assigning addresses, adding or removing devices, routing messages, applying security, and performing route discovery.

UNIT SUMMARY

This unit covers the concepts of synchronous and asynchronous communication, which are fundamental for data transmission between devices. Synchronous communication requires a shared clock signal for timing, ensuring that data is sent and received simultaneously, while asynchronous communication allows data transmission without a shared clock, relying on start and stop bits to signify the beginning and end of a data packet. The unit discusses standard communication protocols, including RS232, which is widely used for serial communication, and SPI (Serial Peripheral Interface) and I2C (Inter-Integrated Circuit), both of which enable efficient data exchange between microcontrollers and peripheral devices. Additionally, it introduces interfacing with modern wireless protocols such as Bluetooth and Zigbee, highlighting their applications in short-range communication and networked devices. This knowledge is crucial for developing systems that require reliable communication in embedded applications.

EXCERCISE

Multiple Choice Question

1. Asynchronous transmission is characterized by:

   A. The transmitter and receiver sending and receiving data at different rates

   B. The transmitter and receiver sending and receiving data at the same rate

   C. The inclusion of start and stop bits before data transmission begins

   D. The transmission clock being synchronized with each bus cycle

2. Which of the following statements best distinguishes between synchronous and asynchronous communication in microcontrollers?

   A. Synchronous communication requires both devices to share a common clock signal, while asynchronous communication uses start and stop bits to frame the data.

   B. Asynchronous communication is faster than synchronous communication because it does not require a clock signal.

C. Synchronous communication is more error-prone than asynchronous communication because it lacks start and stop bits.

D. In asynchronous communication, data is transmitted in real-time without any delay, whereas synchronous communication introduces a delay to synchronize clocks.

3. Which communication protocol is commonly used for short distance communication and requires only two wires for data transmission?

   A. SPI　　B. I2C

   C. RS232　　D. Bluetooth

4. RS232 is an example of:

   A. Synchronous communication　　B. Asynchronous communication

   C. Full-duplex communication only　　D. A high-speed communication protocol

5. Which protocol uses a Master-Slave architecture and can support multiple devices on the same bus?

   A. RS232　　B. SPI

   C. I2C　　D. Zigbee

6. Which communication protocol is most suitable for low-power, wireless mesh networking applications?

   A. Bluetooth　　B. SPI

   C. Zigbee　　D. RS232

7. Which protocol is designed for high-speed communication between microcontrollers and peripherals, with separate data and clock lines?

   A. SPI　　B. I2C

   C. RS232　　D. Zigbee

Short Answer Questions (8 to 12)

8. What is the primary difference between synchronous and asynchronous communication?
9. Describe the main use case of the RS232 communication protocol.
10. What are the roles of the Master and Slave in SPI communication?
11. Explain how I2C allows multiple devices to communicate on the same bus.
12. What is the typical application of Bluetooth in microcontroller-based systems?
13. Explain Multiprocessor Communication in Mode 2 and Mode 3 of serial communication.

Long Answer Questions (13 to 16)

14. How would you configure a microcontroller to communicate with multiple sensors using the I2C protocol? Explain the role of addresses in this configuration. Define an embedded system and list its main characteristics.
15. Explain how you would interface a microcontroller with an SPI-based peripheral, such as an external ADC. What are the key connections and considerations for data transfer?
16. Write an 8051 C program to transfer the message "HELLO" serially at 9600 baud, 8-bit data, 1 stop bit. Do this continuously.
17. Program the 8051 in C to receive bytes of data serially and put them in P1. Set the baud rate at 2400; use 8-bit data, and 1 stop bit.
18. Write an assembly language program to transmit 45H at 9600 baud rate.
19. Derive the timer count value for 4800 baud rate.

MCQ answer

1. (c) 2. (a) 3. (c) 4. (b) 5. (c) 6. (c) 7. (a)

KNOW MORE

Synchronous and asynchronous communication are essential concepts in data transmission; synchronous communication requires a shared clock signal between sender and receiver, leading to faster data transfer with minimal overhead, exemplified by protocols like SPI (Serial Peripheral Interface), which uses separate data and clock lines for high-speed communication, and I2C (Inter-Integrated Circuit), which utilizes two wires for multi-device communication with start and stop bits. In contrast, RS232 is an asynchronous protocol often used for point-to-point connections, typically found in older devices like modems. Interfacing these protocols with wireless communication standards like Bluetooth—which facilitates short-range data exchange—and Zigbee, designed for low-power, low-data-rate applications in IoT and home automation, is increasingly common. Emerging trends include advancements in Bluetooth technology (like Bluetooth 5.0) for greater range and speed, the integration of low-power wireless protocols like LoRaWAN for long-range IoT applications, and a growing emphasis on security and interoperability among devices, highlighting the evolution and complexity of modern communication systems.

REFERENCES AND SUGGESTED READINGS

1. Muhammad Ali Mazidi , Janice G. Mazidi, Rolin D. McKinlay 8051 Microcontroller, The: A Systems Approach: Pearson New International Edition 1st Edition, 2013
2. K. J. Ayala, "8051 Microcontroller", Delmar Cengage Learning, 2004.

QR code for further reading

SPI vs I2C

6 Applications

UNIT SPECIFICS

Through this unit we have discussed the following aspects:

- *LED, LCD and keyboard interfacing*
- *Stepper motor interfacing*
- *DC Motor interfacing*
- *Sensor interfacing*

The topics practical applications are discussed to inspire curiosity, creativity, and enhance problem-solving abilities. The unit includes multiple-choice, short-answer, and long-answer questions, categorized according to Bloom's taxonomy's lower and higher levels, along with assignments involving numerical problems. A list of references and suggested readings is provided for additional practice. QR codes in various sections offer access to further relevant information on topics of interest.

Following the practical content, a "Know More" section is presented. This section is carefully designed to offer supplementary information that is beneficial to users. It covers the initial activity, interesting facts, analogies, and the history of the subject's development, highlighting key observations and findings. Timelines track the subject's evolution from its origins to the present, and its real-life or industrial applications are explored in various contexts. The section also includes case studies on environmental, sustainability, social, and ethical issues where applicable, as well as topics meant to foster curiosity and inquisitiveness within the unit.

RATIONALE

In this unit, students will learn LED, LCD, keyboard, stepper motor, DC motor, and sensor interfacing to develop essential skills in embedded systems. Mastering these interfaces is crucial for designing and implementing systems that interact with both users and the environment. LED and

LCD interfacing focuses on visual communication and output display, while keyboard interfacing facilitates user input. Understanding stepper and DC motor control is key for applications requiring precise movement and automation. Sensor interfacing allows systems to detect and respond to environmental changes, which is critical for real-time monitoring and control. Together, these skills form the foundation for building complex and responsive embedded systems across various domains.

PRE-REQUISITES

C language programming of 8051, Assembly language programming, Basic electronics.

UNIT OUTCOMES

List of outcomes of this unit is as follows:

U6-O1: Demonstrate how to interface LEDs, LCDs, keyboards, motors, and sensors with microcontrollers for simple embedded applications.

U6-O2: Analyze the interaction between various interfaced components (like sensors, motors, and displays) to optimize system performance.

U6-O3: Design and implement an embedded system integrating LED, LCD, keyboard, motor, and sensor interfaces for a specific application.

Unit-6 Outcomes	***EXPECTED MAPPING WITH COURSE OUTCOMES*** *(1-Weak Correlation; 2-Medium Correlation; 3-Strong Correlation)*				
	CO-1	***CO-2***	***CO-3***	***CO-4***	***CO-5***
U6-O1	*2*	*3*	*3*	*1*	*1*
U6-O2	*2*	*2*	*3*	*1*	*1*
U6-O3	*2*	*3*	*3*	*1*	*2*

6.1 Light Emitting Diode (LED) Interfacing

LEDs (Light Emitting Diodes) are increasingly popular across a wide range of applications. When voltage is applied to a PN junction diode, electrons and holes combine at the junction, releasing energy as light (photons). The electrical characteristics of an LED are similar to those of a PN junction diode. In forward bias, free electrons in the conduction band recombine with holes in the valence band, producing light as energy is released. LEDs are commonly used in applications like message display boards and traffic signal lights. The operation of an LED is driven by the movement of charge carriers (electrons and holes) across the P-N junction. When a forward voltage is applied (with the anode positive relative to the cathode), electrons and holes recombine at the junction, releasing energy as photons (light). The semiconductor chip is connected to external terminals, with the anode (+) linked to the P-region and the cathode (-) connected to the N-region.

Interfacing LEDs with the 8051 microcontroller is a basic yet important exercise in embedded system design. It involves controlling the state of the LEDs (ON or OFF) by sending signals from the microcontroller. Here's an overview of how LED interfacing with the 8051 works:

Components Required:

- 8051 Microcontroller
- LEDs
- Current-limiting resistors (220Ω to 1kΩ)
- Connecting wires
- Breadboard

Concept:

LEDs are connected to the I/O pins of the 8051 microcontroller through resistors as shown in Figure 6.1. The resistors used as current limiting resistor prevent from damaging the LEDs. The microcontroller can control the LEDs by configuring the connected pins as output. The state of these pins (HIGH or LOW) determines whether the LEDs are ON or OFF.

Circuit Configuration:

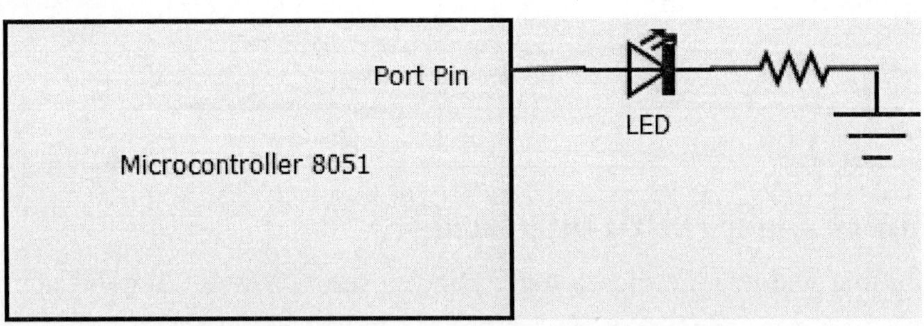

Figure 6.1: LED interfacing with 8051

One terminal of each LED is connected to a port pin (e.g., P1.0, P1.1, etc.) of the 8051 microcontroller. The other terminal of the LED is connected to the resistor. The other end of resistor is connected to the ground (GND).

Working:

When a port pin is configured as output and set HIGH, current flows through the LED, causing it to light up (ON state). When the port pin is set LOW, no current flows, and the LED remains OFF.

Example 6.1 Write C language program of interfacing LED to port pin 1.0 of 8051 microcontroller.

```
#include <reg51.h>
// Define LED pin
sbit LED = P1^0;
// Function to generate a delay
void delay(void) {
   unsigned int i, j;

   // Outer loop for the delay duration
   for(i = 0; i < 500; i++) {
      // Inner loop for additional delay granularity
      for(j = 0; j < 100; j++);
   }
}
// Main program
void main(void) {
   while(1) {
      LED = 1;  // Turn ON the LED
      delay();  // Wait for the specified delay
      LED = 0;  // Turn OFF the LED
      delay();  // Wait again for the specified delay
   }
}
```

6.2 Liquid Crystal Display (LCD) Interfacing

A Liquid Crystal Display (LCD) is highly useful for providing a user interface and for debugging purposes. The most commonly used LCD controller is the HITACHI 44780, which offers an easy interface between the microcontroller and the LCD. The most commonly used ALPHANUMERIC displays are

- 1x16 (Single Line & 16 characters).

- 2x16 (Double Line & 16 character per line).
- 4x20 (four lines & Twenty characters per line).

The LCD requires 3 control lines (RS, R/W, and EN) and either 8 or 4 data lines, depending on the mode of operation. In 8-bit mode, 8 data lines plus 3 control lines are used, requiring a total of 11 lines. In 4-bit mode, 4 data lines plus 3 control lines are needed, requiring only 7 lines. How do you decide which mode to use? It's straightforward: if you have enough available data lines, you can choose the 8-bit mode.

Additionally, if faster display speed is a priority, the 8-bit mode is preferred since the 4-bit mode takes roughly twice as much time compared to the 8-bit mode.

Table 6.1: Pin Descriptions for LCD

Pin	Symbol	Function
1	V_{SS}	Ground
2	V_{CC}	+5 V power supply
3	V_0	Power supply to control contrast
4	RS	RS = 0 to select command register, RS = 1 to select data register
5	R/W	R/W = 0 for write, R/W = 1 for read
6	En	Chip Enable Signal
7-14	DB0-DB7	Data Lines
15	A	Backlight VCC (5V)
16	K	Backlight Ground

Table 6.2: Important Command Codes for 16×2 LCD

S. No.	Hex Code	Command to LCD instruction Register
1	1	Clear display screen
2	2	Return home

S. No.	Hex Code	Command to LCD instruction Register
3	4	Decrement cursor (shift cursor to left)
4	6	Increment cursor (shift cursor to right)
5	5	Shift display right
6	7	Shift display left
7	8	Display off, cursor off
8	0A	Display off, cursor on
9	0C	Display on, cursor off
10	0E	Display on, cursor blinking
11	0F	Display on, cursor blinking
12	10	Shift cursor position to left
13	14	Shift the cursor position to the right
14	18	Shift the entire display to the left
15	1C	Shift the entire display to the right
16	80	Force cursor to the beginning (1st line)
17	C0	Force cursor to the beginning (2nd line)
18	38	2 lines and 5×7 matrix

RS (Register Select):

A 16x2 LCD has two registers: the command register and the data register. The register select (RS) pin is used to switch between these registers. Setting RS=0 selects the command register, while RS=1 selects the data register.

- **Command Register:** The command register holds the instructions sent to the LCD. These commands tell the LCD to perform specific tasks, such as initializing, clearing the screen, setting the cursor position, and controlling the display. All command processing occurs within this register.
- **Data Register:** The data register holds the information to be displayed on the LCD, which is the ASCII value of the characters. When data is sent to the LCD, it is stored in the data register

for processing. Setting RS=1 selects the data register, allowing the characters to be displayed on the screen.

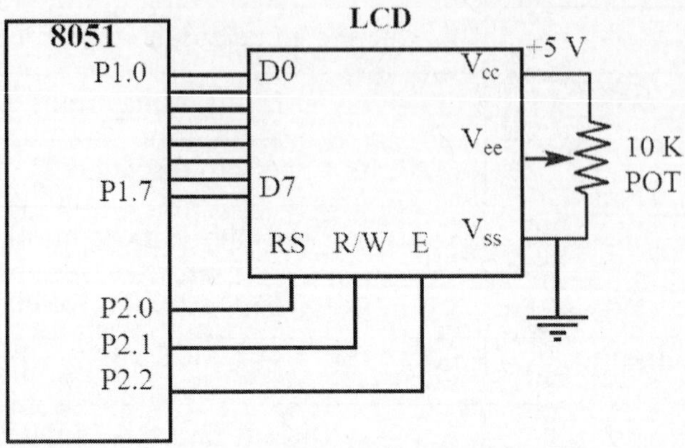

Figure 6.2: LCD interfacing with 8051 [Mazidi, 2013]

Circuit Connections:

- RS (Pin 4): Connect to P2.0 of 8051.
- RW (Pin 5): Connect to P2.1 of 8051.
- E (Pin 6): Connect to P2.2 of 8051.
- D0-D7 (Pins 7-14): Connect to P1.0-P1.7 of 8051 for 8-bit mode.
- VSS (Pin 1): Connect to GND.
- VCC (Pin 2): Connect to +5V.
- VEE (Pin 3): Connect to the wiper of a 10kΩ potentiometer for contrast adjustment.
- LED+ (Pin 15) and LED- (Pin 16): Connect to +5V and GND, respectively, for backlight.

Example 6.1 Print "Hello World" on 16x2 LCD using 4 bit mode.

```
#include <reg51.h>
// Define LCD control pins
sbit RS = P2^0;  // Register Select pin
sbit RW = P2^1;  // Read/Write pin
sbit EN = P2^2;  // Enable pin
// Define LCD data pins for 4-bit mode
sbit D4 = P2^4;  // Data pin 4
sbit D5 = P2^5;  // Data pin 5
sbit D6 = P2^6;  // Data pin 6
sbit D7 = P2^7;  // Data pin 7
// Function to generate a delay
void delay() {
   int i;
   for (i = 0; i < 50000; i++);  // Simple delay loop
}
// Function to send a command to the LCD
void lcd_command(unsigned char cmd) {
   // Send higher nibble first
   D4 = (cmd & 0x10) ? 1 : 0;
   D5 = (cmd & 0x20) ? 1 : 0;
   D6 = (cmd & 0x40) ? 1 : 0;
   D7 = (cmd & 0x80) ? 1 : 0;
   RS = 0;  // Command mode
   RW = 0;  // Write operation
   EN = 1;  // Enable high
   delay();
   EN = 0;  // Enable low

  // Send lower nibble
   D4 = (cmd & 0x01) ? 1 : 0;
   D5 = (cmd & 0x02) ? 1 : 0;
   D6 = (cmd & 0x04) ? 1 : 0;
   D7 = (cmd & 0x08) ? 1 : 0;
  EN = 1;  // Enable high
   delay();
   EN = 0;  // Enable low
}
```

```
// Function to send data to the LCD
void lcd_data(unsigned char data) {
   // Send higher nibble first
   D4 = (data & 0x10) ? 1 : 0;
   D5 = (data & 0x20) ? 1 : 0;
   D6 = (data & 0x40) ? 1 : 0;
   D7 = (data & 0x80) ? 1 : 0;
   RS = 1;  // Data mode
   RW = 0;  // Write operation
   EN = 1;  // Enable high
   delay();
   EN = 0;  // Enable low
   // Send lower nibble
   D4 = (data & 0x01) ? 1 : 0;
   D5 = (data & 0x02) ? 1 : 0;
   D6 = (data & 0x04) ? 1 : 0;
   D7 = (data & 0x08) ? 1 : 0;
   EN = 1;  // Enable high
   delay();
   EN = 0;  // Enable low
}
// Function to initialize the LCD in 4-bit mode
void lcd_init() {
   lcd_command(0x02);  // Initialize LCD in 4-bit mode
   lcd_command(0x28);  // 2 lines, 5x7 matrix in 4-bit mode
   lcd_command(0x0C);  // Display ON, cursor OFF
   lcd_command(0x06);  // Increment cursor
   lcd_command(0x01);  // Clear display screen
   delay();            // Wait for the LCD to process the command
}
// Function to display a string on the LCD
void lcd_display(char *str) {
   while (*str) {
      lcd_data(*str++);  // Send each character of the string to the LCD
   }
}
// Main function
void main() {
   lcd_init();              // Initialize LCD
   lcd_display("Hello, World!");  // Display "Hello, World!" message
   while (1);              // Infinite loop to keep the message on the screen
}
```

This code interfaces a 16x2 LCD with an 8051 microcontroller using 4-bit mode to the control pins RS, RW, and EN, along with data pins D4 to D7, are connected to Port 2. The lcd_init() function initializes the LCD in 4-bit mode, configures it to use two lines, a 5x7 matrix, and turns on the display without a cursor. The lcd_command() function sends commands by first sending the higher nibble, then the lower nibble, with the RS pin set to 0 for command mode. The lcd_data() function operates similarly but sets RS to 1 for data mode, allowing the display of characters. The lcd_display() function iterates through each character in a string, sending it to the LCD via lcd_data(). A delay function is used to ensure stable timing. Finally, in the main() function, the LCD is initialized, and the message "Hello, World!" is displayed. The code runs in an infinite loop, keeping the message visible on the LCD screen.

Example 6.2 Print “Hello World” on 16x2 LCD using 8 bit mode.

```
#include <reg51.h>
// Define LCD control pins
sbit RS = P2^0;  // Register Select pin
sbit RW = P2^1;  // Read/Write pin
sbit EN = P2^2;  // Enable pin
// Function to generate a delay
void delay(void) {
    int i;
    for (i = 0; i < 50000; i++);  // Simple delay loop
}
// Function to send a command to the LCD
void lcd_command(unsigned char cmd) {
    P1 = cmd;  // Send full 8-bit command to Port 1
    RS = 0;    // Command mode (RS = 0)
    RW = 0;    // Write operation (RW = 0)
    EN = 1;    // Enable high
    delay();   // Wait for the LCD to process the command
    EN = 0;    // Enable low
}
```

```
// Function to send data (characters) to the LCD
void lcd_data(unsigned char data) {
   P1 = data;  // Send full 8-bit data to Port 1
   RS = 1;     // Data mode (RS = 1)
   RW = 0;     // Write operation (RW = 0)
   EN = 1;     // Enable high
   delay();    // Wait for the LCD to process the data
   EN = 0;     // Enable low
}
// Function to initialize the LCD in 8-bit mode
void lcd_init(void) {
   lcd_command(0x38); // Initialize LCD in 8-bit mode, 2 lines, 5x7 matrix
   lcd_command(0x0C); // Display ON, cursor OFF
   lcd_command(0x06); // Increment cursor after each character
   lcd_command(0x01); // Clear display screen
   dclay();           // Wait for the LCD to complete the initialization
}
```

```
// Function to display a string on the LCD
void lcd_display(char *str) {
   while (*str) {
      lcd_data(*str++); // Send each character of the string to the LCD
   }
}
// Main function
void main(void) {
   lcd_init();                    // Initialize the LCD
   lcd_display("Hello, World!"); // Display the message on the LCD
   while (1);                     // Infinite loop to keep the program running
}
```

6.3 Keyboard Interfacing

At the most fundamental level, keyboards are arranged in a matrix of rows and columns. The CPU accesses these rows and columns through ports, allowing an 8 x 8 matrix of keys to be connected to a microprocessor using two 8-bit ports. When a key is pressed, a connection is made between a specific row and column; otherwise, no connection exists between them. In IBM PC keyboards, a single microcontroller, which includes a microprocessor, RAM, EPROM, and several ports integrated into a single chip, handles both the hardware and software interfacing of the keyboard. The microcontroller's programs, stored in its EPROM, are responsible for continuously scanning the keys, determining which one has been pressed, and relaying that information to the motherboard. This section examines how the 8051 microcontroller scans and identifies key presses.

6.3.1 Scanning and identifying the key

Imagine a simple 4 x 4 keypad setup, connected to a microcontroller. The keypad's rows are connected to an output port, and the columns are connected to an input port as shown in Figure 6.3. The microcontroller is responsible for continuously checking for any key presses.

- **Initial State (No Key Pressed):** All the rows are initially grounded (set to 0), and the columns are connected to a high voltage (VCC). If no key is pressed, reading the columns will return all 1s, indicating no connection.
- **Detecting a Key Press:** The microcontroller first grounds all rows and then reads the column inputs. If all column values are 1 (e.g., 1111), no key has been pressed, and the scanning continues. However, if one of the columns reads 0 (e.g., 1101), it means a key has been pressed in that column. The microcontroller now knows a key press has occurred but needs to identify the exact row and column.
- **Identifying the Row:** The microcontroller grounds each row one by one while reading the columns: It first grounds row 1 and checks the columns. If all column values are still 1, no key in that row is pressed. It then grounds row 2 and checks again. If there's still no zero, it moves to row 3, and so on. When a row is grounded and one of the column values turns 0, the microcontroller identifies that the key is in that row.
- **Identifying the Column:** Once the row is identified, the microcontroller checks the columns again to determine which one is 0. This tells it the exact column where the key was pressed.

Debouncing of key

Debouncing is important in matrix keyboards because mechanical switches can create multiple signals when pressed or released, which leads to erroneous readings. Debouncing ensures that only a single, clean signal is registered for each key press.

Here are some common techniques for switch debouncing in a matrix keyboard:

1. Hardware Debouncing

RC Circuit: Add a capacitor and a resistor in parallel with the switch to filter out the noise caused by switch bouncing. This low-pass filter smooths out the transitions and eliminates multiple signals within a small-time window.

Dedicated Debouncing ICs: Use chips like the MAX6816 which are designed specifically to debounce switches.

2. Software Debouncing

Software debouncing is more commonly used for matrix keyboards because it's cost-effective and flexible. Here are some methods:

Time Delay Method: After detecting a key press, introduce a short delay (e.g., 10-50 ms) to allow the bouncing to settle before registering the key press.

Example: Let's say you press a key in row 2, column 3 (like pressing "5" on a phone keypad). Here's what happens: Initially, the microcontroller grounds all rows and reads the columns. Suppose it reads 1101, indicating a key press. The microcontroller then grounds row 1 and checks the columns—no change, so it moves on. It grounds row 2 and reads the columns again. This time, it finds a 0 in column 3, meaning the key press is in row 2, column 3. This process happens very quickly, allowing the microcontroller to detect key presses in real time.

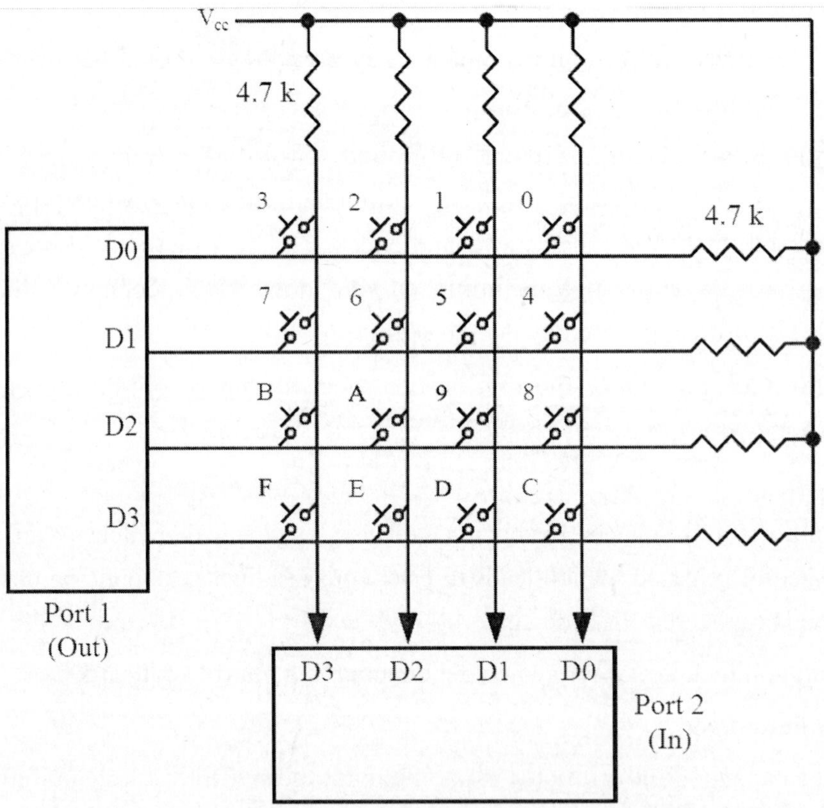

Figure 6.3: Matrix Keyboard

6.3.2 Flowchart of Program

This flowchart represents a typical process for scanning a matrix keypad in embedded systems, step by step. Here is a detailed explanation of each stage:

1. **Start:** The process begins from this point, where the system initiates the keypad scanning.
2. **Ground All Rows:** This step grounds (sets to a low voltage) all the rows of the keypad matrix. This enables the system to detect which row is connected when a key is pressed.
3. **Read All Columns:** After grounding the rows, the system reads the states of all columns. If a key is pressed, the corresponding column will show a low signal.
4. **All Keys Open? This decision box checks whether any key is pressed:** If yes, meaning all keys are open (no keys are pressed), the system will loop back to continuously check until a key is pressed. If no, meaning a key is pressed, the system moves to the next step.
5. **Read All Columns Again:** The system rechecks the columns to ensure a stable keypress. This is to verify that the initial reading was not due to noise.
6. **Any Key Down? This decision box checks if the key is still pressed (to confirm stability):** If yes, meaning a key is consistently pressed, the process moves to the next step. If no, meaning no key is pressed, the system loops back to the beginning.

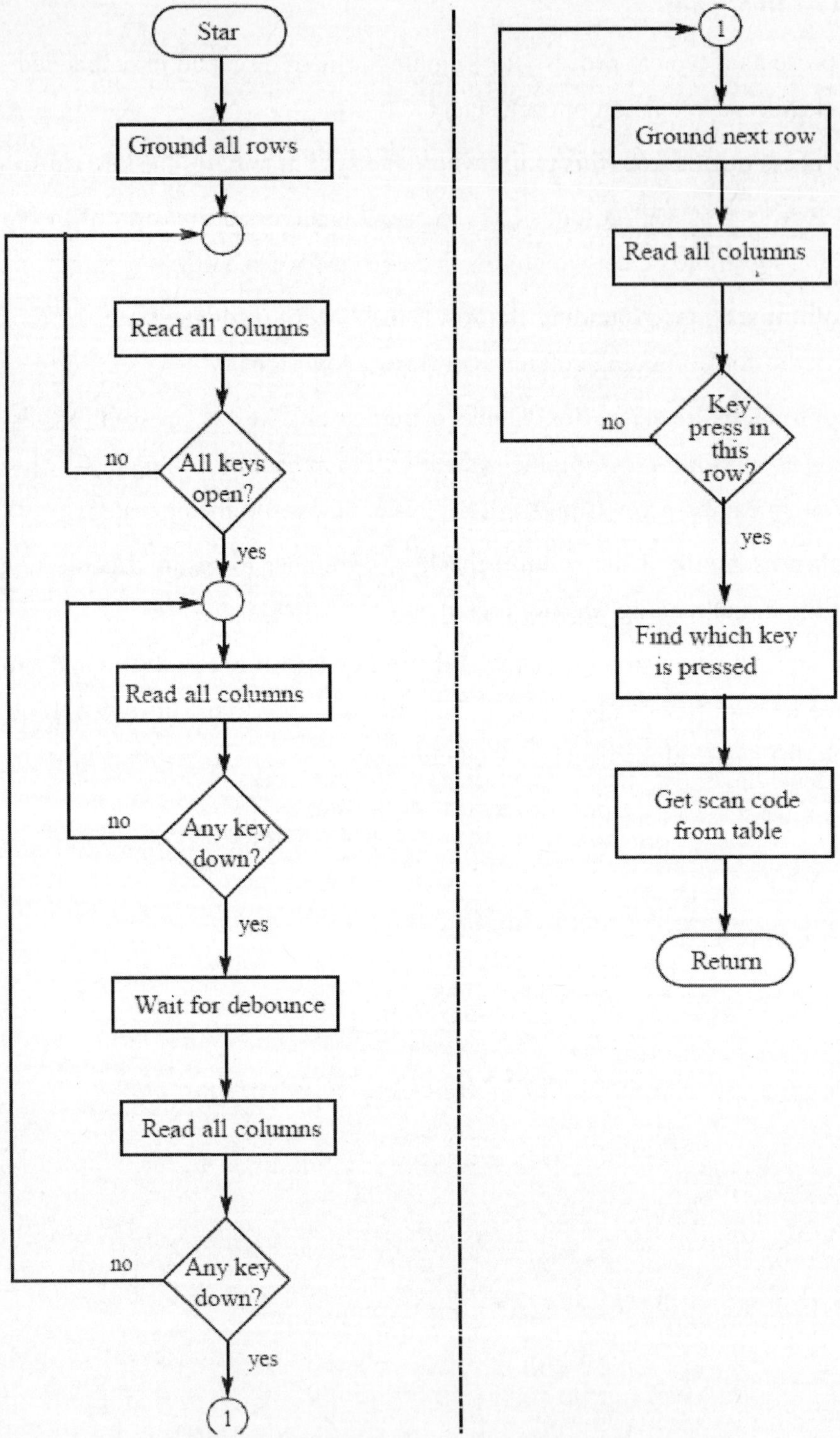

Figure 6.4: Flowchart of Program [Mazidi, 2013]

7. **Wait for Debounce:** This step ensures that any noise or bouncing effects from the mechanical press of the key are eliminated. It waits for a short duration to avoid false detection due to rapid transitions.
8. **Read All Columns Again:** After the debounce wait, the system checks the columns again to ensure that the key is still pressed.
9. **Any Key Down? Once more, the system verifies if the key is still being pressed:** If yes, meaning the key press is confirmed stable, the process moves to the right side of the flowchart. If no, the system loops back to the beginning to start the scanning process again.
10. **Ground Next Row:** The system grounds the next row (one at a time) to identify exactly which row the pressed key belongs to.
11. **Read All Columns:** The system reads the columns again to determine which column corresponds to the pressed key.
12. **Key Press in This Row?:** This decision checks if the key press corresponds to the currently grounded row: If yes, meaning the key belongs to this row, the system proceeds to the next step. If no, the system moves to ground the next row to repeat the check.
13. **Find Which Key Is Pressed:** Once the correct row is identified, the system uses the column information to determine exactly which key in the matrix has been pressed.
14. **Get Scan Code from Table:** The system looks up the scan code corresponding to the pressed key using a predefined table that maps row and column combinations to specific keys.
15. **Return:** Finally, the system returns the scan code of the detected key. The process can now repeat from the beginning to scan for further key presses.

Key points:

1. **Ensuring the Previous Key is Released:** First, the program sets all rows to 0 (grounded) and repeatedly checks the columns until all are high (indicating no key is pressed). Once all columns read high, it waits briefly before moving on to the next stage where it monitors for a new key press.
2. **Detecting a Key Press:** The program then enters an infinite loop, constantly scanning the columns to detect if any key is pressed (indicated by a 0 in one of the columns). The rows remain grounded as set in stage 1. When a key press is detected, the program waits 20 milliseconds to handle any key bounce (a brief fluctuation). It then checks the columns again to confirm the press. If the key is still pressed after the delay, the program proceeds to identify the row where the key is located; if not, it returns to scanning for key presses.

3. **Finding the Row with the Key Press:** The program grounds each row one by one and reads the columns to see where the key press is. If all columns read high, the key isn't in that row, so the program moves to the next row. Once it finds the correct row, it sets up the starting address for a lookup table that stores the scan codes (or ASCII values) for that row, and then moves to the final stage.

4. **Identifying the Key Pressed:** The program checks each column bit, one by one, to see if it's low (indicating the pressed key). When it finds the 0, it retrieves the corresponding ASCII code from the lookup table. If it doesn't find the 0, it moves to the next entry in the table and repeats the process until the key is identified. This process is represented in the flowchart shown in Figure 6.3.

Example 6.4 Keyboard Interfacing with 8051.

```
#include <reg51.h>
#include <stdio.h>
#define ROW P1   // Define the port for rows (P1)
#define COL P2   // Define the port for columns (P2)
// Define the keymap for the 4x4 matrix keypad
unsigned char keymap[4][4] = {
    {'1', '2', '3', 'A'},
    {'4', '5', '6', 'B'},
    {'7', '8', '9', 'C'},
    {'*', '0', '#', 'D'}
};
// Simple delay function
void delay() {
    unsigned int i;
    for (i = 0; i < 30000; i++); // Delay loop
}
// Initialize serial communication at 9600 baud rate
void serial_init() {
    TMOD = 0x20;  // Timer 1, Mode 2 (8-bit auto-reload)
    TH1 = 0xFD;   // Set baud rate for 9600 (for 11.0592 MHz crystal)
    SCON = 0x50;  // 8-bit data, 1 stop bit, REN enabled
    TR1 = 1;      // Start Timer 1
}
```

```
// Send data via serial communication
void serial_write(unsigned char c) {
   SBUF = c;          // Load the data into the serial buffer
   while (TI == 0);   // Wait for transmission to complete
   TI = 0;            // Clear the transmit interrupt flag
}
// Function to read the key press from the keypad
unsigned char read_key() {
   unsigned char row, col;
   while (1) {
      COL = 0xFF;  // Set all columns to high (no key press)
      ROW = 0xF0;  // Ground all rows (set row pins low)
      if (COL != 0xFF) {  // If any column is low, key is pressed
         delay(); // Debounce delay to avoid false triggering
         // Check which row has the pressed key
         ROW = 0xFE;  // Ground Row 1 (P1.0 low)
         if (COL != 0xFF) {
            col = COL;
            row = 0;
            break;
         }
         ROW = 0xFD;  // Ground Row 2 (P1.1 low)
         if (COL != 0xFF) {
            col = COL;
            row = 1;
            break;
         }
ROW = 0xFB;  // Ground Row 3 (P1.2 low)
         if (COL != 0xFF) {
            col = COL;
            row = 2;
            break;
         }
```

```
            ROW = 0xF7;  // Ground Row 4 (P1.3 low)
            if (COL != 0xFF) {
                col = COL;
                row = 3;
                break;
            }
        }
    }
    // Identify the column based on which column is low
    if (col == 0xEE) return keymap[row][0];
    if (col == 0xDE) return keymap[row][1];
    if (col == 0xBE) return keymap[row][2];
    if (col == 0x7E) return keymap[row][3];
    return 0;  // Return 0 if no valid key is pressed
}
// Main function
void main() {
    unsigned char key;
    serial_init();  // Initialize serial communication
    while (1) {
        key = read_key();  // Get the pressed key
        serial_write(key);  // Send the key via serial
        delay();  // Delay to avoid detecting the same key multiple times
    }
}
```

6.4 Stepper Motor Interfacing

A stepper motor is a device that converts electrical pulses into mechanical movement, making it widely used in applications like disk drives, dot matrix printers, and robotics for precise position control.

Structure and Types of Stepper Motors:

- **Permanent Magnet (PM) Stepper Motor:** The most common type, which uses a permanent magnet as the rotor (the shaft that rotates). The rotor is surrounded by a stator with coils.
- **Variable Reluctance Stepper Motor:** Unlike PM motors, these do not have a permanent magnet rotor. They operate based on the magnetic reluctance principle, which creates torque through variations in reluctance in the magnetic circuit.

Unipolar Stepper Motors

A common type of stepper motor is the four-phase or unipolar stepper motor. It typically has four stator windings, each with a center-tapped connection. This configuration allows for easy control by switching the current direction in each coil. The motor has six leads: four for the stator windings and two for the center-tapped commons.

Stepper Motor Working

The stepper motor moves in precise increments, which allows for accurate positioning. The motion is controlled by changing the current direction in the coils, which changes the magnetic polarity of the stator poles. As poles of the same polarity repel and opposite poles attract, the rotor moves accordingly. The direction of rotation is determined by the sequence of current flow through the coils.

Driving the Motor

By applying a specific sequence of power to the stator windings, the rotor rotates in controlled steps. Different stepping sequences can be used, each providing varying levels of precision. For instance, a two-phase, four-step stepping sequence is commonly used to control the rotation of the motor. This sequence determines the smoothness and accuracy of the motor's movement.

Table 6.3: Normal Four-Step Sequence

Clockwis ↓

Step	Coil A	Coil B	Coil C	Coil D
1	1	1	0	0
2	0	1	1	0
3	0	0	1	1
4	1	0	0	1

↑ Anti clockwise

The Table 6.1 represents the normal four-step sequence for driving a unipolar stepper motor. In this sequence, two coils are energized at a time, offering smoother movement and better torque compared to the single-coil version. Let's break down the sequence step-by-step:

Sequence Breakdown

1. Step 1 (Coil A and B On):

Coil A = 1 (On), Coil B = 1 (On), Coil C = 0 (Off), Coil D = 0 (Off):

In this step, both coils A and B are energized, which creates a magnetic field that pulls the rotor to align between these two coils.

2. Step 2 (Coil B and C On):

Coil A = 0 (Off), Coil B = 1 (On), Coil C = 1 (On), Coil D = 0 (Off):

Next, coils B and C are energized, causing the rotor to move to the next position and align between these two coils.

3. Step 3 (Coil C and D On):

Coil A = 0 (Off), Coil B = 0 (Off), Coil C = 1 (On), Coil D = 1 (On):

In this step, coils C and D are energized, making the rotor move to the next step and align between these two coils.

4. Step 4 (Coil D and A On):

Coil A = 1 (On), Coil B = 0 (Off), Coil C = 0 (Off), Coil D = 1 (On):

Finally, coils D and A are energized, pulling the rotor to the next step and completing the cycle.

After Step 4, the sequence repeats from Step 1, causing the motor to rotate continuously in a smooth manner.

Direction of Rotation

Clockwise Rotation: The sequence follows Step 1 → Step 2 → Step 3 → Step 4.

Counterclockwise Rotation: The sequence is reversed, following Step 4 → Step 3 → Step 2 → Step 1.

Stepper Motor Step Angles

The amount of movement corresponding to a single step depends on the internal construction of the motor, particularly the number of teeth on the stator and rotor. The step angle represents the smallest degree of rotation for each step. Different motors have varying step angles. Table 4 presents step angles for various motors. In this table, the term "steps per revolution" refers to the total number of steps required for a complete 360-degree rotation (for example, 180 steps × 2 degrees = 360 degrees).

Table 6.4: Stepper Motor Steps Angles

Step Angle	Steps per Revolution
0.72	500
1.8	200
2.0	180
2.5	144

Step Angle	Steps per Revolution
5.0	72
7.5	48
15	24

The relation between rpm (revolutions per minute), steps per revolution, and steps per second is as follows.

$$\text{Steps per second} = \frac{\text{rpm} \times \text{steps per revolution}}{60}$$

Stepper Motor Interfacing with 8051

The following steps show the 8051 connections to the stepper motor:

1. Using an ohmmeter to measure the resistance between the leads of a stepper motor helps identify which wires are connected to the same winding and which wires are the common (COM) leads. By measuring the resistance between different pairs of wires, you can find pairs with low resistance, indicating they are connected to the ends of the same winding. Then, by checking the resistance between these wires and any other wire, if you find a wire that shows approximately half the resistance, that wire is the COM lead, connected to the center tap of the winding. This process ensures you correctly identify the wiring for proper motor connection.
2. The common wire(s) of the stepper motor are connected to the positive terminal of the motor's power supply, which is often +5V in many motors.
3. The four leads of the motor's stator winding are controlled by four bits from the 8051 microcontroller's port (P1.0–P1.3). However, since the 8051 alone cannot provide enough current to drive the stepper motor windings, a driver like the ULN2003 is necessary to power the stator. While transistors could be used as drivers, they would require additional diodes to handle the inductive current generated when the coil is turned off. The ULN2003 is a better choice because it has built-in diodes to manage the back EMF, simplifying the circuit.

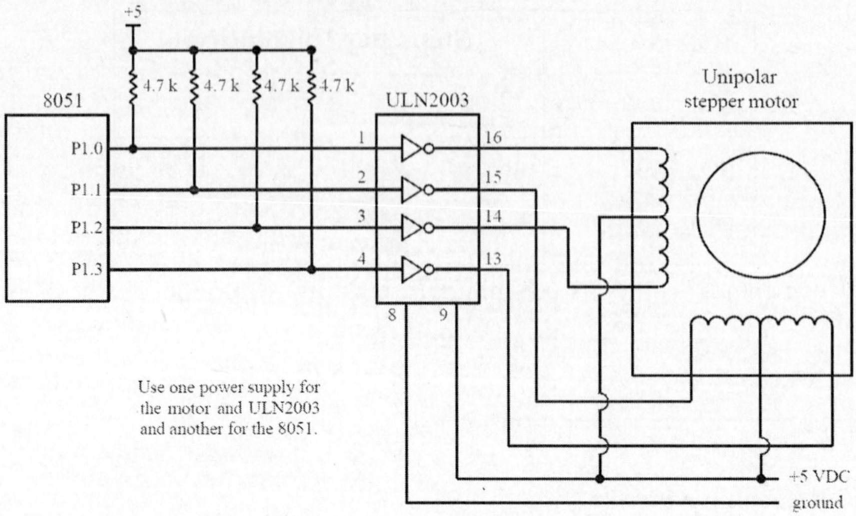

Figure 6.5: Stepper Motor interfacing with 8051 [Mazidi, 2013]

Stepper motor control with 8051 C

```
#include <reg51.h>
void MSDelay(unsigned int delayTime);
void main() { // Main function
  while (1) {
    // Execute the step sequence for the stepper motor
    P1 = 0x0C;  // Step 1: 1100
    MSDelay(100);
    P1 = 0x06;  // Step 2: 0110
    MSDelay(100);
    P1 = 0x03;  // Step 3: 0011
    MSDelay(100);
    P1 = 0x09;  // Step 4: 1001
    MSDelay(100);
  }
}
void MSDelay(unsigned int delayTime) {
  unsigned int i, j;
  for (i = 0; i < delayTime; i++) {
    for (j = 0; j < 1275; j++);  // Inner loop count for fine-tuning delay
  }
}
```

6.5 DC Motor Interfacing

A DC motor converts electrical energy in the form of Direct Current into mechanical energy, specifically producing rotational movement of the motor shaft. The direction of the motor shaft's rotation can be reversed by changing the direction of the Direct Current flowing through the motor. The speed of the motor can be controlled by applying a fixed voltage; varying the voltage will vary the motor's speed. Therefore, by applying a variable DC voltage, the speed of the motor can be adjusted, and by reversing the current direction, the rotation direction can be changed. To vary the voltage, the PWM (Pulse Width Modulation) technique can be used, while reversing the current can be achieved using an H-Bridge circuit or motor driver ICs that incorporate the H-Bridge method or other mechanisms.

Pulse Width Modulation

The speed of a DC motor is influenced by three factors: (a) load, (b) voltage, and (c) current. For a given fixed load, maintaining a steady speed can be achieved using a technique called Pulse Width Modulation (PWM). By adjusting (modulating) the width of the pulses applied to the motor, we can control the amount of power delivered, thereby increasing or decreasing the motor's speed. Although the voltage remains constant in amplitude, the duty cycle varies wider pulses result in higher speeds. PWM is so commonly used in DC motor control that some microcontrollers have PWM circuitry built into the chip. In these microcontrollers, you simply load the appropriate registers with the values for the high and low portions of the pulse, and the microcontroller handles the rest, freeing it up to perform other tasks.

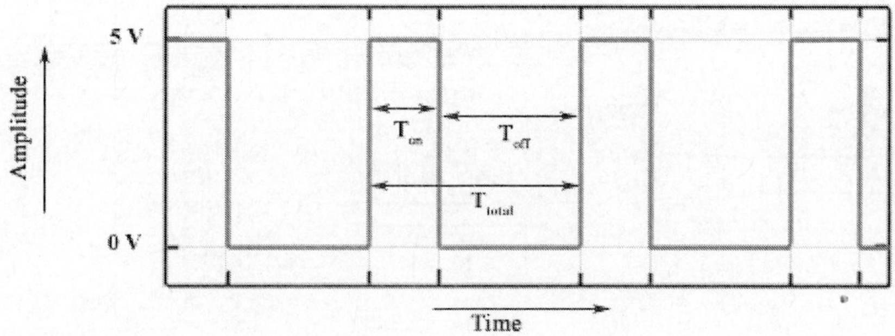

Figure 6.6 Pulse Width Modulation

There are several terms related to PWM:

On-Time: The time signal's duration is high.

Off-Time: The time signal's duration is low.

Period: The total of the PWM signal's on and off times is used to indicate it.

Duty cycle: This is the proportion of time the signal stays on during the PWM signal's duration.

$$\mathbf{D} = \frac{\mathbf{Ton}}{\mathbf{Ton+Toff}}$$

DC Motor control using PWM

We are interfacing a DC motor with the 8051 microcontroller, utilizing an L293D motor driver IC to control the motor's speed and direction. The L293D features an in-built H-bridge, enabling bidirectional control of the motor as shown in Figure 6.7.

In this setup, two toggle switches are connected to pins P1.0 and P1.1 of the AT89S52 microcontroller to adjust the motor speed in increments of 10%. Another toggle switch, connected to pin P1.2, is used to control the rotation direction of the motor. The output direction control is handled by pins P1.6 and P1.7, which are linked to the L293D motor driver's input pins for Motor 1. By changing the polarity of these pins, the motor can rotate either clockwise or counterclockwise.

The speed of the DC motor is modulated through a PWM signal generated on pin P2.0. This PWM signal is created using the 8051 internal timer.

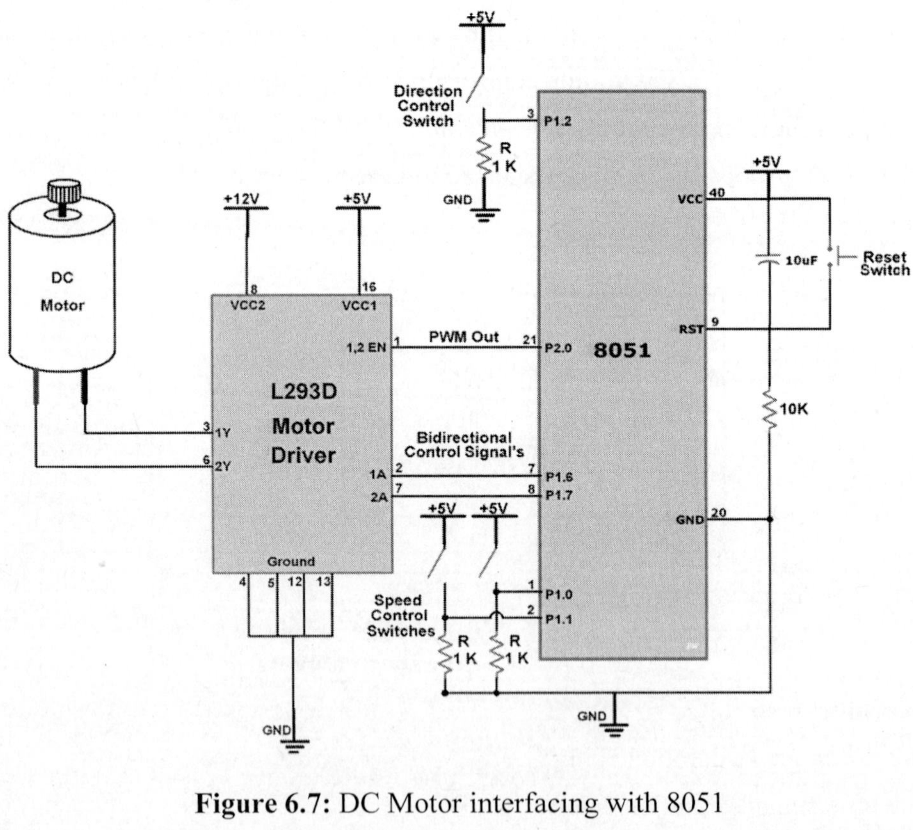

Figure 6.7: DC Motor interfacing with 8051

```
#include <reg52.h>
#include <intrins.h>
#define PWM_PERIOD 0xB7FE  // Value for 20ms PWM period
// Pin definitions
sbit PWM_OUT_PIN   = P2^0; // PWM output for speed control
sbit SPEED_INC     = P1^0; // Speed increment switch
sbit SPEED_DEC     = P1^1; // Speed decrement switch
sbit CHANGE_DIR    = P1^2; // Change rotation direction switch
sbit MOTOR_PIN1    = P1^6; // Motor control pin 1
sbit MOTOR_PIN2    = P1^7; // Motor control pin 2
// Global variables
unsigned int onPeriod, offPeriod;
unsigned char speed = 0;   // Initial motor speed
// Function to provide a 1ms delay at 11.0592 MHz
void delay_ms(unsigned int ms) {
   unsigned int i, j;
   for (i = 0; i < ms; i++)
      for (j = 0; j < 112; j++);
}
// Timer initialization for PWM generation
void timer0_init() {
   TMOD = 0x01;          // Timer0 mode 1 (16-bit)
   TH0 = (PWM_PERIOD >> 8); // Load high byte for 20ms PWM period
   TL0 = PWM_PERIOD;     // Load low byte for 20ms PWM period
   TR0 = 1;              // Start Timer0
}
// Timer0 interrupt service routine for PWM
void timer0_ISR() interrupt 1 {
   PWM_OUT_PIN = !PWM_OUT_PIN;  // Toggle PWM output
   if (PWM_OUT_PIN) {         // Set on-period when high
      TH0 = (onPeriod >> 8);
      TL0 = onPeriod;
   } else {                   // Set off-period when low
      TH0 = (offPeriod >> 8);
      TL0 = offPeriod;
   }
}
```

```
// Function to set PWM duty cycle
void set_duty_cycle(unsigned char dutyCycle) {
   unsigned int period = 65535 - PWM_PERIOD;
   onPeriod = (period * dutyCycle) / 100;
   offPeriod = period - onPeriod;
   onPeriod = 65535 - onPeriod;
   offPeriod = 65535 - offPeriod;
}
// Initialize motor to default state (initial speed and direction)
void motor_init() {
   speed = 0;
   MOTOR_PIN1 = 1;
   MOTOR_PIN2 = 0;
   set_duty_cycle(speed);
}
int main() {
   EA  = 1;  // Enable global interrupts
   ET0 = 1;  // Enable Timer0 interrupt
   timer0_init();
   motor_init();
   while (1) {
      // Increment duty cycle by 10% if SPEED_INC switch is pressed
      if (SPEED_INC == 1) {
         if (speed < 100) speed += 10;
         set_duty_cycle(speed);
         while (SPEED_INC == 1); // Wait for switch release
         delay_ms(200);
      }
      // Decrement duty cycle by 10% if SPEED_DEC switch is pressed
      if (SPEED_DEC == 1) {
         if (speed > 0) speed -= 10;
         set_duty_cycle(speed);
         while (SPEED_DEC == 1); // Wait for switch release
         delay_ms(200);
      }
```

```
        // Change motor rotation direction if CHANGE_DIR switch is pressed
      if (CHANGE_DIR == 1) {
        MOTOR_PIN1 = !MOTOR_PIN1;
        MOTOR_PIN2 = !MOTOR_PIN2;
        while (CHANGE_DIR == 1); // Wait for switch release
        delay_ms(200);
      }
    }
}
```

6.6 Sensor Interfacing

This section will demonstrate how to interface sensors with a microcontroller. While the emphasis is on temperature sensors, the principles discussed here apply equally to other types of sensors, such as light and pressure sensors.

Temperature Sensor LM35 Interfacing with 8051

The LM35 series are precision integrated-circuit temperature sensors with an output voltage that is directly proportional to the temperature in Celsius. The LM35 does not require external calibration because it is internally calibrated. It provides an output of 10 mV per degree Celsius. Table 10 serves as the selection guide for the LM35. Signal conditioning is a critical aspect of data acquisition systems. Common transducers generate outputs in various forms, such as voltage, current, charge, capacitance, and resistance. However, to interface these signals with an A-to-D converter, they must first be converted to a voltage, a process known as signal conditioning (see Figure 20). Signal conditioning may involve converting current to voltage or amplifying the signal. For instance, a thermistor's resistance changes with temperature, but this change must be converted into a voltage to be usable by an ADC.

Consider the example of interfacing an LM35 temperature sensor with an ADC0848. The ADC0848 has 8-bit resolution, resulting in 256 (2^8) discrete steps. Since the LM35 outputs 10 mV per degree Celsius, the input voltage to the ADC0848 can be conditioned to produce a full-scale output of 2560 mV (2.56 V). To achieve this, the reference voltage (Vref) of the ADC0848 should be set to 2.56 V, allowing the ADC's output to correspond directly to the temperature measured by the LM35.

Figure illustrates the connection of a temperature sensor to the ADC0848. A 10 K potentiometer is used, with its voltage fixed at 2.5 V using an LM336-2.5 zener diode. The LM336-2.5 stabilizes the voltage to prevent fluctuations from the power supply, ensuring consistent performance of the signal conditioning circuit.

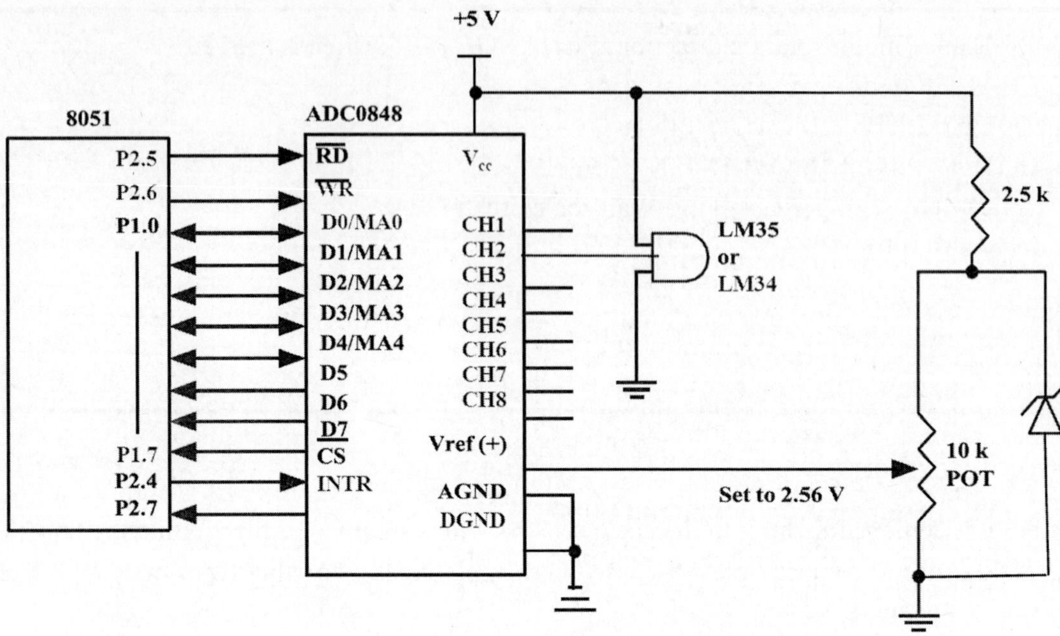

Figure 6.8: 8051 Interfacing with temperature sensor [Mazidi, 2013]

```
//C code to read temp from ADC0848, convert it to
//decimal, and put it on P0 with some delay
#include <reg51.h>
sbit RD = P2^5;       // Read pin for ADC
sbit WR = P2^6;       // Write pin for ADC (start conversion)
sbit INTR = P2^7;     // End-of-conversion (EOC) pin for ADC
sfr ADC_DATA = P1;    // Port P1 connected to D0-D7 of ADC0848 for data transfer
void DisplayOnPort0(unsigned char value);
void DelayMs(unsigned int milliseconds);
void main() {
   unsigned char adc_value;
   ADC_DATA = 0xFF; // Set P1 as input for ADC data
   INTR = 1;        // Set INTR as input
   RD = 1;          // Initialize RD high
   WR = 1;          // Initialize WR high
while (1) {
      WR = 0;       // Send WR pulse to start conversion
      WR = 1;
      while (INTR == 1); // Wait for EOC signal from ADC4
```

```
RD = 0;          // Send RD pulse to read data from ADC
      adc_value = ADC_DATA; // Read value from ADC
      DisplayOnPort0(adc_value); // Display ADC value on P0
      RD = 1;
   }
}
void DisplayOnPort0(unsigned char value) {
   unsigned char hundreds, tens, units;

   hundreds = value / 100;    // Extract hundreds place
   tens = (value / 10) % 10;  // Extract tens place
   units = value % 10;        // Extract units place
   P0 = units;                // Display units digit
   DelayMs(250);
   P0 = tens;                 // Display tens digit
   DelayMs(250);
   P0 = hundreds;             // Display hundreds digit
   DelayMs(250);
}
void DelayMs(unsigned int milliseconds) {
   unsigned char i, j;
   for (i = 0; i < milliseconds; i++) {
      for (j = 0; j < 1275; j++); // Calibrated loop for ~1 ms delay
   }
}
```

The step-by-step explanation of the program is as follows:

1. **Pin Definitions:** The sbit keyword defines single-bit access to specific pins on Port 2 (P2.5 for RD, P2.6 for WR, and P2.7 for INTR). The sfr keyword defines MYDATA as Port 1 (P1), which is connected to the data pins (D0-D7) of the ADC0848.

2. **Function Prototypes:** In the program two functions have declared. ConvertAndDisplay(), Converts the binary value from the ADC to decimal and displays it on Port 0 (P0). MSDelay() function Creates a delay.

3. **Main Function Setup:** MYDATA = 0xFF;: Configures Port 1 (P1) as input since the ADC0848 will send data to it. INTR = 1;: Configures the INTR pin (interrupt pin) as an input

(ready for receiving an interrupt signal from the ADC). RD = 1; WR = 1;: Sets the RD and WR pins high to prepare them for reading and writing to the ADC.

4. **While Loop - Reading Data from ADC:**

   WR = 0; WR = 1;: Sends a "write" pulse to initiate the conversion process on the ADC0848.

   while(INTR == 1);: Waits for the INTR signal (EOC, End of Conversion) from the ADC0848, indicating that the conversion is complete.

   RD = 0;: Sends a "read" pulse to the ADC to retrieve the converted data.

   value = MYDATA;: Reads the 8-bit digital value from the ADC into the value variable.

   ConvertAndDisplay(value);: Calls the function to convert the binary value to decimal and display the result on Port 0.

   RD = 1;: Resets the RD pin.

5. **Convert and Display Function:**

   x = value / 10;: Divides the binary value by 10 to separate the higher decimal places.

   d1 = value % 10;: Calculates the least significant digit (units place).

   d2 = x % 10;: Calculates the middle digit (tens place).

   d3 = x / 10;: Calculates the most significant digit (hundreds place).

   P0 = d1;: Displays the least significant digit (units) on Port 0.

   MSDelay(250);: Delays for 250 ms before displaying the next digit.

   P0 = d2;: Displays the middle digit (tens) on Port 0.

   P0 = d3;: Displays the most significant digit (hundreds) on Port 0.

UNIT SUMMARY

This unit focuses on interfacing various peripheral devices with microcontrollers, emphasizing the integration of LEDs, LCDs, and keyboards. It explains how to control LEDs for visual indicators, utilize LCDs for displaying information, and connect keyboards for user input, highlighting the necessary wiring and control signals. The unit further explores stepper motor interfacing, detailing how to control the precise movement of stepper motors for applications requiring accurate positioning. It also covers DC motor interfacing, focusing on driving motors for tasks like motion control and automation. Additionally, the unit addresses sensor interfacing, which includes connecting various sensors (such as temperature, humidity, and motion sensors) to microcontrollers for data acquisition and environmental monitoring. This comprehensive understanding of interfacing techniques is essential for building interactive and responsive embedded systems.

EXERCISES

Multiple Choice Questions (1 to 8)

1. Which of the following statements is true about interfacing an LED with a microcontroller?

   a) The LED should be connected directly to the microcontroller pin without a resistor.

   b) The LED requires a current-limiting resistor to prevent damage.

   c) The LED must be connected in series with the microcontroller pin.

   d) An LED can only be connected to the microcontroller through an external driver circuit.

2. What is the typical number of data lines required to interface a 16x2 LCD in 4-bit mode with a microcontroller?

   a) 16 b) 8

   c) 4 d) 6

3. Which of the following commands is used to clear the screen of a 16x2 LCD?

   a) 0x01 b) 0x02

   c) 0x80 d) 0x0C

4. In a matrix keyboard interfacing, how are the rows and columns connected to the microcontroller?

   a) Rows to input ports, columns to output ports.

   b) Rows and columns are both connected to input ports.

c) Rows to output ports, columns to input ports.

d) Both rows and columns are connected to output ports.

5. Which of the following control sequences is typically used for full-step operation in a unipolar stepper motor?

a) 1 1 0 0, 0 1 1 0, 0 0 1 1, 1 0 0 1
b) 1 0 0 0, 0 1 0 0, 0 0 1 0, 0 0 0 1
c) 1 0 1 0, 0 1 0 1, 1 0 1 0, 0 1 0 1
d) 1 1 1 1, 0 0 0 0, 1 0 1 0, 0 1 0 1

6. What is the primary purpose of using an H-Bridge circuit when interfacing a DC motor with a microcontroller?

a) To regulate the speed of the motor.

b) To allow the motor to rotate in both directions.

c) To increase the voltage applied to the motor.

d) To provide isolation between the motor and the microcontroller.

7. Which of the following is used to control the speed of a DC motor in a microcontroller-based system?

a) PWM (Pulse Width Modulation)

b) ADC (Analog to Digital Converter)

c) DAC (Digital to Analog Converter)

d) UART (Universal Asynchronous Receiver/Transmitter)

8. Which type of sensor typically requires an ADC (Analog to Digital Converter) for interfacing with a microcontroller?

a) Digital temperature sensor
b) Push-button switch
c) LDR (Light Dependent Resistor)
d) Reed switch

Short Answer Questions (9 to 15)

9. Describe the steps required to initialize a 16x2 LCD in 4-bit mode.

10. How does a microcontroller detect a key press in a 4x4 matrix keyboard?

11. What is the advantage of using a matrix keyboard over individual key inputs?

12. What is the purpose of using a driver circuit when interfacing a stepper motor with a microcontroller?

13. Why is an Analog-to-Digital Converter (ADC) necessary for interfacing certain sensors with a microcontroller?

14. Explain the steps to connect and control an LED using GPIO pins of a microcontroller.
15. Explain the difference between 4-bit and 8-bit modes in LCD interfacing.

Long Answer Questions (16 to 19)

16. How is a stepper motor connected and controlled using a microcontroller and a driver circuit?
17. Provide code examples and real-world applications of stepper motors in embedded systems.
18. Explain how PWM (Pulse Width Modulation) is used for speed control.
19. How is data from an analog sensor (like a temperature sensor) processed using an ADC?

MCQ answer

1. (b) 2. (d) 3. (a) 4. (c) 5. (b) 6. (b) 7. (a) 8. (c)

KNOW MORE

Recent advancements in LED, LCD, and keyboard interfacing have focused on improving power efficiency, miniaturization, and integration with IoT platforms. LEDs are now commonly used in smart lighting systems with PWM-based dimming and remote control. LCD advancements include OLED and touch-sensitive displays with enhanced clarity and responsiveness. Keyboards now often feature capacitive touch or membrane technologies with haptic feedback, particularly in wearable and mobile devices. In stepper motor and DC motor interfacing, new driver ICs with micro stepping and regenerative braking capabilities provide smoother and more precise control, especially in automation and robotics. Sensor interfacing has evolved with smart sensors that integrate more processing power for data analysis, edge computing, and wireless connectivity, playing key roles in IoT, smart homes, and industrial automation.

REFERENCES AND SUGGESTED READINGS

1. R. S. Gaonkar, ", Microprocessor Architecture: Programming and Applications with the 8085", Penram International Publishing, 1996
2. Muhammad Ali Mazidi , Janice G. Mazidi, Rolin D. McKinlay 8051 Microcontroller, The: A Systems Approach: Pearson New International Edition 1st Edition, 2013

QR Code for further reading:

8051 Online Reference

COURSE OUTCOME ATTAINMENT TABLE

Course outcomes (COs) for this course can be mapped with the programme outcomes (POs) after the completion of the course and a correlation can be made for the attainment of POs to analyse the gap. After proper analysis of the gap in the attainment of POs necessary measures can be taken to overcome the gaps.

Table for CO and PO attainment

Course Outcomes	**Expected Mapping with Programme Outcomes** *(1- Weak Correlation; 2- Medium correlation; 3- Strong Correlation)*											
	PO-1	**PO-2**	**PO-3**	**PO-4**	**PO-5**	**PO-6**	**PO-7**	**PO-8**	**PO-9**	**PO-10**	**PO-11**	**PO-12**
CO-1												
CO-2												
CO-3												
CO-4												
CO-5												
CO-6												

The data filled in the above table can be used for gap analysis.

INDEX